Young Feminisms

Praise for this book

'This fresh, inspiring collection comes to us at a time when the pressing global challenges we face require urgent, innovative and paradigm-shifting solutions that disrupt the status quo. Highlighting young feminist voices from across the globe is key to this endeavour, and to igniting change.'

Rebecca Fries, CEO, Value for Women

'This important book shines a spotlight on the strategies of resistance and resilience being pioneered by young feminist leaders. It is relevant for a wide audience – from activists looking to be inspired and learn from the experience of peers, to institutions and funders wanting to understand how to better support the inherently political work of the young feminists fighting for equality and rights today.'

Abigail Hunt, Research Fellow, Overseas Development Institute

Young Feminisms

Edited by
Imogen Davies and Caroline Sweetman

Practical ACTION PUBLISHING

OXFAM

Published by Practical Action Publishing in association with Oxfam GB

Practical Action Publishing Ltd
27a Albert Street, Rugby, Warwickshire, CV21 2SG, UK
www.practicalactionpublishing.com

ISBN 978-1-78853-133-7 Paperback
ISBN 978-1-78853-134-4 Hardback
ISBN 978-1-78853-136-8 eBook

Citation: Davies, I. and Sweetman, C. (eds) (2021) *Young Feminisms*,
Rugby, UK: Practical Action Publishing and Oxford: Oxfam GB.
http://dx.doi.org/10.3362/9781788531368

Since 1974, Practical Action Publishing has published and disseminated books and
information in support of international development work throughout the world.
Practical Action Publishing is a trading name of Practical Action Publishing Ltd
(Company Reg. No. 1159018), the wholly owned publishing company of Practical
Action. Practical Action Publishing trades only in support of its parent charity
objectives and any profits are covenanted back to Practical Action (Charity Reg. No.
247257, Group VAT Registration No. 880 9924 76).

Oxfam is a registered charity in England and Wales (no 202918) and Scotland
(SC 039042). Oxfam GB is a member of Oxfam International.

Oxfam GB,
Oxfam House, John Smith Drive,
Oxford, OX4 2JY, UK
www.oxfam.org.uk

Cover photo shows young women marching to end violence against women in
Montevideo, Uruguay, 2017
Credit: UN Women / Sahand Minae

Contents

Working in Gender and Development

The *Working in Gender and Development* series brings together themed selections of the best articles from the journal *Gender & Development* and other Oxfam publications for development practitioners and policy makers, students, and academics. Titles in the series present the theory and practice of gender-oriented development in a way that records experience, describes good practice, and shares information about resources. Books in the series will contribute to and review current thinking on the gender dimensions of particular development and relief issues.

Other titles in the series are available from www.practicalactionpublishing.com and include:

Gender-Based Violence
HIV and AIDS
Climate Change and Gender Justice
Gender and the Economic Crisis
Gender, Faith and Development
Gender, Monitoring, Evaluation and Learning
Gender, Business and Enterprise
Gender, Development and Care
Gender and Inequalities
Working with Men for Gender Equality
Gender and Water, Sanitation and Hygiene

For further information on the journal please visit:
www.genderanddevelopment.org

CHAPTER 1

Introduction:
Development and young feminisms

Imogen Davies and Caroline Sweetman

This book focuses on young feminisms. This theme is inspired by the convergence of three key areas in the current moment. These are: increasing development sector interest in young people, as a result of peak youth populations in the global South; a vibrant 'fourth wave' of feminism, often focusing on sexual violence, pioneering online forms of collective action, and feminist ways of working that reject hierarchy and domination; and the emergence of young women activists mobilising around the world in response to current onslaughts on women's rights.

There are more young people today than ever before, with almost 1.8 billion people aged 10–24 – 24.6 per cent of the world's population of 7.3 billion (UNFPA 2014, 3). Almost nine out of ten of these live in less developed countries (*ibid.*). Many countries in the global South have youth populations which comprise well over half of the total: for example, 56 per cent of the population in Guatemala is under the age of 25; this figure is 63 per cent in Afghanistan and 67 per cent in Mali (CIA 2018).

As present and future workers, citizens, leaders, parents and carers, young people need development that works for them. Yet, they have traditionally been marginalised from formal power and decision-making in most cultures worldwide. In response, young people are to be found questioning authority, challenging injustices, championing change, and asserting their right to play a full part in shaping today and tomorrow. During the past decade alone, young activists have agitated for change through powerful social movements including the global Occupy Movements, the Arab Spring, the Umbrella Revolution in Hong Kong, Los Indignados in Spain, Y'en en marre in Senegal, le Balai Citoyen in Burkina Faso, and Lucha in the Democratic Republic of Congo, to name just a few.

In these movements, young women are to be found alongside young men, agitating for change seen as positive for both. But as feminists have pointed out, not all activists are equal. In a gender-unequal world, activism carries particular risks and costs for women. Change takes a very long time and in 2018, men are still widely seen as natural leaders. The audacity of young women marching on the streets, demanding space and voice, is punished and policed through harassment and violence – not only from men who oppose them, but from men 'on their side'. Feminist political scientists studying social movements have long pointed out that mixed-sex political action does not result in all the changes women need to see. To further those interests they share with other women but not with men – 'gender interests' – feminist activism is necessary (Molyneux 1985). We are living through an era of stalling human rights and freedoms, as many authors in this book point out. For the current generation of feminists, taking risks to further and protect women's rights is a daily fact of life.

This book is based on an issue of *Gender & Development* that came out at the height of the #MeToo movement[1] which is transforming public narratives on sexual violence, assault and harassment. #MeToo is spreading to other sectors, including journalism, advertising, industry – and most notably, for this journal with its focus on international development, the aid sector, with #AidToo revelations in early 2018 in high profile INGOs including Oxfam, Save the Children and UN agencies. Young feminists are leading voices in this activism.

Of course, #MeToo is not the only game in town: it is simply the most globally publicised. In India, following widespread protests in 2012 after the violent rape of a young woman in Delhi, young women have been leading campaigns such as the 2016 #IWillGoOut protest, calling for legal protections from sexual assault. In Latin America, the 2017 ACTÚA, detén la violencia campaign is addressing violence in young people's relationships in Bolivia. In Argentina and more broadly in the region, the 2015 #NiUnaMenos campaign calls for no more femicides, as well as demanding an end to all forms of oppression experienced by women, lesbians and trans people – from extreme violence to unpaid care work, and from unsafe abortions to daily street harassment. In their activism, these feminist campaigns are pioneering and 'politicising the use of technologies' (Alcaraz 2017, n.p.) for mass reach. While not every cyberfeminist is young, these technologies are second nature to the young women online who are using social media as a catalyst for new ways of organising both on and off-line.

As chapters in this book show, young feminists are developing innovative responses to resurgent patriarchal power. They are outing sexual violence while holding perpetrators to account, asserting sexual and reproductive rights, and campaigning for political, economic and social empowerment – working as part of a wider movement for social justice which understands power and powerlessness from an awareness of inclusivity and intersectionality[2]. Their work is founded on principles of participation, empowerment, collaboration, power-sharing, and feminist leadership.

Young feminists are highly critical of international development for its reductive vision of development as economic growth, and its top-down, hierarchical ways of working. They come from a generation that is too young to have been at the Fourth World Conference on Women at Beijing in 1995, and too young to remember the agenda of 'gender mainstreaming' as it started: a radical feminist concept. Authors in this book highlight the failings of international development to take on the messages of feminists at that time, and since. In their work, they respond to women's realities in ways that international development does not.

In this Introduction, we explore these themes in more detail, and introduce the chapters published here. In the next section, we start by tracing evolving perspectives on youth in international development.

Youth and international development: evolving perspectives from welfare to rights

There is no universally agreed end to childhood and start of young adulthood, though many legal systems focus on 18 as the age of legal majority, when a range of rights is realised. The UN has adopted the definition of a 'young person' as being between the ages of 15 and 24 (General Assembly A/36/215 and Resolution 36/28, 1981). However, definitions change between countries and cultural contexts – the African Youth Charter (African Union Commission 2006), for example, defines young people as those between the ages of 15 and 35.

Children and adolescents have long been a focus of international development initiatives, focusing on health and education. In 1992, the UN Declaration of the Rights of the Child reflected growing recognition of the distinct rights of children to these and other services and resources, but recognition of their agency too. Child and youth participation in the decisions affecting them is increasingly seen as 'a fundamental human right' (Viviers and Lombard 2013, 7). This way of seeing the relationship between the young and older people in society is profoundly different from the time-honoured view of children and younger adults as 'minors' to be guided by older decision-makers. Principles of youth participation, leadership, agency and empowerment are gradually being recognised.

The UN first acknowledged young people as a constituency in the 1965 'Declaration on the Promotion Among Youth of the Ideals of Peace, Mutual Respect and Understanding Between Peoples' (General Assembly A/res/20/2037). It continued to promote youth rights and participation through the creation of the International Youth Year in 1985; the adoption of the UN youth agenda – the 'World Programme of Action for Youth' – by member states in 1995; the observation of International Youth Day from 2000; and proclaiming the year commencing 12 August 2010 as the International Year of Youth. Thinking about youth as a distinct constituency in development – as opposed to children – has gained traction much more recently, as a result of increasing awareness of burgeoning youth populations in the global South. Development agencies such as USAID and the UK Department for International Development (DFID), for example, published their first youth agendas and policies within the last few years, in 2012 and 2016 respectively.

Perspectives and policy approaches on youth in international development have followed a very similar trajectory to those on women in development. An initial focus on welfare and awareness of needs has developed into a more sophisticated understanding of the right to equality and to play a full role in determining human development, in both cases. The UN's launch of the 'Youth 2030' strategy recognises the need for young people to lead on the 2030 Agenda for Sustainable Development, both as an end in itself to fulfil their potential, and to ensure that its goals are realised (UN 2018).

Agenda 2030, the Sustainable Development Goals (SDGs) and the 'Leave No One Behind' agenda[3] reflect growing current awareness of the importance of participation and leadership of marginalised groups – including youth and women – in international development. The SDG process reflected an unprecedented level of consultation and input from civil society, including women's rights and youth organisations. The SDGs have been credited as being more attuned to youth activists' identity as global active citizens than the MDGs[4]. SDG 17, which aims to 'strengthen the means of implementation and revitalise the global partnership for sustainable development', has tackling systemic global injustice at its core, promoting solidarity and mutual support between those struggling against inequality around the world, and rejecting the traditional view of development as the transfer of knowledge and funding from North to South. This has been welcomed by many youth rights activists for its rejection of the idea of 'white saviours' leading development, on behalf of passive populations in need of charity in the global South.

Peaks, bulges, and dividends: young people as drivers for development

Today, recognising the opportunities which the phenomenon of the 'youth bulge' in many populations provides, governments and international development actors are focusing on youth. A major motivation is growing realisation of the potential young people offer to generate wealth. They want to take advantage of what some youth organisations have defined as 'Peak Youth' (Restless Development 2015). Young people are seen as engines of economic growth, with development agencies outlining the most effective ways to 'harness' young people's potential to 'reap' the 'demographic dividend' (UNFPA 2014, 24). This policy approach echoes the focus on women in the 1980s onwards as governments realised the potential they represented for economic growth, if their role in paid production could be increased.

A second motivation for current agendas on youth is the fear of elites made insecure by rising economic inequalities both within and between nations – and the global communications revolution which makes these inequalities so obvious to all of us. Elites throughout history have feared the energy and passion of young people rising up against inequality, poverty and marginalisation[5]. They can be seen as a ticking time bomb (Ighobor 2013). Power-holders ponder the threats presented by youth unemployment, violent extremism, rural-to-urban migration, and mass international migration in search of a better life. Some see the idea of allowing increased youth voice and political participation as a threat to stability (Pereznieto and Hamilton Harding 2013).

But for others, keen to move beyond instrumentalisation, genuine child and youth participation can deepen insights, increase ownership and legitimacy and 'transform ... young people and their relationships with their communities' (Cheney 2011, 166).

Andries Viviers and Antoinette Lombard (2013) see the marginalisation of child and youth voice as comparable with women's rights struggles. Development programming now needs to take on the new focus on youth, while still struggling to integrate gender justice and women's rights. In their chapter, Pushpita Saha and her fellow authors provide a case study of how this is happening in an Oxfam programme in Bangladesh. On the face of it, programming to support young women into training and employment sounds positive. Yet, as this chapter shows, without an understanding of feminist critiques of 'economic empowerment' and a focus on rights and equality, programming is going to be of limited worth to the young women it seeks to support. In the rush to increase young women's economic value, youth employment initiatives risk repeating the mistakes of previous women's 'economic empowerment' projects: failing to understand the political, social and economic factors that need to be challenged and changed to support women's empowerment, and vastly over-stating the power of top-down development programming to deliver the radical change women need.

Beyond economic empowerment and the 'girl effect'

In her chapter, Catherine Nyambura focuses on the idea of the 'demographic dividend' and the policy approach that comes from it, from her perspective as a young African feminist involved in the pan-African network FEMNET. As she points out, according to UN statistics, there were 226 million young African people aged between 15 and 24 in 2015: that is, 19 per cent of the global youth population (UN DESA 2015). By 2030, it is projected that the number of youth in Africa will have increased by 42 per cent, and it is expected to continue to grow throughout the remainder of the 21st century, more than doubling from current levels by 2055 (*ibid.*). These statistics attest to the potential power of young African women and men to change their societies. However, for young women to be able to play a full part in this work, gender inequality needs to end.

The connections between lack of choice for young women and a lifetime of poverty and underachievement are so clear that a whole sub-section of international development has grown up around the need to break the chain. Narratives perpetuate stereotypes of backward developing country communities. These are accompanied by slick and clever online marketing promises to turn small donations from benevolent Western givers into seemingly miraculous life changes for young rural women. Feminist critiques of such programming have highlighted the dangers of focusing narrowly on increasing the agency and choices of young women without a parallel focus on challenging the discrimination they face from key institutions that shape their lives (Chant and Sweetman 2012). As Catherine Nyambura writes in her chapter:

> These discourses are focused on the contribution young people, and women, may make to economic growth, rather than focusing on their rights and the gender and social justice issues that are relevant to them. These are questions that must be addressed if young people and women are to fulfil their potential for themselves, and for society.

In her chapter, Rosie Walters focuses on the UN Foundation's Girl Up campaign which has, as she discusses, received criticism by feminist scholars and activists for perpetuating patronising discourses that see women and girls in the global South as awaiting 'rescue' by the North. This chapter draws on focus group data with Girl Up club members in the UK, US and Malawi, to explore how they are adapting the aims of the campaign to better fit their own vision of empowerment. Cheeringly, she finds evidence of young women involved at both 'ends' of the programme subverting 'discourses of empowered Northern saviours and passive Southern girls in need of rescue'.

In her chapter, Ruvani Fonseka turns to another key area of development programming that aims to support the empowerment of young women, but which often falls short of that goal: education. She, too, emphasises the need for participants to have the freedom to identify the key issues that require addressing. Programming designed to empower young women needs to be designed by them if it is to fulfil its aim. Ruvani Fonseka's case study focuses on an NGO offering rural youth education and employment in the up-country tea plantations of Sri Lanka. The chapter shows an approach which enables participants in the project to take their activities in directions they see themselves as critical, and outlines the various strategies that youth within the programme use to challenge prevailing gender norms that limit their potential. These strategies include: postponing early marriage; identifying employment opportunities for young women; challenging gender segregation and gendered divisions of labour; and increasing the number of female leaders.

Feminist politics as a basis for development that works for young women

The voices of young feminists writing in this book – from research institutions, from development organisations, from feminist movements – reflect a backstory of continuous struggle over the past 40 years to keep the feminist politics in international development, in particular since the agenda of 'gender mainstreaming' was embraced by women's movements nearly 25 years ago at the UN Fourth World Conference on Women at Beijing in 1995. Gender mainstreaming was, as Catherine Nyambura's chapter highlights, originally an approach developed by feminists, drawing on an intersectional understanding of gender, race and class to explain poverty and marginalisation. All feminists working in development policy and practice will be familiar with the constant challenge it is to further this most radical of agendas.

Young feminists highlight the depoliticisation of the feminist perspectives on international development that informed the Beijing Platform for Action. We live in a world where feminist terms like 'empowerment' and 'agency' have been stripped of their radical power, where the language of 'gender' and 'diversity' has replaced 'women's rights'. Christine Homan, Divya Chandran, and Rita Lo share their experience of working in the Coalition of Feminists for Social Change (COFEM), a collective of feminists working in humanitarian and development settings on violence against women and girls (VAWG). They highlight the tendency to approach this most critical of political issues in ways that fail to understand the need for radical change to power relations.

This failure to hold on to the feminist politics in gender and development practice is particularly problematic at this time of global rollbacks in human rights. Despite a focus on 'women's rights' being a priority for most INGOs, many are partly or completely silent on the current crisis for women that the rising phenomena of fascisms and fundamentalisms represents. This reflects a bias towards focusing on economic aspects of gender inequality at the expense of political and social aspects, as well as depoliticising the economic issues by focusing on increasing the earnings of individual women within the existing grossly unequal global economic system. These feminist politics have formed the foundation of young women today fighting for gender justice worldwide.

In the next section, we explore some of the prominent themes and concerns that emerge from the young feminist realities featured in this book.

Young feminists in the fourth wave: priority issues and innovative strategies

In their chapter, Gopika Bashi and fellow authors from FRIDA | The Young Feminist Fund consider the ways in which every generation of feminists faces the particular challenges of a time and a location. As they note, every generation builds upon the work of previous generations. Their chapter, and other chapters here, present a snapshot of young feminisms at the time of writing – late 2018. These accounts show young feminists analysing their realities, pondering how they work and what they work on, and discussing their experience, in the current moment.

Much of what the young feminist authors in this book say about their priorities and the strategies they are trialling will resonate with older feminists (and with other young social justice activists involved in other rights movements). Fourth-wave feminism is notable for its renewed and more energised social and political activism around third-wave issues of intersectionality, trans inclusion and reproductive rights, and a re-politicisation of second-wave politics rejected by the third wave, including 'human trafficking, socialism, anti-capitalism, patriarchy, pornography, rape and rape culture, slut-shaming, body shaming, and sex positivity' (Zimmerman 2017, 57). A focus on intimate social relationships and the family is also a defining feature of young women's activism today (Kimball 2017).

Intersectionality as a means of analysis, and a basis for activism

The concept of intersectionality – the idea that different axes of oppression intersect – is central to young feminist organising. While prominent third-wave feminist thinkers such as bell hooks (1987), Audre Lord (1984) and Angela Davis (1981) have long criticised the exclusionary nature of mainstream feminism, this idea has become embedded in the discourses of much young women's activism (Schuster 2016). In gender and development policy and practice, the idea that it is not only gender, but race and class, that disadvantage women in poverty in the global South is familiar and well-accepted by the feminists who began the field, but it has never yet been fully accepted by international development – as argued earlier in this Introduction. Now may be the moment of reckoning, with the idea of intersectionality finally breaking through, driven by young feminist activists.

Tegan Zimmerman (2017) argues that intersectionality is the dominant framework being employed by fourth-wave feminists, and that this is most in evidence on social media, particularly Twitter. While hierarchies of power which favour the discourses of white, middle-class feminists are of course evident in fourth-wave feminism, online activism has highlighted the combined injustices of racism and sexism experienced by women of colour, and enabled them to hold white feminists to account on issues of racial privilege. Activist Mikki Kendall did this most notably with her Twitter hashtag #SolidarityIsForWhiteWomen in 2013, which has been the foundation of much debate on mainstream feminist spaces which exclude marginalised voices.

Social media reflects how important intersectionality is to fourth-wave feminism: the phenomenon of 'privilege checking' draws on feminist concepts of reflexivity and positionality, reminding people that they are not able to speak on behalf of others (Munro 2013), and is dominant in social media discourses. The embedding of intersectionality is also evident in the offline sphere, with research into young feminist movements by FRIDA and the Association for Women's Rights in Development (AWID) (2016, 3) finding that young feminist organisations across the globe represent diverse feminist identities and social movements. These included 'youth, climate justice, sex workers, LGBTQI, indigenous, sexual reproductive rights, grassroots women, human rights defenders, health and disability rights'. Young feminists are integrated within and organising across these diverse movements in an intersectional way, both within and between countries.

Sexualities, gender identities and intimate relations

Research by Anna-Britt Coe (2015) in Ecuador and Peru found that while youth activists mobilised around the same issues of gender-based violence and sexual and reproductive rights as 'professionalized adult feminists'[6], there was a stronger focus on intimate relationships and gender dynamics in the family and household sphere.

Sexual rights – including trans rights and the inclusion of sexual minorities – are central to young feminist discourses. Using social media, fourth-wave feminists are popularising discussions on sex, gender identity, and the fluidity of gender binaries, with vocabulary such as 'cis' (denoting people whose gender and sexual identities align) and TERF (trans-exclusionary radical feminist) becoming common parlance in these spheres (Munro 2013). Young feminist activists across the world are using the new opportunities digital offers for communicating and campaigning.

In their chapter, Isabel Marler, Daniela Marin Platero, and Felogene Anumo draw on their work for the advocacy and campaigning organisation AWID to highlight current threats to young women, girls, and gender-non-conforming people. In 2016 research, FRIDA and AWID (2016) identified young feminists' priority issues as gender-based violence, sexual reproductive health and rights, LGBTQI and political and economic empowerment for women. This chapter draws on case studies from two contexts: Kenya, where young feminists are organising to protect and advance the rights of LGBTQI+ people, and Brazil, where young Afro-Brazilian feminists are asserting their religious rights in a context of racism, evangelical fundamentalism, and a political shift to the right. Offering support and solidarity to women's rights defenders and feminist organisations has never been more important, and international development actors could play a vital role.

Online spaces: activism in a digital world

A powerful driver of young feminist activism currently is the opportunity to engage online with issues of political, social and economic justice – which can stay as a single retweet, or continue into engagement over days, weeks or months with a movement mobilising around a key issue of concern. Millions of young women are encountering feminist politics in this way. Many young women are coming into activism as a result of encountering others on social media, and movements evolve organically from these encounters. Some commentators have emphasised that fourth-wave activism is not solely in the online sphere; rather, it is 'an alliance between technology, social networks, and people on the streets', constantly oscillating between the web and the street to take full advantage of both domains (Alcaraz 2017).

Gender & Development journal published an issue on ICTs in July 2018 in which young feminist experiences of using online to counter these new and evolving forms of VAWG was a major focus. It is clear that online has dramatically changed activism. Indeed, some commentators have argued that the internet is what actually distinguishes third-wave from fourth-wave feminism, with some theorists questioning whether there are clear ideological differences between the two waves, or whether the fourth wave is rather defined by its medium (Zimmerman 2017). Young women activists today are able to share ideas and information, discuss political ideas, and mobilise for collective action in ways that were unfeasible for previous generations (Schuster 2013).

At a moment where space for dissenting – and progressive – voices is closing in many contexts, and women promoting feminist ideals are often particularly demonised and hounded, online represents an alternative space which, at best, can enable women to raise their voices comparatively safely. For Tegan Zimmerman (2017, 56), this is one of the defining ideological features of the fourth wave: 'it reaches and connects mass audiences in rapid speed and, in doing so, it collapses the binary between the online and the offline to the extent that the online and offline are not, and perhaps never were, separate spheres'.

Reclaiming participation as a radical concept

Recently, proponents of youth rights have called for a 'youth-centred' approach (IPPF 2016), whereby young people are at the heart of any initiatives which affect them, shaping programmes and interventions from their own perspectives to ensure that they are relevant, inclusive and effective. The 'ladder of participation' developed by Roger Hart (1992) has formed the theoretical basis of development practice on youth participation. Child and youth engagement may remain as 'non-participation' on the three bottom rungs – 'manipulation', 'decoration' and 'tokenism' – when they are seen through an instrumentalist lens. The top three rungs of Hart's ladder denote young people leading and initiating action, and sharing decision-making with adults as partners and as agents of change.

However, the tendency of international development to depoliticise concepts which start out as radical ideas has been noted above. While participation and empowerment were terms picked up readily by international development organisations of all kinds in the 1990s, they morphed to become 'buzzwords and fuzzwords' (Cornwall 2010), and lost their political edge. Many theorists note the discrepancy between the rhetoric of women's empowerment through participation, and the practice of many mainstream NGOs which 'enlist people in pre-determined ventures and secure their compliance with pre-shaped development agendas' (Cornwall 2003, 1327). But young feminist organisations have been revisiting and reclaiming the radicalism of participatory principles, leading through consensus decision-making models to ensure that youth experience is at the forefront of decisions, and that marginalised young women's voices are heard (FRIDA and AWID 2016).

Rethinking leadership and organisational form

A major critique of international development currently is its failure to challenge profound inequalities that were created in the eras of conquest and colonialism. During the 1970s, a generation of NGOs informed by left-wing politics critiqued mainstream development for rolling out a top-down, technical model of development that failed to address the true causes of poverty in the 'Third World'. In the current era, young feminists are highlighting what they see as a slow but steady drift away from those radical politics on the part of international NGOs. In their chapter, Devi Leiper O'Malley and Ruby Johnson discuss this phenomenon. They show how their own funding organisation, FRIDA, is pioneering new ways of working and thinking about its role, to push back against this tide. Theirs is a fascinating and important account of a real alternative to mainstream international development visions and processes.

Among other things, they share their experience in FRIDA of using the possibilities of online to realise a new kind of organisation that reflects feminist commitment to equalities and rejects hierarchies and 'power-over', to the extent that FRIDA's leadership model itself is collaborative and its 'office' has no physical location, rather existing in virtual space to enable access for all.

As Devi Leiper O'Malley and Ruby Johnson point out, young feminists are also recognising the power and agility that can sometimes be found in remaining outside formal institutional spaces. Unlike more established women's rights organisations, young feminist activists are often not registered, and operate in non-formalised spaces, for a variety of reasons. These can include a desire to distinguish themselves from 'professionalised' feminists operating in mainstream spaces, without the radical agenda or the intersectional perspectives that are important to them. Young feminist movements may not want to be registered so that they can operate outside of monitored spheres, or they may be excluded by expensive or overly administrative processes. Many young feminist groups favour informal or collective structures, which allow them to work on specific campaigns and issues when these arise, while remaining comparatively dormant at other times.

Challenges faced by young feminists

Chapters here also focus on the challenges faced by young feminists currently. We focus on two most critical challenges here.

Feminist human rights defenders in a hostile world

As well as sexual abuse and harassment at the forefront of the #MeToo and #AidToo revelations, targeting and persecution by governments is a reality for many young activists campaigning on feminist issues which challenge vested interests, with FRIDA and AWID (2016) finding that more than half of survey respondents regularly feel unsafe or threatened because of the work they do.

Those advocating on issues such as gender equality, sexual and reproductive health rights, and gender-based violence often face backlash from religious and political leaders, from conservative members of their communities, or from partners and family members. Young LGBT people are also experiencing conservatism and violence in countries with oppression of homosexuality and a rejection of gender binaries (FRIDA and AWID 2016; Coe 2015). And even those involved in less obviously political initiatives, such as young women's employment projects, may experience violence or threats to their well-being as increased income, mobility or social standing challenge existing power dynamics and gender roles.

In this book, the reality of risk and danger is present throughout the accounts of young feminist activism in different locations throughout the world. In their chapter, Poe Ei Phyu, Agatha Ma, and Catriona Knapman discuss the experiences of women activists in Myanmar, where women experience a range of gender- and age-related factors that constrain their political participation in a context where much is currently being made of civil society space opening up, yet young women's participation is still highly contested. Their respondents spoke of regular harassment focusing on their bodies and behaviour, from male activists as well as political opponents and members of the public. Another chapter, by Esther Moraes and Vinita Sahasranaman, draws on their first-hand experience gained in the YP Foundation in India. Here, too, young women are 'still fighting to be seen as political entities'.

Safety is a particular concern in online spaces, where content is harder to monitor and impossible to withdraw once in the public sphere – and where much young feminist activism takes place. Technology-based violence against women and girls is a growing problem for women who write, work, contribute and campaign in online spaces. Cyberstalking, online harassment and trolling are daily realities for young feminist activists, with much abuse sexualised to discourage their participation in the digital sphere – including comments on women's appearance, rape threats, and the distribution of private and sexual images without consent (JASS 2015).

Funding young feminist agendas

Devi Leiper O'Malley and Ruby Johnson's chapter, first mentioned earlier, also focuses on another key issue for many young feminist organisations: how to find funding for their activism. Accepting money from mainstream development funders can result in small local organisations delivering programming developed thousands of miles away, which does not match women's own agendas (Mannell 2012). To stay true to their grassroots constituencies and their desire to challenge inequalities of race and class as well as gender, feminist organisations face a dilemma when they look for the resourcing they need.

As a result of a struggle for funding and reluctance to sell out or dilute their agendas, young feminist organisations typically have very low incomes, even compared to women's rights organisations. They often rely on diverse funding streams to finance their campaigns, or use umbrella movements to access income and capacity-building opportunities (FRIDA and AWID 2016). FRIDA is a funder that seeks to respond to young feminist organisations in ways that live out its values. Devi Leiper O'Malley and Ruby Johnson's chapter offers lessons from FRIDA's experience of funding small feminist organisations. They focus in particular on approaches to resource mobilisation focused on autonomous organising, strong anti-capitalist politics, volunteer models, and self-generated income, and on the other hand the reality of the unequal distribution of the resources and that activists need a living wage to survive and sustain their work.

These new ways of working and the radical rejection of current development they reflect are challenging reading for development policymakers and practitioners. The critiques mounted by young social justice activists of mainstream international development are stringent, and sometimes devastating. As Devi Leiper O'Malley and Ruby Johnson discuss in their chapter, INGOs are seen by young feminists as having lost their way, morphing from the relatively small, rights-based organisations of the 1970s and 1980s into enormous organisations which have become part of the very system of inequality that they originally challenged. Until this critique is heeded, a focus on gender justice or youth rights will not result in programming that responds to the needs and interests of young women.

Conclusion

Development processes must ensure 'appropriate, meaningful and authentic' participation for youth (Viviers and Lombard 2013, 8). But as we have argued here, youth rights activism has frequently been gender-blind. The developing thinking about youth participation urgently needs to link up to feminist analysis of development. Young women's movements require support to survive and thrive, offering a model of political, intersectional work to guide and re-politicise international development. Young feminists are challenging international development policymakers and practitioners, national governments, and development donors of all kinds to recognise their right to shape development itself.

Notes

1. The phrase #MeToo was originally coined by activist Tarana Burke as far back as 2006 to promote 'empowerment through empathy' among women and girls – particularly those of colour – who had experienced sexual abuse (Ohlheiser 2017). It was popularised by actress Alyssa Milano, who in late 2017 encouraged survivors to tweet #MeToo, and was joined by other Hollywood survivors of sexual assault, later spawning the #TimesUp movement.
2. Intersectionality refers to a political analysis of the reasons for particular individuals to be excluded and marginalised from power, arising from multiple systems of discrimination and oppression including, critically, gender, race, and class (Crenshaw 1989). As a field, gender and development (GAD) draws on a similar analysis coming up from the experience of poor women in the global South (Sen and Grown 1987).
3. For more information and analysis from a feminist perspective of Agenda 2030, the SDGs and 'Leave No-one Behind', see Gender & Development 21(1), The Sustainable Development Goals.

4. This point was made by youth activist Heena Qamar, of First Aid Africa, at the 2018 Scottish International Development Alliance annual conference, during a panel discussion on how young people can use the SDGS to campaign for the change that they want to see.

5. Ironically, the world's current youth generation – often called Generation Y or Millennials – are often demonised in public discussions as selfish, consumerist and apathetic and such ageist prejudices against the young are nothing new for humanity. Generation Y and the Millennials are terms used to refer to people born between 1980 and 2000. They are part of a series of characterisations of 'generational demographic cohorts'. They are generalisations that reflect biases from globalised, largely affluent (and heavily Western-influenced) cultures, at odds with the realities worldwide of vibrant activism in this generation.

6. Coe (2015, 889) describes 'professionalized adult feminism' as a sector of women's movements deriving from middle-class, educated women in the 1970s in Ecuador and Peru, which was the first to self-identify as feminist in contemporary history. Professionalisation began in the 1980s to provide training and support to low-income women's groups, further developing in the 1990s when adopting policy advocacy to effect legal changes. These feminists have provided gender training to mobilise a younger generation of activists in the new millennium.

Notes on the editors

Imogen Davies is Gender Lead for CARE Deutschland. She was previously Global Adviser on Youth, Gender and Active Citizenship at Oxfam GB.

   Caroline Sweetman was previously Editor of *Gender & Development*.

References

African Union Commission (2006) African Youth Charter, Addis Ababa: African Union Commission, http://www.un.org/en/africa/osaa/pdf/au/african_youth_charter_2006.pdf (last checked 30 August 2018)

Alcaraz, Maria Florencia (2017) '#NiUnaMenos: Policitising the Use of Technologies', *GenderIT.Org*, 4 September, https://www.genderit.org/feminist-talk/special-edition-niunamenos-politicising-use-technologies (last checked 30 August 2018)

Chant, Sylvia and Caroline Sweetman (2012) 'Fixing Women or fixing The World? "Smart Economics", Efficiency Approaches, and Gender Equality in Development', *Gender & Development* 20(3): 517–29, https://policy-practice.oxfam.org.uk/publications/fixing-women-or-fixing-the-world-smart-economics-efficiency-approaches-and-gend-251931 (last checked 30 August 2018)

Cheney, Kristen E. (2011) 'Children as Ethnographers: Reflections on the Importance of Participatory Research in Assessing Orphans' Needs', *Childhood* 18(2): 166–79

CIA (2018) 'The World Fact Book', https://www.cia.gov/library/publications/resources/the-world-factbook/ (last checked 30 August 2018)

Coe, Anna-Britt (2015) '"I Am Not Just a Feminist Eight Hours A Day": Youth Gender Justice Activism in Ecuador and Peru', *Gender & Society* 29(6): 888–913

Cornwall, Andrea (2003) 'Whose Voices? Whose Choices? Reflections on Gender and Participatory Development', *World Development* (31): 1325–42

Cornwall, Andrea (2010) 'Introductory overview' in Cornwall, A. and Eade, D. (eds), *Deconstructing Development Discourse: Buzzwords and Fuzzwords*, Rugby, UK: Practical Action Publishing

Crenshaw, Kimberle (1989) 'Demarginalizing the Intersection of Race and Sex: A Black Feminist Critique of Antidiscrimination Doctrine, Feminist Theory and Antiracist Politics', *University of Chicago Legal Forum* 1989(1): 139–67

Davis, Angela Y. (1981) *Women, Race & Class*, New York: Random House

DFID (2016) 'Putting Young People at the Heart of Development: The Department for International Development's Youth Agenda', London: UK Department for International Development, https://www.gov.uk/ government/publications/dfids-youth-agenda-putting-young-people-at-the-heart-of- development (last checked 30 August 2018)

FRIDA | The Young Feminist Fund and the Association for Women's Rights in Development (AWID) (2016) *Brave, Creative, Resilient: The Global State of Young Feminist Organizing*, Toronto: FRIDA and AWID, https://www.awid. org/sites/default/files/atoms/files/frida-awid_field-report_final_web_issuu. pdf (last checked 30 August 2018)

Hart, Roger A. (1992) *Children's Participation: From Tokenism to Citizenship*, Innocenti Essays No. 4, Florence: UNICEF

hooks, bell (1987) *Ain't I a Woman: Black Women and Feminism*, London: Pluto Press

Ighobor, Kingsley (2013) 'Africa's Youth: A 'Ticking Time Bomb or an Opportunity?', *Africa Renewal*, May, https://www.un.org/africarenewal/ magazine/may-2013/africa%E2%80%99s-youth-%E2%80%9Cticking-time-bomb%E2%80%9D-or-opportunity (last checked 30 August 2018)

International Planned Parenthood Federation (2016) *Young at Heart: How to be Youth-centred in the 21st Century. An Introduction*, London: IPPF, https://www. ippf.org/sites/default/files/ippf_youngatheart_english.pdf (last checked 30 August 2018)

Just Associates (JASS) (2015) *ICTs for Feminist Movement Building Toolkit*, Washington, DC: JASS, https://justassociates.org/en/resources/icts-feminist-movement-building-activist-toolkit (last checked 30 August 2018)

Kimball, Gayle (2017) *Brave: Young Women's Global Revolution*, Volume 1: Global Themes; Volume 2: Regional Activism, Chico, CA: Equality Press

Lorde, Audre (1984) 'The Master's Tools Will Never Dismantle the Master's House', in Audre Lorde, *Sister Outsider: Essays and Speeches*, Berkeley, CA: Crossing Press, 110–14

Mannell, Jenevieve, (2012) '"It's Just Been Such a Horrible Experience": Perceptions Of Gender Main-Streaming By Practitioners in South African Organisations', *Gender & Development* 20(3): 423–34

Molyneux, Maxine (1985) 'Mobilization Without Emancipation? Women's Interests, the State, and Revolution in Nicaragua', *Feminist Studies* 11(2): 227–54

Munro, Ealasaid (2013) 'Feminism: A Fourth Wave?', *Political Insight* 4(2): 22–5

Ohlheiser, Abby (2017) 'The Woman Behind "Me Too" Knew the Power of the Phrase When She Created it – 10 Years Ago', *The Washington Post*, 19 October, https://www.washingtonpost.com/news/the-intersect/wp/2017/10/19/the-woman-behind-me-too-knew-the-power-of-the-phrase-when-she-created-it-10-years-ago (last checked 30 August 2018)

Pereznieto, Paola and James Hamilton Harding (2013) 'Youth and International Development Policy: The Case for Investing in Young People', ODI Project Briefing No. 80, London: Overseas Development Institute

Restless Development (2015) 'Peak Youth', *Restless Development*, 12 June, http://restlessdevelopment.org/news/2015/06/12/peak-youth (last checked 30 August 2018)

Schuster, Julia (2013) 'Invisible Feminists? Social Media and Young Women's Political Participation', *Political Science* 65(1): 8–24

Schuster, Julia (2016) 'Intersectional Expectations: Young Feminists' Perceived Failure at Dealing with Differences and Their Retreat to Individualism', *Women's Studies International Forum*, 58: 1–8

UN (2018) 'Youth2030: UN SG Launches Bold New Strategy for Young People "To Lead"', *United Nations Youth*, 25 September, https://www.un.org/development/desa/youth/news/2018/09/youth2030/ (last checked 30 August 2018)

UN DESA (2015) 'Population Facts 2015/1, May: Youth Population Trends and Sustainable Development', New York: UN Department of Economic and Social Affairs, Population Division

UNFPA (2014) *State of the World's Population 2014, The Power of 1.8 Billion: Adolescents, Youth and the Transformation of the Future*, New York: United Nations Population Fund

USAID (2012) *Youth in Development: Realizing the Demographic Opportunity*, Washington, DC: US Agency for International Development

Viviers, Andries and Antoinette Lombard (2013) 'The Ethics of Children's Participation: Fundamental to Children's Rights Realization in Africa, *International Social Work* 56(1): 7–21

Zimmerman, Tegan (2017) '#Intersectionality: The Fourth Wave Feminist Twitter Community', *Atlantis* 38(1): 54–70

CHAPTER 2

Reclaim, resist, reframe: re-imagining feminist movements in the 2010s

Esther Moraes and Vinita Sahasranaman

Abstract

The study analyses the intersection of youth movements and feminist movements that has emerged in India since the 2010s. Focusing on five movements and campaigns, the study analyses the commonalities across them in terms of their mobilisation, methods of protest, and their goals. With their sites of mobilisation spanning online and offline spaces, these movements have had significant impact on public discourse on women's rights and bodily autonomy, and systemic inequality and discrimination against women in university spaces. The study argues that we are currently seeing the real-time development of a wave of young feminist movements in India that is distinct in its methods and spaces of mobilisation, protest strategies, and membership, and has rapidly grown from feminism 'lite' into one that is highly political and conceptually nuanced in the face of significant backlash from oppositional forces as well as potential supporters.

Keywords: Feminist; youth; movement; India

Introduction

The YP Foundation[1] is a youth-led and -run organisation founded in 2002, and aims to raise the political consciousness and promote the feminist leadership of young women and young people. The YP Foundation is built on a belief that for young people to develop their own perspectives on social justice issues, the creation of safe, analytical spaces for analysis is essential. These spaces enable individuals to think through complex social problems, and unravel – for themselves – the intersecting manner in which privilege and discrimination manifest. The YP Foundation also aims to advance the rights of young women, girls, and other marginalised adolescents in the areas of health, governance, and education.

In this chapter, we reflect on the experience of young feminist activism in India, focusing in particular on five examples from 2010 to 2017. The primary author and researcher for this chapter is Esther Moraes. She works on movement-building and feminist leadership within the organisation alongside the secondary researcher, Vinita Sahasranaman, who was also at The YP Foundation until 2017. Both of us have been strongly involved in feminist movements in university spaces and outside, and some of the insights in this chapter come from this wider experience.

The context and content of youth activism in India

In the 15 years since The YP Foundation came into being, the context in which youth activism is taking place has changed, and so have the strategies. Right now, in 2017, we realise that young people in India (and elsewhere) receive and experience political apprenticeship[2] in diverse ways and spaces, even outside the university structure.

College campuses have traditionally been the first space within which young people rally around political issues, and India has a rich tradition of student activism (Altbach 1968). Due to a strong wave of conservatism that is sweeping across educational institutions affecting students' rights, experiences of education, and daily lives on campus, in a range of ways, there has been a significant resurgence in student activism. College campuses in India have thus exploded as sites of protest on a number of issues, such as the systemic discrimination faced by Dalit students (the protest in response to Rohith Vemula's death, 2016[3]) and the clampdown on free speech in the name of patriotism (#istandwithjnu, 2016–2017[4]), but also issues such as sexual harassment (#hokkolorob in 2015) and the control of women's mobility in the guise of 'safety' (Pinjra Tod in 2015). The emergence and widespread acceptance of women's rights-focused student initiatives is new and has developed over the last eight years.

Outside universities, young people, and especially young women, are still fighting to be seen as political entities (Matiyani 2017). Consequently, while antecedents of student activism have nurtured the emergent feminist politics in campus spaces, young feminist activists outside university spaces continue to fight for legitimacy, and face significant resistance and backlash, even while they influence change in perspectives.

A key focus for many of these initiatives led by young women is the question of bodily autonomy, love, and desire. Mostly organised initially via Facebook, many of them – e.g. the Pink Chaddi Campaign and the Society of Painted and Dented Ladies, #happytobleed, Pinjra Tod, #iwillgoout, and most recently, #MeToo and the LoSHA[5] – have gone viral and transformed public discourse around these issues. They are also causing change within feminist discourse, sometimes even disrupting it and causing important internal debates (Kapur 2012).

Young people, and especially young women, are thus addressing similar issues inside and outside universities – that is, young people's experience of marginalisation due to gender or sexuality, shaped by different systems of discrimination and differentiation.

This kind of analysis and the activism arising from it is referred to as 'intersectionality' (Crenshaw 1994). As we show in this chapter, young activists are drawing on their understandings of intersectionality as a political struggle and also as a means of analysing power and inequalities. They are fundamentally calling for a reshaping of the social and material conditions under which they live. They aim to equalise power shared by young people and authority figures, or gatekeepers, in their lives.

Another important development in youth activism in the 2010s is the use of online spaces as important sites for connecting, networking, and mobilising. Many youth-led movements, and especially young feminist initiatives, have expanded and developed using the potential the online world offers for connecting, networking, and mobilising. Initial online engagement on political issues, often via social media, has translated into increased mobilisation of women and other young people on-ground. They have developed connections across and between universities, as well as connecting with non-university-based movements and initiatives.[6]

Looking at these developments online and on-ground, we can see that there is a wave of active young people – across identities including gender, class, religion, and sexual orientation – using innovative methods to mobilise around issues that are at the core of feminist and social justice movements. More importantly, they are effecting real social and behavioural change, even as they face continuous resistance from authorities of all kinds (both outside movement spaces, as well as within them).

While these kinds of initiatives are certainly not entirely new or 'firsts', given the rich history of social movements in India, they do indicate that we are in an especially interesting time, when strategies and rules of agitation[7] are witnessing some renewal (Kapur 2012). They exemplify new ways in which young women, fed up with the increasing policing and regulation of their mobility, expressions, relationships, and desires are mobilising, collectivising, and agitating. Despite these changes, there are very few articles or documents that put forth a collective analysis of them and explore whether a young feminist movement exists in India. In documenting and analysing these movements, then, one of the aims of this study is to contribute to our current understanding of feminisms and feminist activisms.

Methodology and scope

We conducted a broad-based review of literature on youth activism taking place between 2010 and early 2017. Our review took place between August 2016 and January 2017. It included academic writing, but also media sources, as well as online informal writing on social media. This literature review defined the scope of a mapping study and informed the selection of five initiatives that we have highlighted and analysed in granular detail below.

We also draw here on the insights of activists involved in many different initiatives. These insights came from a range of conversations and discussions, and we attribute various points to particular individuals in the sections below. Where these are named, they have given permission for these to be used, and we state when and where they were interviewed. Others are anonymous. While our primary focus was on organisers or participants in these move-ments, we also included, within the scope of our research, information and views of individuals who are involved in political mobilising and youth activ-ism across movements, and/or have chronicled many of these movements and have online platforms that provide a voice to these movements. We also spoke to those who are well known for their contributions to the women's rights movement and to feminist perspectives across all fields (including law and film). They were involved in initiatives around gender and sexuality in the 1970s to 1990s, and their reflections have also shaped the structure of this study, as have many other initiatives, too numerous to mention in this short chapter.

A snapshot of five movements

The initiatives in this section offer a powerful narrative of how student movements – and the young feminist movements they intersect with – have furthered transformative social change.

#hokkolorob

#hokkolorob began as a student body response to Jadavpur University's treat-ment of a sexual harassment complaint (Ghoshal 2014). Jadavpur University is a state university located in Kolkata, West Bengal. While this could have remained an internal issue had it been addressed as per process, it turned into a national movement with global support against sexual harassment and victim-blaming on university campuses (interview with Devjyot Ghoshal, New Delhi, December 2016).

This escalation of the issue occurred because the university and state response to the sexual harassment incident exacerbated a more generalised frustration and anger that had been building in West Bengal, and particularly Kolkata, around a political transition process, from the CPM (Communist Party of India – Marxist) to TMC (Trinamool Congress) (interview with Devjyot). However, despite this widening of participation and focus, the sex-ual harassment case and the subsequent sexual assault that the students faced in the protests ultimately stayed central to the movement (*ibid.*).

Offline, #hokkolorob looked similar to student movements that preceded it – there was a gradual escalation in the protesters' activities, from peaceful meetings, to sit-ins, to the *gherao* (surrounding the premises thus blocking entrance and exit), and eventually the protest rallies which took to the streets. What was different with #hokkolorob was how it took off online, leading to global coverage and support (Chhinkwani 2014). Online and offline mobilising quickly became diffcult to separate, with both feeding into each other – those who were at 'ground zero' continuously contributed to online updates, while online mobilising sustained the energy among the students and in the university. Students and participants across the world shared images of the events, keeping up the momentum of the movement (as one respondent said, 'the revolution begins with a meme').

Even financially, #hokkolorob stayed independent of all political parties, with all of its funding acquired from participants in the form of voluntary donations, which were collected in boxes at the protests and rallies (*ibid.*). The movement itself died down after the Vice-Chancellor was removed from his position in January 2015 at the behest of the combined efforts of students on hunger strike, the parents of the students, and Jadavpur University teachers.

Why Loiter

Begun as an experiment in 2014, Why Loiter has now grown into a movement around the same issues as the Besharmi Morchha.[8] Unlike the latter, however, Why Loiter developed an online presence gradually. It was begun after three young women were inspired by the book *Why Loiter? Women and Risk on the Streets of Mumbai* (Phadke *et al.* 2011) to rethink their understanding of safety in the city. Young women stepped out of their houses and into public spaces without books, headphones, or another person to shield them from public scrutiny (interview with Neha Singh, New Delhi, December 2016). The movement encourages women to get into public spaces, like the city's roads, specifically to 'occupy' the space and thus question what prevents them from doing this on a regular basis (*ibid.*). Online, at http://whyloiter.blogspot.com, the group chronicles their episodes of loitering and the experiences of the loiterers.

Over the last three years, Why Loiter has become a movement, a 'collection of personal mini-revolutions' (*ibid.*), and a space to explore gender identity. It has also made links with similar collectives from other cities in India, including Blank Noise, and often runs joint events on occupying public space and street harassment (*ibid.*).

#HappytoBleed

#HappytoBleed was a viral campaign for women's rights, the breaking of menstrual taboos, and religious discrimination against women. It was a response to a re-affirmation of an archaic mandate at the Sabarimala Ayyappa temple in Kerala, which disallows women between the ages of 10 and 50 from entering the temple premises because they are understood to be 'impure'. The President of the Board of the temple refused to change this mandate, stating that he would only do so if he had a machine that could scan women to ensure that they were not menstruating (*International Business Times* 2015). This statement drew angry reactions from many women across the country, but one young woman, Nikita Azad, wrote an open letter that strongly critiqued the temple mandates (Azad 2015). In a matter of hours, other young women began registering their support for the letter through the hashtag #happytobleed, with pictures of themselves with sanitary products. It went viral within two days, exploding the stigma associated with menstruation and bringing it into the public sphere. Within a few months, a series of campaigns around menstrual taboos emerged, leading to 2015 being widely described as the 'year of menstruation' (Shastry 2016). Happy to Bleed has developed into a field-based research study on menstrual taboos in Punjab (interview with Nikita Azad, New Delhi, October 2016).

Pinjra Tod (break the cage)

Pinjra Tod emerged in response to Jamia Milia Islamia University, Delhi, cancelling nightouts (a fixed number of nights a student is allowed to stay outside the hostel) for female students in July 2015. At a march organised in response, a group of individuals from various colleges and institutions in Delhi came together to write and publish collectively an open letter to the Delhi Commission of Women. This letter pointed out the issues that female university students, particularly those living on campus, face on a regular basis, including moral policing (defined in the last section), higher-priced accommodation, shorter curfews, and lack of redress of sexual harassment complaints.

By September 2015, Pinjra Tod had developed a significant online presence (Mogul 2015). Its Facebook page became an important chronicle of university women's experience of hostels and curfews, and it was through this that they connected with allies and other women living in hostels in Delhi. This Facebook page also chronicled the movement's offline mobilising events. The impact of Pinjra Tod was increasingly felt as graffiti and posters began showing up on college campuses across Delhi. Student parties across universities began to show support for their cause, and an increasing number of female students were posting on the Facebook page their experiences of gender-based discrimination in student hostels. As one of our interviewees said, the Facebook page eventually developed into a strong offline collective of young women from universities across Delhi, who advocated for equality in educational institutions.

Since its inception, Pinjra Tod has rapidly evolved geographically. It is active across the country, with significant effect. Protests, sit-ins, and campaigns emerged in Punjab, Benaras, and Kerala, across universities and colleges of varying scale, where women have raised their voices against systemic gender discrimination and demanded their right to freedom on campus (Borpujari 2016). Pinjra Tod now refers to itself as an autonomous women's collective (interview with Pinjra Tod respondent, New Delhi, February 2017) which is spread across the country. The collective continues to campaign for the abolition of unequal curfews and the overall unequal treatment of men and women in the university space. In the analysis that inspires and informs its activism, Pinjra Tod has evolved into a movement against societal institutions through which patriarchy operates. These include the notion of the family, the relationship between brothers and sisters and parents, and the infantilisation of women that occurs in educational institutions.

Pinjra Tod has also grown in terms of its reach and impact. It has developed very strong connections with other student groups across Delhi and consciously reaches out to student movements across the country through public statements and displays of support. They have formed links with workers' movements through developing online chronicles of movement history (Pinjra Tod 2016), and have also made links with issue-specific or location-specific collectives or through membership in these collectives. A respondent from Pinjra Tod asserted that members are part of, or connected to, political student groups like Collective in Jawaharlal Nehru University (JNU), and Saheli, a decades-old women's group. They have also actively made connections with workers' movements and strikes by writing articles that highlight women's workers' strikes across the country (*ibid.*), and the 2017 Maruti Suzuki Workers' Strike (Venkat *et al.* 2017).

Occupy UGC

While Occupy UGC is not a movement that centred on issues of gender or sexuality, it is unique in the feminist frameworks and analysis that it espoused. It was an important moment when a coalition was formed between a range of groups. Occupy UGC erupted in late 2015 in response to a statement by India's University Grants Commission about a drastic reduction in the number of fellowships available for MPhil and PhD students. This decision would adversely impact over 35,000 students, a very serious issue since the stipend is their primary source of sustenance (Pisharoty 2016). In addition, the stipends in question (Rs 5,000 for MPhil students and Rs 8,000 for Doctorates; Shankar 2015) are laughably small, barely covering their cost of living (Qazi 2017). Students protested against this by 'occupying' the space in front of the UGC office for over three months between October 2015 and January 2016. As of the writing of this study, there continues to be a lack of clarity around the issue and the fear of losing UGC funding continues to plague university campuses across India, as the steady move towards privatising education persists (Pisharoty 2016).

While the Occupy demonstrations were largely housed at UGC premises in New Delhi, the scope of the protests was not limited to the issues above, or targeted only at UGC. Rather, activists were critiquing a wider concern: the government's move to privatise education (a move that the current regime has continued from the previous government). Consequently, the Occupy group also orchestrated demonstrations against India's position within the World Trade Organization on privatising education.[9]

As student voices continued to be ignored, protesters persisted in occupying the space in front of the UGC buildings. Resistance to the protesters continuously escalated as well – one of our respondents told us that police officials began preventing them from ever leaving the space – even to relieve themselves (interview with Sayan Chaudhuri, New Delhi, January 2017). When a large-scale march to Parliament was held, physical violence, water cannons, and tear gas shells were deployed to keep the students at bay (Rahul 2015). The continual pressure caused the Ministry of Human Resource Development minister to announce on social media that the fellowships would continue; however, no official announcement or statement was released (Pisharoty 2015). While the movement dissipated in three months, many felt the impact on student mobilising, which was the coming together of multiple student groups (both political and otherwise) with diverse focus areas (interview with Sayan Chaudhuri).

Those who were part of the Occupy UGC movement strove to be as intersectional in their understanding of the issues as possible, pointing out how the UGC resolution would affect people from different genders, socio-economic classes, and other marginalised groups (*ibid.*). Occupy UGC brought together groups from across universities and campuses, allowing trans-university groups, like Pinjra Tod, to come together over common agendas, and transforming university-specific groups into issue-specific pressure groups. Other student groups that were part of Occupy UGC include two from JNU in New Delhi: BAPSA (Birsa Ambedkar Phule Students' Association, a group whose primary focus is minority issues – caste, gender, or sexual orientation) on campus, and YFDA (Youth Forum for Welfare and Discussion Activities, which describes itself on its Facebook page as a non-political group for Muslim students in JNU).

While the Occupy UGC protest did not centre only on issues related to gender and sexuality, it is a pertinent example of the power of student movements in how they sharpen their political analyses. Even though the issue at hand that initially catalysed Occupy UGC was the decision around stipends, Occupy UGC went on to delve deep into questions of privilege and discrimination within education. The movement reflected upon the divides amongst the student community on the lines of gender, caste, class, and other indices. It asked pertinent questions on how students from marginalised communities face systemic oppression in educational institutions.

Across the movements studied, several interesting commonalities and analyses emerge for us, in terms of what kind of issues that were/are raised; the methods of mobilisation and strategies of protest; and the ways in which these challenge and often subvert existing discourse, stereotypes, and mind-sets. We summarise some of these observations in the sections below.

Defining boundaries and reconceptualising concepts: leadership and membership

The potential that online spaces offers to grow movements is very important when understanding today's campaigns and movements and their trajectories from inception, which are typically very fast-growing, morphing from a few like-minded individuals encountering each other and sharing an opinion, to something involving tens, hundreds, or thousands of people.

In today's campaigns and movements, digital spaces – specifically for most of them, a Facebook page – serves as a first port of call for individuals interested in their cause and activism. The page serves as an important chronicle of all offline and online events, allowing a narrative to emerge about the movement's beginnings and the evolution of its own positions and analyses of issues. This has implications for ideas of leadership and membership familiar to earlier generations of activists.

Leadership

When Hokkolorob exploded, the protest coalesced around '#hokkolorob' rather than specific leaders or political groups. The Hokkolorob Facebook page was, in fact, not run by students at Jadavpur University – it was created by a group of individuals who were remotely engaging with the news from Jadavpur University (Chhinkwani 2014). Social media-led activism encourages decentralised leadership – or perhaps more properly challenges the whole notion of leadership. For many feminists and social justice advocates, this is a positive, helping with a carefully maintained lack of hierarchy, undermining ideas of 'power over' which are often seen by feminists as negative (Rowlands 1995). Pinjra Tod does have a distinction between those who founded the group and those who joined after, but this is primarily for logistical purposes (interview, February 2017). In Why Loiter, too, there is a 'leader' who frequently organises the loitering events and meetings; but other members can take up this responsibility and are encouraged to do so (interview with Neha).

This is clearly a break from traditional political activism in India where movements have had spokespersons, and/or clearly identified leaders, who are recognised outside the movement as well. From our discussions with respondents who had direct experience of the above initiatives, we learnt that while there were/are some individuals who were primary drivers, it was fairly common for them to remain anonymous, or lowprofile. Such movements do not have individuals to be their 'face' to the external world. Our respondents made it clear that this was often a deliberate strategy to protect individuals from opposition, minimising risk to them, while simultaneously asserting the collective identity of the campaign or movement. Similarly, an online presence, rather than a physical 'office space', means greater physical security in an era of great risk for feminist activists.

Most of the online campaigns that we spoke to explained that their initiatives became larger than originally intended primarily because people on Facebook picked up their ideas and ran with it themselves. This has implications for the intellectual ownership of the campaign, recalling the issues of leadership raised above. Nikita Azad had no idea her open letter to the Sabarimala temple, along with an image of her wearing sanitary pads saying 'happy to bleed', would go viral – let alone that other women would join her with their own versions of 'happy to bleed' signage (interview with Nikita Azad, New Delhi, November 2016).

Even while groups maintain minimal hierarchy, there are still key members who drive them forward. This is one issue that campus-based groups like Pinjra Tod will have to tussle with as members graduate from university.

Membership

Membership is also being reconceptualised. Membership in most of the initiatives discussed in this chapter is a fairly open process. For the online campaigns, 'membership' is not a category that is relevant – e.g. one could participate in #happytobleed even just by sharing images and posts from the Facebook page itself. This was true of Hokkolorob as well: one respondent observed:

> [Hokkolorob made] such a universal demand ... It was something that a lot of people could get behind, or thought about, or dealt with. (Interview with Devjyot)

Thus, the concept of 'membership' is not as important as explicitly expressing support. For Hokkolorob, individual people did this through social media by sharing updates from those present at the protests, and individuals from across the world sent collective public messages of solidarity. In effect, participation in Hokkolorob was not limited to Kolkata, but was actually global.

With collectives like Why Loiter and Pinjra Tod, membership as a category flows along the continuum of 'supporter' to 'organiser', and is only loosely tracked through WhatsApp groups, which are an important forum on which the collectives organise themselves. The openness of these collectives allows them to be unconsciously inclusive, welcoming all people to consider themselves members if they identify with the same principles. It is perhaps this inclusivity that has allowed women across the country to identify with the collectives discussed above, and use the same slogans and calls in their own demonstrations.

This became clear to us while in conversation with individuals involved in #HappytoBleed – our respondent, Nikita, mentioned that she considers herself a member of Pinjra Tod, even while it continues to be primarily based in New Delhi (interview with Nikita). At the same time, however, the openness of these groups does lead to some issues – e.g. Pinjra Tod was appropriated by student political parties during election time, when female candidates have claimed to be members despite never having engaged with the group.

Yeh Dosti (This Friendship): the power of strong alliances

Many of our respondents expressed strong support for each other's initiatives, and spoke of the strength they derive from sister movements. This is shown by #happytobleed's self-identification with Pinjra Tod, and from the frequent collaborative events Why Loiter organises with groups like Blank Noise (interview with Neha). Social media is important for building and nurturing connections across cities and collectives. Neha pointed out:

> [social media] inspires you and motivates you because there are people in other cities and parts of the world that are moving in similar directions as you and you see them as a support and feel encouraged to not stop doing what you're doing. It's a great thing, and social media is very powerful for people like us.

Across the movements mentioned above, there is a strong sense of allyship and solidarity that enables them to support and inform each other's work. In the case study of Pinjra Tod, we emphasised the ways in which it has evolved in terms of reach and impact, as well as geographically and in relation to the focus of its activism. This evolution has allowed the collective to act in multiple capacities simultaneously: in forming cross-movement links, Pinjra Tod has come to act as a trans-college pressure group for gender issues and discrimination, providing a strongly feminist lens to systemic issues in educational institutions; in their consistent defiance of right-wing student groups on campus (Acharya 2017), their lobbying with university officials, and engagement with student politics, they seem to present as a student party in the making; and in the way they have spread across the country (Borpujari 2016), they are an emergent movement that is young, feminist, and constantly striving for intersectional analyses within themselves.

In the eyes of a Pinjra Tod respondent, the openness and flexibility of collectives like theirs is both a strength and a weakness. They are very wary of being appropriated by student parties that have begun to recognise the political value of supporting women's rights on campus. This has frequently been an issue they have to address, which our respondent mentioned, and can sometimes be difficult to do so given that well-established student parties have much louder voices on campus.

As suggested earlier, Occupy UGC was another important moment in youth mobilising, as groups who were otherwise separate from each other came together as a larger coalition. Pinjra Tod, YFDA, BAPSA, and other groups came together to articulate a position that took into account each of their perspectives and issues. By bringing together multi-university and multi-interest groups, it exemplified an important feminist and intersectional moment in movement building. Additionally, these groups also learned from each other through this process and sharpened their political analyses, visible in, for instance, the changed articulation in Pinjra Tod's positions.

The notion of alliances is also important for considering the role of men in supporting feminist activism, and activism around LGBTQI+ rights. While understanding the nature of allyship in movements, some of our respondents mentioned that the role of heterosexual cisgender[10] men in feminist action can be hard to delineate. For Why Loiter, their goal is clear – loitering is a revolutionary act for women and does not have the same import for men. Their loitering groups are necessarily all-women groups; to have even one cis-man in the group would completely change the experience for women as well as for onlookers.[11] Cis-men are encouraged to be passive supporters to the Why Loiter movement and have only been 'allowed' to be active partners in loitering when they have done it in drag. These particular loitering events have been experimental and few in number, but have had healthy participation. One of these events was 'Walk Like a Woman', held in Mumbai in April 2015 (Pasricha 2015).

Pinjra Tod is still in the process of delineating the role of male-identifying allies within the collective. They do have a few cis-male members who are welcome at their public events and their organisational meetings, but are left out of some spaces like their WhatsApp groups. Since Pinjra Tod is an autonomous women's collective, this stance is logical, in principle. However, it has two separate negative outcomes: it can be logistically confusing and unintentionally exclusionary when the individual in question moves beyond being a supporter to being an enthusiastic participant and organiser. At the time of writing, in one Delhi University college, for example, the primary Pinjra Tod member is a cis-male individual who carries out a significant amount of the collective's work; however, he is still not part of the WhatsApp group (interview with Pinjra Tod respondent).

'If you sexist me, I will feminist you, OK?': using humour and popular references in protest culture

Bigger initiatives like #hokkolorob and Pinjra Tod were and are conducted in ways that are similar to their predecessors, calling back to tactics traditionally used by the left: protest marches, sit-ins, speeches by important figures (usually well-known left-leaning academics), etc. The slogans and chants used by the initiatives are very similar to those traditionally used, in terms of the use of repetition, the cadence, and the calls to revolution (*'nahi sahenge, nahi sahenge'* ('we won't tolerate this, we won't tolerate this'), and *'inquilab zindabaad, zindabaad zindabaad'* ('long live the revolution, long live, long live'). These chants are staples of left-leaning protests, and have been instinctively employed by these movements as well – but this is also strategically very powerful. In implicitly linking these protests to the larger left protest tradition, they get immense credibility and garner support among seasoned activists, and young participants feel like they are part of the larger left tradition.

The use of music, dance, and humour is also well established as part of protest culture, and particularly feminist protest culture in India. These movements have built on this tradition in their own unique way: the 2009 Pink Chaddi Campaign's method of protest was to send pink underwear to the Sri Ram Sena headquarters; Pinjra Tod's meetings and public rallies use heteronormative Bollywood songs with the lyrics changed to be more topical (*'tod do taala, zamana kya kahega'* ('break the locks, so what if society cares'), sung to the tune of *'Chhod Do Anchal'* ('Let Go of Me'), a famous Bollywood song).

They heavily employ meme-language and internet humour in their offline mobilising and protests, particularly in their posters and slogans. By making a mockery of sexist diktats and statements by eminent political leaders, protesters subvert violent threats, making them objects of ridicule.

Many demonstrations that have been on the streets, particularly marches, have an almost carnivalesque atmosphere, and seem to channel the celebratory, party-like energy of the Pride Parades and other movements, like the Carnivals Against Capitalism (John 2008). One such example of this is the 2017 student-led march against a right-wing student party (Akhil Bhartiya Vidyarthi Parishad or ABVP – the student wing of the Bhartiya Janata Party), and their violent thuggery on campus – protesters called out slogans like 'ABVP, why so creepy?', and held up posters enforcing that message.

Online, humour is the most effective way in which people trade ideas and thoughts (Holton and Lewis 2011); this is something that these initiatives have embraced completely and have taken into their on-ground mobilising. Pinjra Tod aggressively used these tactics against ABVP when the latter's threats against the former escalated (Acharya 2017). They particularly targeted the masculine identity that ABVP projects and their president, Satender Awana, who has accused Pinjra Tod members of being 'loose' women: *'Haaye Awana, tu hai kitna mardaana!'* (Oh Awana, you're so masculine!)

Memes and meme-esque humour, a mix of laugh-out-loud humour and cutting sarcasm, have been used repeatedly, reaching a larger audience very quickly. Memes also move offline: a Pinjra Tod member told us that they deliberately use memes, humour, and Hinglish in their posters and social media posts because 'we know it will trend. Students and other young people almost universally understand memes, and that's important'.

These movements and initiatives have thus seamlessly taken internet language, memes, and other 'milliennialisms' off the internet and into college campuses through 'protestivals', public meetings, rallies, and their presence in other movement spaces.

These tactics are powerful and effective ways of mobilising young people, particularly around women's rights and gender rights. Through the use of millennial-talk and social media lingo, they turn what might be an 'apolitical' language into a shorthand for protest, challenging the norm, and a refusal to be cowed by the authoritarian figures or by fear and anger. The emphasis on laughter also drives home the completely non-violent nature of these movements, in direct opposition to the violence and aggression that they emerge in response to.

What's in a name? Protest culture currency

The importance of naming is well understood by each of these initiatives. A lot of the organisers are young women, and some of our respondents mentioned that they are not connected to political organisations or Indian feminist movement spaces in any substantial sense, nor do they see themselves as political;

however, they have an implicit understanding of the importance of linking themselves with older or more established movements.

Many movements have used their names to tap into the existing imagination and gain protest culture currency, as it were. The use of the word 'Occupy' in the name of the Occupy UGC protests is an example of this. In an interview with one of the organisers of Occupy UGC, we were told that this move was consciously made in order to draw implicit links between the issues, strategies, demands, and atmosphere of the Occupy protests and the protests against the UGC (interview with Sayan Chaudhuri). This is true as well of the SlutWalk, Take Back the Night, and I Will Go Out protests, all of which are strongly connected to the long history of marches by women occupying 'unsafe' spaces.[12]

Even while they have an eye on making connections with the existing protest culture, they also assert their uniquely irreverent identities. This is an important aspect of how they project themselves: from the Pink Chaddi Campaign that primarily focused on humour and silliness, which transforms into provocation with Happy to Bleed and Why Loiter, and further morphs into an out-and-out challenge with names like SlutWalk arthaat Besharmi Morchha (Slutwalk, meaning the March for Freedom from Shame), Hokkolorob, We Will Go Out, Take Back the Night, and Pinjra Tod.

In discussing the use of language in the SlutWalk, and the accompanying furore among both opposition (Goswami 2011) and supporters (Roy 2011) alike, a respondent said '[I] wasn't sure whether [the word 'slut'] was something I wanted to identify with ... That said, however, I do think that there is a growing acceptance of youth culture and the language of protest that we have adopted' (interview, New Delhi, December 2016). Similarly, another respondent asserted that '[We]'ve got to use terminology that this generation uses. We can't hold back. Just as technology is evolving, so is [the use of] language' (interview with Anshul Tiwari, New Delhi, February 2017).

An example of the most effective employment of both language and technology is Hokkolorob. The hashtag 'became the leitmotif [of the movement]' (interview with Devjyot). Within a day or two of its emergence, everyone who was at the protests or reporting on it was using '#hokkolorob'. Supporters also used it to link their posts to the movement. The hashtag allowed everyone's voices to join the discussion and reporting on the protest, leading to the creation of an entirely spontaneous, uncontrolled, crowdsourced chronicle of events.

> [T]he JU [Jadavpur University] students were able to use social media in a way that I hadn't seen before. Hokkolorob is from an old Bangladeshi song, and the hashtag just turned up and became really emblematic somehow. It also shows how the protest culture has evolved in JU ... the entire gamut of social media assets were used, and perhaps wasn't conscious ... but it contributed massively to the movement. (*ibid.*)

From our own perspective, however, these instances are examples of the conscious use of the democratising power of the internet and social media, which is utilised to the fullest extent by youth organisers of movements. As one respondent mentioned: 'the competence that young people have today for mobilisation is phenomenal. They are using all kinds of media [and] using both technology and different spaces … really smartly at the right moment' (interview with Anshul, 2017).

Engaging with backlash within and without

The backlash activists involved in these movements have faced ranges from the insubstantial to the relevant. Much of this comes from, unsurprisingly, authority figures and 'gatekeepers', including the police and political parties (such as ABVP, mentioned earlier).

With Why Loiter, it has been in the form of admonishments from 'well meaning' onlookers and police officers, who advise young women participants in the actions not to be out at late hours if they want to be seen as 'good women' (interview with Neha). Women from Pinjra Tod have been criticised for looking too 'posh' at protests, and are singled out for their outfits. This, however, is small fry in comparison to the very real threats of violence that many women from Pinjra Tod have faced, both online and offline. While members of Why Loiter spoke of engaging in gentle debate with their gatekeepers, when threats against Pinjra Tod escalated on campus, they responded with a strong show of force both online and offline, and effectively called out their harassers' threatening behaviour. While these strategies were major successes, activists said they continue to face on-campus harassment.

One of our respondents pointed out how backlash also comes from within the activist community, and particularly from the older generation of activists. They recalled an incident from a rally at a major movement, where senior activists asked a group of young to leave the protest because of their 'cavalier' approach that 'disrespected the protest and what it stood for' – the young people had used face paint as part of their participation in the protest (interview, December 2016).

The same person mentioned that the 'traditional' protest spaces that they were in 'seemed to constantly erase class and gender (even though we were all perhaps from the same milieu); my performance of gender was definitely not "appropriate" there, there is only a very particular type of gender performance that's allowed' (*ibid*.). This kind of criticism seems to assert that there is both a 'right' way to protest, as well as a particular '*dharna* (protest) etiquette' to maintain while doing so!

Initiatives likes the SlutWalk, the Pink Chaddi Campaign, Kiss of Love, and Shuddh Desi Romance have been critiqued for not being 'substantial enough', even while they were responding to important issues. The Besharmi Morcha, for instance, received a significant amount of mistrust and suspicion for the use of the word 'slut' and '*besharam*' (which literally translates to 'without shame').

These movements do have to fight for legitimacy even within movement spaces and feminist spaces. They are critiqued for their focus on middle-class, upper-caste issues. For some of the more recent movements, these problems are in-built in their framework, and how they project themselves; Happy to Bleed was exclusively for those who have regular access to the internet (and by extension social media), while Why Loiter is necessarily geared towards women who are of a very narrow class, caste, and age bracket.

For many of these initiatives, criticism about the language they employ, their analytical perspectives and brand of feminism, as well as their engagement and response to all of it can be seen happening in real time. This is because quite a few first emerged in the public eye of the internet – as a result, their political education and progress has been documented quite publicly (interview, 2016). This is a unique phenomenon – that a group or movement can be publicly critiqued even while in the process of germination.

On the other hand, this has also led to the rapid development of nuance within a lot of these initiatives: the SlutWalk, for instance, officially became Besharmi Morchha within the month that it first emerged to become more strongly relevant to its context. Still other movements like Pinjra Tod and Occupy UGC have rapidly, and very publicly, developed an increasingly intersectional perspective within their movement, and have made strong efforts to address a variety of issues that inform gender inequalities on university campuses, including caste and class. Pinjra Tod particularly has made consistent efforts to engage with the women's movement and academia through public meetings with key figures in both spaces. Access to academia is important for both Occupy UGC and Pinjra Tod, both of which espouse significantly more nuanced and articulate politics than initiatives like Happy to Bleed and others. Non-university-based initiatives are more atomised and cut off from the larger Indian feminist movement (a strong bastion of which is academia itself), and have developed their politics through engagement with other online initiatives, both globally and locally.

It is in their articulation of their agendas that we see the 'substantiveness' of these movements. Whether in university spaces or outside, most of them acknowledge patriarchal, capitalist, and exploitative institutions, and collectively put together a node of movement building, which strongly have sexuality, feminist perspectives, and ultimately, pleasure, at their core. In their analysis, they demonstrate how the control of love, desire, and sexuality, especially of young people and young women, is connected to the larger discourse that manufactures and protects the systems of inequality and discrimination centred on women's bodies.

Conclusion: where do we go from here?

Ratna Kapur describes the SlutWalk and the Pink Chaddi Campaign as 'feminism "lite". These are not revolutionary moments, but hold within them powerful critiques of dominant feminist positions and operate as space clearing mechanisms for other analytical possibilities to emerge' (Kapur 2012, 7).

Together, the movements and initiatives discussed here demonstrate an important, revolutionary moment in both youth movements and feminist movements. Whether online or offline, the power of collective action is evident across all initiatives – many of these movements, including #hokkolorob, Occupy UGC, and Pinjra Tod, witnessed online anger as well as offline action in the form of hundreds of people marching the streets and braving violence.

Many of our respondents mentioned that their online engagement with each others' movements and initiatives led to further interrogation of the ways in which discrimination and inequality operate in their own contexts. This engagement with each other's movements and the consequent introspective analysis has led to, or contributed to, the starting of other initiatives. These initiatives are learning from each of their individual moments of disruption, and are taking forward feminist ideals in a way that is distinct from established feminist movements – in terms of their strategies, membership, and primary goals.

Together, we think that they are calling for and developing new analytical possibilities within the feminist movement, within institutions, and within public discourse.

Notes

1. Before we registered as an organisation in 2007, we were 'The Youth Parliament Foundation'. Since then, our title has been officially truncated to 'The YP Foundation'. For more information, see www.theypfoundation.org.
2. This term typically connotes an apprenticeship in political offices or parties wherein one learns about the workings of political bodies. Here, the term connotes a wider understanding of political apprenticeship – that is, opportunities to build or expand one's perspective on the politics of social change. Inherent to the word 'apprenticeship', therefore, these opportunities also allow young people to experience the convergence of their own theoretical knowledge with on-ground practice and skills.
3. For more information, see 'Outrage over Rohith Vemula suicide', *The Times of India*, https://timesofindia.indiatimes.com/outrage-over-dalit-scholar-rohith-vemula-suicide/liveblog/50634069.cms?curpg=2 (last checked 2 October 2018).
4. For more information, see '#JNU row: why I stand with JNU', *India Times*, www.indiatimes.com/news/world/jnu-row-why-i-stand-by-jnu-317348.html (last checked 2 October 2018).
5. The LoSHA is a List of Sexual Harassers in Academia that emerged on Facebook in late October 2017 as a response to the #MeToo movement online. It was inspired by Christine C. Fair's article, '#HimToo: a reckoning', that first appeared on the *Huffington Post* (21 October 2017), but later moved to *BuzzFeed*, see www.buzzfeed.com/christinefair/himtoo-a-reckoning?utm_term=.snLvLorxz#.aqE4W1K96 (last checked 2 October 2018).

6. However, connecting online is a challenge in many rural areas and this affects engagement with the forms of activism that rely on this (Shukla 2017).
7. We are using this phrase to refer to the methods of mobilisation, organising, issues addressed, and protest strategies that are employed.
8. The Besharmi Morcha (March of the Shameless) (2011) was the Indian leg of the SlutWalk. The name was changed after much discussion around the term 'slut' – which is described in further detail in later parts of this study.
9. For more information, see Pisharoty (2015).
10. The term 'cisgender' refers to a person whose gender identity matches the sex assigned at birth, i.e. a man who has male sex characteristics and identifies comfortably as a man in his particular society.
11. An additional point that we noted as researchers was that, in our conversation with Why Loiter, the focus was unconsciously, but surely, on the participation of exclusively cisgendered women.
12. From the Reclaim the Night website, see www.reclaimthenight.co.uk.

Notes on contributors

Esther Moraes works at The YP Foundation on communication and public advocacy around issues of health, rights, and youth leadership with a focus on young girls and adolescents.

Vinita Sahasranaman has worked with community-based, women-led organisations to build grassroots feminist leadership over the last 15 years. She currently works with the Children's Investment Fund Foundation, Delhi.

References

Unless otherwise stated, all online references were last accessed by editor 10 September 2018

Acharya, Ilina (2017) '"ABVP Kaahe So Creepy?": Hear Students of Delhi University from the "Save DU March"', *Indian Cultural Forum*, 4 March, http://indianculturalforum.in/2017/03/04/abvp-kahe-socreepydelhi-university-save-du-ramjas/ (last checked 2 October 2018)

Altbach, Philip (1968) 'Student Politics and Higher Education in India', *Daedalus* 97(1): 254–73

Azad, Nikita (2015) 'A Young Bleeding Woman Pens An Open Letter To The Keepers Of Sabrimala Temple', *Youth Ki Awaaz*, 20 November, https://www.youthkiawaaz.com/2015/11/open-letter-to-devaswom-chief-sabrimala/ (last checked 2 October 2018)

Borpujari, Priyanka (2016) 'How "Pinjra Tod" spread its wings', *LiveMint.com*, 30 December, https://www.livemint.com/Leisure/z6E69WRoNJAyUuGU5yYwXO/How-Pinjra-Tod-spread-its-wings.html (last checked 2 October 2018)

Chhinkwani, Nishant (2014) 'Molested at the protest against molestation: How a revolution is brewing in Jadavpur University', *Youth Ki Awaaz*, 18 September, https://www.youthkiawaaz.com/2014/09/jadavpur-university-protest-molestation-police-crackdown/ (last checked 2 October 2018)

Crenshaw, Kimberlé Williams (1994) 'Mapping the Margins: Intersectionality, Identity Politics and Violence Against Women of Color', in Martha Albertson Fineman and Roxanne Mykitiuk (eds.) *The Public Nature of Private Violence: The Discovery of Domestic Abuse*, New York: Routledge, 93–118

Ghoshal, Devjyot (2014) 'A brief history of #hokkolorob, the hashtag that shook Kolkata', *Quartz.com*, 9 October, https://qz.com/india/269774/hokkolorob-the-hashtag-thats-defining-an-indian-student-protest-against-violence/ (last checked 2 October 2018)

Goswami, Seema (2011) 'SlutWalk? No Thanks!', *Hindustan Times*, 27 June

Holton, Avery E. and Seth C. Lewis (2011) 'Journalists, social media, and the use of humor on Twitter', *The Electronic Journal of Communication* 21(1&2)

International Business Times (2015) 'Kerala Devaswom chief wants machine to scan women for purity at Sabarimala', 16 November, https://www.ibtimes.co.in/kerala-devaswom-chief-wants-machine-scan-women-purity-sabarimala-654925 (last checked 2 October 2018)

Kapur, Ratna (2012) 'Pink Chaddis and SlutWalk Couture: The Postcolonial Politics of Feminism Lite', *Feminist Legal Studies* 20(1): 1–20

Matiyani, Manak (2017) 'How the social sector is failing India's youth', *India Development Review*, 13 July, http://idronline.org/social-sector-failing-india-youth/ (last checked 2 October 2018)

Mogul, Priyanka (2015) 'Delhi universities sexism row divides Indian society as female students call for greater freedom', *International Business Times*, 25 September, https://www.ibtimes.co.uk/delhi-universities-sexism-row-divides-indian-society-female-students-call-greater-freedom-1521089 (last checked 2 October 2018)

Pasricha, Japleen (2015) 'Walk Like A Woman! Men Wear Women's Clothes To Support Why Loiter', *Feminism in India*, 6 April, https://feminisminindia.com/2015/04/06/walk-like-a-woman-men-wear-womens-clothes-to-support-why-loiter/ (last checked 2 October 2018)

Pinjra Tod (2016) '4 Instances When Women Workers Marched For Their Rights, And Kicked Ass', *Youth Ki Awaaz*, 1 May, https://www.youthkiawaaz.com/2016/05/labour-day-womens-movements/ (last checked 2 October 2018)

Phadke, Shilpa, Sameera Khan and Shilpa Ranade (2011) *Why Loiter? Women and Risk on Mumbai Streets*, New Delhi: Penguin

Pisharoty, Sangeeta Barooah (2015) 'What Lies Behind the "Occupy UGC" Protest', *The Wire*, 24 November, https://thewire.in/education/what-lies-behind-the-occupy-ugc-protest (last checked 2 October 2018)

Pisharoty, Sangeeta Barooah (2016) 'Uncertainty for TISS Adivasi Researchers as UGC Drops Institute from Fellowships List', *The Wire*, 18 February, https://thewire.in/education/uncertainty-for-tiss-adivasi-research-scholars-as-ugc-drops-institute-from-st-fellowship-list (last checked 2 October 2018)

Qazi, Musab (2017) 'Researchers left high and dry: Mumbai University scholars have not received fellowships for last 6 months', *Hindustan Times*, 26 April, https://www.hindustantimes.com/mumbai-news/mumbai-university-scholars-haven-t-received-monthly-fellowships-for-last-six-months/story-6oDnGqOgnbFw8iLrE8Vb1L.html (last checked 2 October 2018)

Rahul, M. (2015) 'Loose Cannons: How Student Protesters Were Attacked And Detained By The Police In Central Delhi', *The Caravan*, 10 December, http://

www.caravanmagazine.in/vantage/loose-cannons-student-protestors-attacked-detained-police-central-delhi (last checked 2 October 2018)

Rowlands, Jo (1995) 'Empowerment Examined', *Development in Practice* 5(2): 101–7

Roy, Nilanjana S. (2011) 'Ready or not, New Delhi gets a women's street protest', *New York Times*, 14 June

Shankar, Aranya (2015) '"Occupy UGC" movement intensifies after crackdown', *The Indian Express*, 28 October, https://indianexpress.com/article/cities/delhi/occupy-ugc-movement-intensifies-after-crackdown/ (last checked 3 October 2018)

Shastry, Sharmada (2016) 'Why 2015 Was the Year When Periods Won', *Menstrupedia*, http://menstrupedia.com/blog/2015-year-review/ (last checked 3 October 2018)

Shukla, Vandana (2017) 'Is # feminism elitist in India?', *The Tribune*, 5 March

St. John, Graham (2008) 'Protestival: Global Days of Action and Carnivalized Politics in the Present', *Social Movement Studies* 7(2): 167–90

Venkat, T., Srividya Tadepalli and Thomas Manuel (2017) 'The Life of Labour: Maruti Suzuki Violence in Manesar – a Retrospective', *The Wire*, 19 March, https://thewire.in/labour/maruti-suzuki-violence-judgement-case-details (last checked 2 October 2018)

CHAPTER 3

Repoliticising women's rights in development: young African feminisms at the cutting edge

Catherine Nyambura

Abstract

Twenty-five years on from the UN Conferences in Cairo (1994) and Beijing (1995) with their radical vision of women's rights – including sexual and reproductive rights – this chapter considers the challenges to women's rights from the perspective of young feminists connected to FEMNET. It draws on recent research with FEMNET members, partners, allies, and staff at the secretariat in Nairobi, Kenya. The chapter has been developed through collaboration and feminist sisterhood with the ATHENA Initiative, a feminist collective working on gender equality, HIV/AIDS, and sexual and reproductive health and rights. The chapter reflects in particular on the role of young African feminists in reclaiming the women's rights agenda from political actors who many of us consider to have hijacked the concept and language of 'women's rights' and 'gender equality', to further different goals. These concepts have been depoliticised and professionalised, at a time when many of the rights of young women are increasingly under threat.

Keywords: Youth; feminism; Africa; politicisation; sexual reproductive health and rights; women's rights

Introduction

It is such an exciting time for young feminism in Africa and the world over. Young women are standing up for their lives, for their voices, standing up for their freedom to choose and to exercise their rights to learn, to thrive, to decide when and if to have children and to access reproductive health care. This generation continues to see a feminist movement that has been imbued with a spirit of fierce defiance, a spirit carried by its youngest voices who no longer ask for a seat at the table but create their own platforms, harnessing the power of social media and community movements to tell their story and dismantle patriarchy. (Imungu Kalevera, Advocacy Intern at FEMNET, 9 May 2018)

According to United Nations (UN) statistics, there were 226 million young African people aged between 15 and 24 in 2015: that is, 19 per cent of the global youth population (UN 2015). By 2030, it is projected that the number of youth in Africa will have increased by 42 per cent, and it is expected to continue to grow throughout the remainder of the 21st century, more than doubling from current levels by 2055 (*ibid.*). Yet despite discussions about the potential 'demographic dividend' (UN OSAA 2017) that young people might offer to international development, development remains largely silent about the specific contribution and role of young women in the development of Africa. Currently, young women and girls are left outside mainstream discussions about youth and development. In its critique of the demographic dividend agenda, FEMNET points out that young women's

> voices are considered peripheral and their bodies constructed as sites to be acted on by policy prescriptions developed by others for them. (FEMNET 2017, 4)

These discourses focus on the contribution young people may make to economic growth, rather than focusing on their rights and the gender and social justice issues that are relevant to them. These are questions that must be addressed if young people – and in particular young women – are to fulfil their potential for themselves, and for society.

This chapter draws on my own personal experience as a young African feminist activist and professional working in a women's rights organisation, and specifically on my expertise on sexual and reproductive health and rights (SRHR), and the experiences of others. It considers the challenges we are faced with at this moment, and highlights how young feminists and especially young African feminists provide hope for building a better future for young women in Africa. I think we can do this by furthering young women's interests, arguing for their rights, and reinvigorating an inclusive and diverse feminist movement in Africa. While it is critical for young women to be a part of youth movements to secure the range of rights they require to be upheld as a generation, I believe a strong young *feminist* movement is key. We need to be part of leading, co-creating, and articulating collective feminist narratives and developing action to further women's rights and social justice in the women's movements that exist throughout the world.

We are at an important moment. In 2020, it will be a quarter-century since the Fourth UN World Conference on Women was held at Beijing. Its outcome was the Beijing Platform for Action (1995), which laid out a wide and radical vision of women's rights. At Beijing, there were delegations of political leaders from all 54 African countries. Beijing was held one year after another landmark conference for women: the International Conference on Population and Development (ICPD), held in Cairo in 1994. The ICPD Program of Action gave the world leadership and political commitment on SRHR.

At the time of Cairo and Beijing, the world's attention was on women's rights among other broader social, economic, political, cultural, and environmental rights. The governments and international decision-makers were challenged to respond to the demands of feminist activists for women's political, economic, and social rights to be realised. The interests of young women in particular were recognised at Beijing and in the Platform for Action in a focus on the 'girl child' as one of 12 critical areas of concern. This provided a policy framework to acknowledge the gendered dimensions of problems that affect female children. Examples are harmful practices such as female genital mutilation, child and 'early' marriages, and the burden of unpaid care work. Other critical areas of concern also had obvious importance for young women and girls – among them, education and training, and women and health. Under the critical area on women's health is a commitment to sexual and reproductive rights (UN 1995, paragraph 96) that remains the only globally agreed language on sexual rights.

The quarter-century that has passed since Cairo and Beijing is a moment to reflect on progress since. What are the challenges and setbacks that we have encountered, and the narratives about women's rights that different stakeholders are using today? Young feminists – in common with the entire feminist movement – find ourselves in a deeply troubled and complex political context: one that is deeply shaken up by roll-back and backlash against women's rights and gender equality. It is a critical moment for the feminist to re-imagine herself, her work, and the spaces she occupies, including asking critical questions on the status of the movement. Parallel to these grave challenges and barriers to women's rights, we are seeing the opportunities of 'fourth-wave feminism' sweeping over the world, with new forms of activism – notably using digital and ICTs to enable us to 'meet' and organise. While second- and third-wave feminists were involved in the activism around the UN Conferences of the 1980s and 1990s, today's fourth-wave feminists have not had the opportunities for face-to-face encounters that the Conferences and parallel NGO Forums made possible for earlier generations.

There are many different important challenges facing me and other young African feminists at this time. I will discuss some of them here, bringing varied perspectives and insights from my own experience and that of other young feminists. For this chapter, I conducted research including interviews in March 2018, in Nairobi, Kenya. My aim was to gain personal perspectives of FEMNET members, as well as information from staff, members, and allies. FEMNET[1] is a pan-African women's rights organisation that was started in 1988 by African feminist activists. It is also known as The African Women's Development and Communication Network: a name that clearly shows the commitment of the organisation to feminist organising and networking through solidarity around shared objectives. Today, FEMNET has a presence in 48 African countries across all five sub-regions of Africa and with 630 members.

Other feminists whose insights appear in this chapter have been part of the #WhatWomenWant campaign by the ATHENA initiative.[2] The ATHENA initiative is a global network made up of individuals and organisations that has been leading efforts to ensure that gender equality is central to the HIV response since 2006. Through campaigns such as #WhatWomenWant and #WhatGirlsWant, ATHENA has provided spaces for young feminists to articulate their policy priorities boldly.

My sources of information for this chapter

I carried out research for this chapter during April and May 2018. I carried out one-to-one interviews with young feminists actively working in or involved in various aspects of social justice work. I also draw on presentations given at the January 2018 Gender is My Agenda campaign,[3] online feminist information, and campaigns such as the #WhatWomenWant website and the ATHENA website, and FEMNET's (2012) organisational story, published as *Herstory – Our Journey: Advocating for the Rights of African Women.*

As stated above, I also draw on personal experience gained in FEMNET, which I joined as a member in 2014. FEMNET has an organisational vision of an African society where gender equality is achieved, and women and girls enjoy all their rights and live in dignity. At the time of writing in August 2018, it currently has 650 members in 48 countries, 15 staff, and a Board to direct the organisation. Members participate in FEMNET in many ways, including shaping the vision of the organisation through programmatic priorities articulated in the strategic plan. Additionally, members are crucial in implementing this vision through joint implementation and co-creation of activities and especially collective advocacy at different decision-making decisions.

I became a staff member at the FEMNET secretariat in 2016, first as the Advocacy Program Associate, and now as the Advocacy Officer. My most critical and important perspectives come from my own personal and professional experience leading FEMNET's thematic programming on SRHR, and young women's engagement. In addition, I am proud to have worked with the ATHENA initiative on the young feminist blog series which collated young feminist perspectives ahead of the UN High Level Meeting on AIDS in New York in 2016. Through ATHENA, I also supported the broader framework of the #WhatWomenWant campaign. All these initiatives provide a space for young feminists to connect working on SRHR, HIV/AIDS, and violence against women, in all of their diversity. It has been refreshing to see the strong political analysis which comes out in their work and their priorities.

In the next section, I give a brief historical account of feminist activism around Beijing, before considering the context we find ourselves in today as young African feminists.

Women's rights and feminisms in African contexts: Beijing as a catalyst for action

At Beijing, global decision-makers encountered the women's rights movements from all regions of the world, with diverse priorities but a shared vision of equality and rights. A process of influencing and consciousness-raising – or 'conscientisation' – developed in the earlier UN Conferences, including Nairobi in 1990 – went on as the civil society groups, movements, and organisations lobbied the official delegations. The aim was to achieve a strong articulation of feminist visions for women's rights as human rights (Correa and Reichmann 1994) in the Beijing Platform for Action. This would provide a framework for feminist activism, urging governments all over the world, furthering and supporting women's rights in partnership with women's movements.

In the lead-up to Beijing, feminist activism experienced a surge: organisations that had existed previously grew and developed, and new ones were inspired to begin. Many feminists have been active in the years since – not only in women's organisations, but also in politics and governance. They have worked to implement mainstreaming by integrating gender analysis into research, planning, and policymaking, and to transform the institutions that women should be able to depend on to advance and support their full and equal rights. At the parallel NGO Forum held at Huiairou, feminists from all over the world met to network with each other, hold dialogues and discussions on shared concerns, and influence the official delegations, as well as holding side events of many different kinds. Many of the encounters between them developed subsequently into longer engagement and collaborations. A statement by FEMNET stated our hope that African women would be empowered to challenge both gender- and race-based inequalities:

> we the African women will reclaim, reconstruct and transform Africa, on the basis of gender equality, giving credence to the principles of democracy and human rights; mobilizing and utilizing human and other resources; and take our rightful place in the global arena, on the basis of equality with other nations, from now into the future, in partnership with our men, girls and boys. (FEMNET 2012, 36)

This statement not only gives a broad perspective of what issues were a priority for African women and girls but also reflects the diversity of African women and girls and their aspirations for sustainable development.

Young African feminists were trailblazers in the African feminist movement. Platforms such as the African Women's Leadership Initiative Akina Mama wa Afrika[4] created a focus for activism.

Young women were present at Beijing as members of wider feminist organisations, and also as leaders of their own specifically young feminist-focused organisations. In the Beijing Platform for Action, they found their interests addressed in various ways. Though the outcome document had no specific commitments on young women, its recognition of the diverse and intersecting identities of women was a cause for celebration. Many of the policy priorities outlined through the 12 critical areas in the Platform for Action – including the focus on education – had a strong focus on young women and girls. Education was articulated both as a human right and an essential tool for achieving the goals of equality, development, and peace, ensuring that both young women and men have an equal chance at upward mobility in life.

Much of the passion and politics that informed the Beijing Platform for Action was lost in the years after Beijing, as feminists struggled to get elites in government and international agencies to accept a complete transformation of development as they understood it. As a means to attempt to do this, the 'gender mainstreaming' approach emerged from a critique of the Women in Development (WID) policies and programming of the 1980s (Jahan 1995). At Beijing, battles were fought to get a strong Platform for Action, with right-wing and conservative factions challenging the language and framing of the Platform (Baden and Goetz 1997). Feminists evolved the concept of 'gender mainstreaming' (UN 2001) – that is, analysing the implications for women of all state actions to ensure 'inequality is not perpetuated ... the ultimate goal is to achieve gender equality' (*ibid.*, 1).

Current challenges facing young feminists in Africa

To some extent, the international development agenda – including both state institutions and NGOs – has adopted Beijing's language and policy commitments to gender equality. There has been significant progress on a range of issues affecting women's rights and gender equality through the past 30 years, including education (UNFPA 2014) and maternal mortality (Cha 2017). Political participation has increased, and African countries have seen female political leaders, including Liberia, Mali, Mozambique, Senegal, and Namibia. Rwanda leads the world regarding gender parity in parliament.

However, the process of gender mainstreaming has actually been seen by many as having depoliticised the feminist visions that inspired women's activism at Beijing. Much has been said and written about the lack of real political commitment to change. To take the example of increasing numbers of women in formal political leadership, this does not necessarily translate into real change for women. Twenty-five years on from Cairo and Beijing, the challenges remain to get real transformative change to power relations on many of the most difficult and profound aspects of gender inequality.

At this moment, 25 years after Beijing, we are faced with many challenges to our movements from right-wing politics and increasingly fragile states, to religious fundamentalisms, to failures to eradicate poverty and growing inequalities, and depoliticisation of gender equality and women's rights work. We are also seeing that the foundational values and principles which ignited and formed the premise for women's rights organising are being threatened. From the local community level right up to the global platforms, we are experiencing backlash where there has been previous progress, and a deepening of inequalities where no progress had yet been made. Renewed sexism and homophobic waves are sweeping across the continent, threatening a new world 'disorder' that calls for urgent redress. It is almost as if all the feminist ideologies we have been pushing for in the past three decades are directly under attack!

Historically, women's organisations and movements have seen SRHR as central to our agendas. This remains the case, but so many other issues are pressing at this moment of crisis across a range of women's rights, and the capacity of feminist movements to respond on all of them is seriously under threat. Threats to reproductive health care are intensifying due to policies seeking to constrain and cut their access to these essential resources and services, including Donald Trump's intensification of the Global Gag policy (O'Brien 2017). Faced with these threats to SRHR, women of reproductive age – and the youngest among them most of all – risk unplanned pregnancies, diseases, and permanent damage and deaths from unsafe abortion.

Repoliticising the women's rights discourse in Africa

We have an enormous task facing us: to shake up the status quo and re-politicise the women's rights discourse on the African continent. I see the need for young African feminists to take a deliberate and disruptive approach towards shaking the prevailing status quo, and seeding progressive change anchored on inclusive, pluralistic, and a bold political agenda for women's rights. Across Africa and more widely in the global South, young feminists are developing a powerful agenda that arises from their daily lived realities. The challenges and the current context call for a re-imagination and deeper reflection on the narratives we are anchoring our feminist work on to help us to organise better politically. If we want to make progress, this will involve deliberately and carefully focusing on the simple concepts of choice, voice, and agency.

Feminist organising turns the choices, voices, and agency of individuals into a powerful collective voice. The young feminists active today were children at the time of Beijing. Yet the 'herstory' of African feminisms and African feminists is important, to bear witness to previous struggles, to learn from the battles lost and won over the years, and to ensure our current struggles as young African feminists are as informed as possible by prior experiences and lessons.

In 1988, at the time of FEMNET's formation, there were many debates around the concept of feminism, its origins, and its relation to the realities of gender inequality and gendered poverty experienced by African women in a post-colonial era. Debates included different perspectives on the political strategies open to African women to advance their interests. Women's rights were sometimes addressed using different framings which aimed to be more appropriate to different African cultural, political, and economic contexts. In the global South, women's rights activism is intertwined with wider liberation movements fighting to liberate countries from the evils of conquest and colonialism. Feminism was, as is, sometimes perceived in the media in Africa (as elsewhere) as a culturally imposed and hence alien and 'Western' set of ideas and ideals.

However, many African women's rights activists have welcomed the possibilities of alliances and joint agendas with other women's rights allies elsewhere and saw no difficulties with self-identifying as feminists. Women's rights activism and resistance to patriarchal structures and practices existed in many forms in sub-Saharan Africa, prior to conquest and colonialism. Indeed, the colonial experience and the imposition of Western-style political and economic institutions and social norms has been argued by some African feminists as harmful to women's position in societies in this continent, as it codified gender inequality and shaped and worsened the marginalisation of women from power and resources in many contexts.

For organisations such as FEMNET, it is clear that a rights-based model of activism focusing on gender equality and social justice is the pathway forward. As laid out in the Strategic Plan (2014–18), FEMNET's work currently aims to ensure that African women's organisations, lobby groups, decision-makers, like-minded organisations, as well as men, take action to create an environment that supports gender equality and social justice. This aligns with the aspiration to have African women's rights recognised in key policy and development frameworks and as change agents in the role they play towards sustainable development. While international development often restricts its vision to the factors seen as holding women back in terms of their role in production – e.g. education and training to enable them to become paid workers in the formal economy – a feminist vision focuses on the political, economic, and social dimensions of gender inequality and understands the need to advance women's full and equal human rights.

As an organisation founded on principles of organising and networking around women's rights, FEMNET supports members to hold governments to account and currently focuses on the following priority areas: harmful practices with specific reference to female genital mutilation and early marriage; violence against women and girls; women in political leadership and decision-making; SRHR; and women and the economy. FEMNET works by supporting its members to link national-, regional-, and global-level activities strategically to contribute to enabling women in Africa to be better informed, able to engage in and influence processes meaningfully at all levels, using cutting-edge communication tools and platforms to tell and document their stories and contribute to the body of knowledge on women's rights. FEMNET does this by strengthening the capacity of women's organisations to access information and manage knowledge. We also create and manage platforms to share information, ideas, strategies, and experiences for cross-learning and implementation, and support members to do this via digital technologies as well as traditional means of communication.

FEMNET is slowly building and integrating a conscious focus on young feminist issues in its activism and analysis. For example, we are challenging and broadening the concept of the demographic dividend. This is discussed in more detail in the next section, where I offer insights on some key issues in the context that we face as young feminists in Africa, and share some of our experiences and strategies.

The context of young feminist organising in Africa: insights into key issues

The critical importance of intersectionality for young African feminisms

I began my own journey as a young feminist consciously in 2008, even though I like to think of myself as always being a feminist. During a feminist leadership class in 2013, I was able to articulate my own personal feminist vision and conviction. During this period as a feminist, I have worked on various exciting topics, including abortion rights in a criminalised context, working towards policy reform and addressing abortion stigma. Having worked and focused my professional expertise on SRHR has definitely grounded my feminist journey and perspectives. This experience, in addition to my own personal experience growing up as a girl in one of the biggest slums in Nairobi, gave me insights into what intersectionality means. Intersectionality (Crenshaw 1991) is a complex concept but put at its simplest, it is an analysis of power and powerlessness focusing on multiple disadvantages linked to gender, race, and class, which suggests a radical agenda for change.

To achieve real change for young women in sub-Saharan Africa requires creative ways of mobilisation, communication, and advocacy. Young feminists have to grapple with a dynamic context, one where they are afforded new tools and platforms for organising, but also the urgent need to articulate an intersectional agenda. It is not enough to focus on 'gender' separately from issues of poverty, race, class, and other critical aspects that underpin our marginalisation and oppression. Young feminist organising has been built on pushing a radical agenda, using exciting and new methodologies of organising to disrupt the status quo and challenge patriarchal norms. All this while advancing broad agendas with a deep political analysis of issues such as access to safe abortion, LGBTQIA+ rights, confronting inequality that is – literally – man-made, and demonstrating what inclusive and non-hierarchical movements look like.

These issues – and many of our ways of working too – are always deemed controversial, because we are confronting and boldy challenging patriarchy. With creativity, boldness, and inclusive organising, young feminists continue to seek a path to overcome all the stumbling blocks facing young women in our homes, communities, and societies, and we are guided by the simple awareness of the need for engagement between the feminist and youth movements, and the intersectional space in which we work. We recognise the need to link to both movements because of the strength of political allies and coalitions. Where a collective agenda can be set and articulated, and collective action can be undertaken, faster and wider impact can be achieved.

The demographic dividend agenda and its 'use' of young women

As highlighted at the start of this chapter, young people are attracting the attention of governments and international development policymakers, but the approach taken is very problematic. The demographic dividend agenda essentially sees Africa's youth instrumentally, as 'key forces of sustainable development' (UN OSAA 2017, 3). This thinking is encapsulated in the African Union roadmap for harnessing demographic dividend through investments in youth (African Union 2017).

FEMNET launched an advocacy brief titled 'Young Women and the Demographic Dividend' at the sidelines of the July 2017 29th African Union Summit in Addis Ababa, Ethiopia. The brief was initiated at the 28th African Union summit in January 2017, in consultation with African young women. The brief aimed to provide a nuanced gender and human rights analysis of the demographic dividend discourse, highlighting its lack of attention to power and politics (FEMNET 2017). The demographic dividend agenda does not seek to empower young women or men, or to challenge the current model of development in which decision-making is taken by older decision-makers who are still predominantly men. Instead, it limits its focus to recognising young people for their large numbers, and the potential energy and skills can be harnessed to help deliver existing development goals. The approach outlines four very broad areas of investment: health, education, employment, and governance.

Demographic dividend thinking on sexual and reproductive health is anchored on a population and development premise, rather than principles of agency, choice, and control over one's own body. This is highly problematic for women and girls, as it sees them as a means to the end of economic development. If policymakers are only focusing on young women in an instrumentalist way, they will fail to understand the importance of responding to different interests and needs and, above all, recognising and affirming their rights. A further problem with such narratives is their failure to recognise the fact that young people exist in a spectrum of diversity (by gender, but also by disability, by religion, by wealth or poverty, and beyond). This diversity fails to be recognised in the somewhat homogenous approach taken by governments and international development agencies in youth programming and policymaking.

The FEMNET 2017 analysis was framed as a contribution to the technical enrichment of the concept of the demographic dividend, but also to outline clearly the alternative priorities and investment pathways for African governments to take if they are to achieve sustainable development by involving youth in their diversity, and in particular young women. A feminist youth agenda would be focused on recognising the agency and rights of young people, to whom governments must and should be accountable.

The High Level Meeting on AIDS 2016 from a young feminist perspective

Milestone meetings are useful catalysts for feminist organising, as well as targets for our advocacy. Overall, the process around the High Level Meeting on AIDS in 2016 is widely perceived by young feminists as having demonstrated a commitment to values of co-creation, collaboration, and accountability to young women. In my research for this chapter, this High Level Meeting, and its preparation and follow-up, was seen by many participants – and by me! – as a key process that has advanced SRHR in our region, given the disproportionate burden of HIV/AIDS in Africa.

At the time of the meeting in 2016, the world was beginning to recognise that adolescent girls and young women were at particularly high risk of HIV infection. In sub-Saharan Africa, adolescent girls and young women accounted for 25 per cent of new HIV infections among adults, and women accounted for over half (56 per cent) of new HIV infections among adults (UNAIDS 2016, 8). Factors cited as responsible were: harmful gender norms and inequalities, insufficient access to education and sexual and reproductive health services, poverty, food insecurity, and violence (*ibid.*).

The recognition these issues received around the 2016 High Level Meeting created opportunities for women's rights organisations to feed into planning a gendered HIV response, and to emphasise the importance of young women's participation and young feminist perspectives. This has happened via initiatives such as the ATHENA initiative, and through engagement with UNAIDS to create a gendered HIV response.

HIV/AIDS has provided strategic entry points into much wider feminist debates and activism on a wide range of key topics. Hence, this experience was an important moment for young feminisms in Africa. Ahead of this meeting, the ATHENA initiative launched the #WhatWomenWant campaign, a vehicle to advance gender equality within and outside the HIV response. Through it, ATHENA seeks to amplify women's voices, highlight their realities and power collective solutions by creating a platform for women, including young women, to influence global policy discourse that does not require an invitation, or a visa.

Through the campaign platforms and especially, the Young Feminist Blog Series (ATHENA 2016), young feminists from across the globe shared their own voices and those of the constituencies they serve to highlight solutions for programming, policy, and funding priorities. The Blog Series spans 16 countries and territories. It is authored by activists and feminists working across HIV prevention, care, and treatment for diverse population, law and policy, and academia. Showing the widening of the agenda beyond HIV and AIDS, topics covered within this series include SRHR, contraception, youth-friendly services, finance and legal issues, LGBTI issues, gender-based violence, trans rights, implementation, and follow-up and review of the 2030 Agenda for Sustainable Development.

A double-edged sword: the digital revolution

The internet has opened up spaces for new forms of harassment, abuse, surveillance, censorship, control, and violence against women, but it has also had the positive impact of creating new political spaces for young people including young women. It has become one of the most effective ways to engage and disseminate information to young people. Yet despite the rise of the internet as a democratic space, barriers to accessing the internet are deeply entrenched along gender, socio-economic, and rural–urban divides which further advance inequalities among young people. The internet is a phenomenal and huge opportunity for young feminist organising and especially social media as an empowering tool for democracy. It is, however, important to remember that it is not readily available, or affordable, to all young feminists. Owning a personal computer, laptop, or cell phone remains a luxury for many, and yet in high-level spaces and engagements it is often an unspoken assumption for participation.

While there is a digital gender gap – or more accurately, a digital gap that reflects intersectional analysis of disadvantage (O'Donnell and Sweetman 2018), young African women are going online in ever-increasing numbers. Digital technologies are creating spaces for dialogues with policymakers such as #TheAfricaWeWant that mobilised young people towards contributing to the #Agenda2063 and continues to be the preferred hashtag for the African Union and others keen on advancing a pan-African agenda. #JusticeForLiz was a dynamic advocacy hashtag platform launched by FEMNET and partners in 2012, to seek justice for a victim of sexual violence in Kenya and to challenge normalised rape culture. This platform was launched by a young FEMNET staff member through a petition, driven by outrage and the need to draw attention to inequality.

Other examples include the #FeesMustFall movement in South Africa, where young people demanded equal access to education opportunities, and the #BringBackOurGirls movement that called on the Nigerian government to take action in rescuing girls abducted by militia groups.

In the next section, I briefly consider challenges to current feminist activism, organising, and movement building that emerge from the experiences of feminists in sub-Saharan Africa.

Barriers to feminist activism, organisation, and movement building

The first challenge to be mentioned is the shrinking civic space mentioned earlier. The African Union declared 2016–2025 as the Decade of Human Rights, yet civic space across the continent is rapidly shrinking. According to the International Center on Non-Profit Law's (2016) Survey of Trends Affecting Civic Space, since the beginning of 2015, more than 64 countries across the world adopted restrictive laws and other punitive measures, if not fully prohibiting non-government and civil society organisations (*ibid.*, 2). States are using their legislative and executive powers to pass laws designed to restrict and/or criminalise public assembly or protest; to empower states to dramatically increase digital surveillance of their citizens; and/or to regulate civil society activity (*ibid.*).

There is an obvious gender dimension to this. Civic, or public, spaces are often highly contested areas, where politically active women can face abuse, sexual harassment and violence. This is one of the biggest challenges for young women engaging in politics (Kabwato 2013). As part of the broader under-representation of women in leadership positions, young women are rarely elected to leadership positions in mainstream young people's networks and hence end up coalescing among themselves and not feeding into mainstream civil society discourse (*ibid.*).

Another challenge is restrictions on freedom of movement that hinder regional and global connections. Visa restrictions affect travel even within the African continent. Barriers to young African women going to work, live, or even visit different continents are high and rising, with racism and xenophobia worsening in many contexts. This is seen from global media daily referring to policy discussions in the global North aiming to curtail migration. This is a huge deterrent to building solidarity between young feminists across Africa and the world. They are denied the opportunity to connect with others, but also denied the opportunity to share their work and cross-pollinate. Recently, a number of young women FEMNET members were denied US visas to attend the UN Commission on the Status of Women (CSW 62).[5]

For Africa's young feminists, there are serious challenges to developing strong cross-movement social networks. Young feminist organising tends to remain fragmented from wider social justice movements. This is a common problem in civil society. Arriving at and working on common agendas with constituencies representing different groups can be very difficult. This can be seen with the SRHR and HIV movements, whose core agendas and constituencies are overlapping, but where agendas and activities are often not synergised.

Another issue that emerged from discussions for this chapter – and from my experience as an activist – is that language used in high-level policy processes includes a lot of jargon and technical or theoretical terms. These not only lock out many young women (and men) – even when they are educated – but tends to reinforce elitist views and perceptions. It is important that we spend time de-mystifying high-level policy processes and jargon to ensure the language that we use is understandable, respectful, and accessible to everyone in all aspects, including young women. This is illustrated by concepts such as the demographic dividend, discussed earlier. This is a very technical concept representing a very important set of practical and policy issues.

A key issue I have discussed at length in this chapter is the need for an intersectional approach. Instead, many development organisations fail to address our issues because of a ghettoisation and division of it into 'gender' and 'youth' work.

Funding is absolutely critical to ensuring that young women become equal actors in political, economic, and social life in Africa as elsewhere. Most young feminist-led organisations and movements are powered by volunteer labour. There are enormous barriers to accessing the funding we need from governments or development donors. A report launched by FRIDA and AWID (2016), *Brave, Creative, Resilient: The Global State of Young Feminist Organizing*, used a combination of quantitative and qualitative methods to document funding trends, challenges, and opportunities for young women, girl, and trans* youth-led organisations. The report highlighted that young feminist-led organisations have an average budget of $5,000 per annum for their work (*ibid.*, 73), and most operate without core funding. This often means that their work is project-based, and funding is not aimed at building and sustaining young feminist movements (*ibid.*).

A final fundamental challenge to movement building that affects the participation of the most marginalised women relates to poverty and lack of time. An unequal gender division of labour places a huge burden on young women and girls, in particular those living in poverty. Unpaid care was recognised as a human rights violation by the UN Special Rapporteur on Extreme Poverty in 2013 (Esquivel 2014).

Conclusion

> Barack Obama once said: 'the best way to not feel hopeless is to get up and do something!' As a young feminist, this is my mantra. There is so much that young women and girls have to battle with daily especially in regards to Sexual & Reproductive Health & Rights (SRHR) issues. Although there has been progress made, there is still a long way to go. I believe that the role of young feminists right now is to take action and to amplify our voices. (Akushika Odunton, Advocacy Mentee at FEMNET, 9 May 2018)

As a young feminist, I believe we have proven that our #FeministFuture is a world where women and girls in all of their diversity enjoy the benefits of gender equality and human rights. Young women involved in feminist action are taking the initiative for all. This includes the young women who are not immediately involved or privy to our work, due to various limitations, faced with various barriers that hinder them from organising around equality and rights as they experience them. We all need to find the avenues and resources we need if we are going to take political action and try to deliver our imaginings of a better world.

As we look back on 25 years from Beijing and Cairo amid today's unique challenges to women's rights and political action, the obligation to the global feminist movement is to ensure that we honour the work of all feminists, affirm their struggles and our own, and harness the power of a collective movement. If we succeed, we shall live in a world where girls and women in all of their diversity have the power, choice, voice, and agency to make and enact their own decisions regarding their sexual and reproductive health rights and well-being, and to claim their human rights.

Notes

1. For more information, see www.femnet.org (last checked 3 September 2018).
2. For more information, see https://whatwomenwant.format.com/ (last checked 3 September 2018).

3. For more information, see www.genderismyagenda.com/ (last checked 3 September 2018).
4. For more information, see www.akinamamawaafrika.org (last checked 3 September 2018).
5. See   www.nation.co.ke/news/Campaigners-take-on-US-embassies/1056-4338598-m4xfd6z/index.html (last checked 3 September 2018).

Notes on contributor

Catherine Nyambura is an international development expert and independent consultant working with feminist networks, philanthropic foundations, and grassroots movements on global health, advocacy, and feminist movement building across Africa and beyond. Catherine is a program advisor for the Strategic Initiative for the Horn of Africa, one of the largest feminist networks in East and Horn of Africa, and is the chair of the regional activities working group for COFEM. She is a Mandela Fellow (2016), Royal Commonwealth associate fellow, and 120 under 40 winner, and was named one of the five young African women changemakers to know in 2015 by *This is Africa* magazine.

References

African Union (2017) *AU Roadmap on Harnessing the Demographic Dividend Through Investments in Youth*, https://au.int/sites/default/files/pages/33794-file-au_2017_dd_roadmap_final_-_eng.pdf (last checked 2 October 2018)

ATHENA (2015) 'What Women Want', https://whatwomenwant.format.com/feministblog (last checked 10 September 2018)

Baden, Sally and Anne-Marie Goetz (1997) 'Who needs [sex] when you can have [gender]? Conflicting discourses on Gender at Beijing', *Feminist Review* 56(1): 3–25

Cha, Seungman (2017) 'The impact of the worldwide Millennium Development Goals campaign on maternal and under-five child mortality reduction: "Where did the worldwide campaign work most effectively?"', *Global Health Action* 10.1, https://www.ncbi.nlm.nih.gov/pmc/articles/PMC5328361/ (last checked 3 September 2018)

Corrêa, Sonia and Rebecca Lynn Reichmann (1994) *Population and Reproductive Rights: Feminist Perspectives from the South*, London: Zed Books

Crenshaw, Kimberlé (1991) 'Mapping the Margins: Intersectionality, Identity Politics, and Violence against Women of Color', *Stanford Law Review* 43(6): 1241–49

Esquivel, Valeria (2017) 'What is a transformative approach to care, and why do we need it?', *Gender & Development* 22(3): 423–39

FEMNET (2017) 'Young Women and the Demographic Dividend: Advocacy Brief', http://femnet.org/2017/06/young-women-and-the-demographic-dividend-advocacy-brief/ (last checked 3 September 2018)

FEMNET (2012) *Herstory – Our Journey: Advocating for the Rights of African Women*, http://femnet.org/wp-content/uploads/2015/11/livre-Femenet-Her-Story-en-20131209.pdf (last checked 10 September 2018)

FRIDA | The Young Feminist Fund and the Association for Women's Rights in Development (AWID) (2016) *Brave, Creative, Resilient: The Global State of Young Feminist Organizing*, https://www.awid.org/publications/brave-creative-and-resilient-state-young-feminist-organizing (last checked 2 October 2018)

International Center on Non-Profit Law (2016) *'Survey of Trends Affecting Civic Space 2015-6'*, http://www.icnl.org/research/trends/trends7-4.pdf?pdf=trends7-4%20volume%207,%20issues%204%20page%202-21 (last checked 3 September 2018)

Jahan, Rounaq (1995) *The Elusive Agenda: Mainstreaming Women in Development*. London: St. Martin's Press

Kabwato, Linda (2013) 'Young Women in Political Participation, Final Report', https://idl-bnc-idrc.dspacedirect.org/bitstream/handle/10625/52638/IDL-52638.pdf (last checked 10 September 2018)

O'Brien, Jon (2017) 'As a Catholic, I find Donald Trump's anti-abortion legislation disgusting', *The Independent*, 23 January, https://www.independent.co.uk/voices/catholic-global-gag-rule-donald-trump-risks-womens-lives-foreign-aid-abortion-a7542601.html (last checked 18 October 2018)

O'Donnell, Amy and Caroline Sweetman (2018) 'Introduction: Gender, development and ICTS', *Gender & Development* 26(2): 217–29

UN (2015) *Fact Sheet: Youth Population Trends and Sustainable Development*, http://www.un.org/esasocdev/documents/youth/fact-sheets/YouthPOP.pdf (last checked 26 June 2018)

UN (2001) 'The Development of the Gender Mainstreaming Strategy', http://www.un.org/womenwatch/osagi/pdf/factsheet3.pdf (last checked 2 October 2018)

UN (1995) 'Beijing Declaration and Platform for Action', http://www.un.org/womenwatch/daw/beijing/pdf/BDPfA%20E.pdf (last checked 2 October 2018)

UNAIDS (2016) *'Global AIDS Update 2016'*, Geneva: UNAIDS, http://www.unaids.org/sites/default/files/media_asset/global-AIDS-update-2016_en.pdf (last checked 3 September 2018)

UNFPA (2014) *Framework of Actions for the Follow Up to the Programme of Action of the International Conference of Population and Development Beyond 2014: Report of the Secretary-General*, https://www.unfpa.org/sites/default/files/pub-pdf/ICPD_beyond2014_EN.pdf (last checked 2 October 2018)

UN Office of the Special Adviser on Africa (OSAA) (2017) *The New Urban Agenda and Demographic Dividend: Investments for Africa's Youth*, http://www.un.org/en/africa/osaa/pdf/events/2017/20170325/Report-the_New_Urban_Agenda_and_Demographic_Dividend_Investments_for_AfricasYouth_final.pdf (last checked 10 September 2018)

CHAPTER 4

Young feminists' creative strategies to challenge the status quo: a view from FRIDA

Gopika Bashi, Lucia Martelotte,
Boikanyo Modungwa and Maria Eugenia Olmos

Abstract

Young feminist organising is springing up in all corners of the globe – from Mexico to Morocco to Malaysia – powered by brave young women, girls and trans* youth who are creating the change the world needs. FRIDA | The Young Feminist Fund – is a young feminist-led organisation that began in 2010. It aims to provide young feminist leaders with the resources they need to amplify their voices and initiatives as well as bring attention to their work. This chapter offers a view from four young feminists involved in FRIDA's work, sharing some of the innovative and creative strategies currently being used to challenge the status quo.

Keywords: Activism; strategies; feminism; youth; funding

Introduction

The feminist movement worldwide is a key force for change, fuelling important shifts in power to ensure the rights of the most marginalised. Young feminist organisers across the global South are building on past decades of intense work to play a critical role within the movement as it exists today. They are using creative and innovative strategies to strengthen movements, to increase awareness, build capacities, and advocate for gender, climate, socioeconomic, and political justice worldwide. They are responding to key needs within their communities and are often forced to be innovative, due to challenging and generally hostile environments. For example, the insights and mobilisation of young feminists, in particular, have fostered the emergence of movements like #NiUnaMenos ('Not One Woman Less') (Gordon 2016; LATFEM 2017) or #MiPrimerAcoso ('My First Harassment') (Paulier 2016) in Latin America.

Every generation of feminists faces the particular challenges of their time. They are also operating, organising, and strategising in an environment which offers them new opportunities. An obvious one for today's 'fourth-wave' feminists is the new ways of communicating, networking, and harnessing collective power offered by digital technologies and the use of new media. Today, the young feminist movement is growing, and the youth represent a greater proportion of the world's population than ever before. As the global population grows younger, governments and development organisations focus on this reality and what young people can do for the existing economic and political system – referring to this as the 'demographic dividend'. Yet feminists argue that the current system is inherently unequal, unjust, and unsustainable, and young feminists have not bought into the vision of the demographic dividend, but an alternative vision of social, economic, and political justice.

While young feminists continue to innovate in difficult, and sometimes extremely repressive environments, the need to support and strengthen their work is important now more than ever, as the evidence we present in this chapter will show. The chapter will share examples of some of this pioneering work from across young feminist movements, capturing the work that they do, their perspectives on their approach, as well as some of the innovative and creative strategies that young feminists employ to overcome challenges that they face. In addition, the chapter presents key recommendations on how the international community, specifically civil society and international development actors, can best support and collaborate with these groups.

The chapter takes as its starting point some of the key findings of a 2016 report *Brave, Creative, Resilient: The Global State of Young Feminist Organizing* published by FRIDA | The Young Feminist Fund (FRIDA)[1] and the Association for Women's Rights in Development (AWID)[2] (FRIDA and AWID 2016). Our aim in producing this chapter was to build on existing data about the state of young feminist organising, and gather in-depth information about how young feminists are innovating at the grassroots to tackle many of the structural and systemic issues they face. The chapter, therefore, captures the experiences of young feminist activists who come up against significant challenges, in their own words, and captures key intersectional issues that arise from their struggle for justice within the broader context of the feminist movement.

Where are we now? Young feminists in an increasingly polarised world

What kind of world have young feminists inherited in 2018? Globally, while countries make commitments to ensure the achievement of the Sustainable Development Goals, there has been a systematic erosion and violations of fundamental human rights by state and non-state actors: from the ongoing ethnic cleansing of Rohingya people in Myanmar (Al-Jazeera and News Agencies 2018) by a belligerent government, to systematic discrimination against LGBTI communities (UN 2018), merely because of their sexual orientation and gender identity.

According to Amnesty International's (2018, 12) 'Report on the State of the World's Human Rights', 'Assaults on the basic values underpinning human rights – which recognize the dignity and equality of all people – have assumed vast proportions. Conflicts, fueled by the international arms trade, continue to exact a cataclysmic toll on civilians, often by design'. This has, of course, meant that the rights of the most marginalised and vulnerable, including women, girls, trans*, and non-binary communities, have suffered the most.

Women are facing enormous challenges linked to the advancement of conservative and opposition groups, as well as religious fundamentalisms. The reinstatement of The Global Gag Rule (formally known as the Mexico City Policy)[3] has meant the curtailing of basic reproductive rights across the developing world. It is almost too obvious to say, but those personally affected most acutely by this development are women who face reproductive choices, although the impact of not recognising women's basic bodily rights affects the whole of society. Feminist activists won an enormous victory regarding repro-ductive rights at the UN Conference on Population and Development, held a generation ago in Cairo, and it is the next generation of women and girls who are now at the sharp end of the reversal of progress on reproductive rights. Additionally, the proliferation of extractive megaprojects and the implemen-tation of macro-economic models informed by neo-liberal thinking that sees development as economic growth (Trucchi 2016) fuel the criminalisation of protest against these and other violations of human rights. These have an impact on all generations of women, in different ways, depending also on the extent of marginalisation and the intersecting forms of discrimination that women face.

In recent years, there has been a rise in the systematic targeting and kill-ing of women human rights defenders (WHRDs), whose critical work is at the frontlines to uncover serious violations of human rights by states that are often carried out with impunity. The year began with the cold-blooded murder of Marielle Franco, prominent Brazilian feminist and human rights defender and activist (Phillips 2018); not very long after, Indian journalist and human rights defender Gauri Lankesh was shot dead outside her home in September 2017 (Deb 2018). According to Global Witness, 60 per cent of the murders of human rights defenders took place in Latin America, and in 40–50 per cent of the cases, the targets were indigenous, rural, peasant, and/or Afro-descendant populations (Freijó 2018, 67). In Central and Eastern Europe, the significant backlash against WHRDs working on intersectional discrimination has led to severe security threats for them, even when they are merely travel-ling to meetings (Global Fund for Women 2016).

Many women and survivors of sexual and gender-based violence who had been silent, or silenced because of fear, stigma, and mistrust in the justice system, have found their voices through the public conversation generated by #MeToo, a movement that was founded in 2006.[4] While, on the one hand, the virality of #MeToo has served as a powerful reminder of the sheer scale of violence against women and girls, it has also led to reactionary and often violent retaliations against those who choose to speak out. Online has become a critical space for women to come together, as noted earlier, but it is also a space of violence, enabling hostile and aggressive individuals to find each other and take action against progressive voices, with little or no regulation by companies or governments.

Currently, young feminists are emerging as a force to represent the future face of a complex and changing wider feminist movement. This is composed of feminists from around the globe facing many different and complex manifestations of the trends we have outlined in this section. They are young, mid-life, and old. They started out in the second and third wave, as well as today's fourth wave. But young women are our focus here, as the seeds that are sprouting out in what has been called a 'feminist spring' (Lanza 2018). Young feminists are challenging and shifting public discourse about women, gender roles and relations, and gender itself – and doing so at community, regional, national, and international levels. They are showing their ability to organise intersectionally (that is, recognising and respecting differences between them arising from race, class, caste, disability, and other aspects of identity), with often extremely limited resources and support from their own communities.

Young feminists are proving brave, creative, and resilient. They are developing and innovating tactics to fight the forces of rising conservatism, violence from state and non-state actors, and restricted mobility and freedom of speech. It is important to analyse and share their specific experience. Feminists have consistently come together down the decades to challenge dominant patriarchal structures and narratives in their particular time and location. Women's personal experience of gendered oppression and discrimination differs according to their age and life-stage. Young women and trans* youth have the right to education, to laws that further their human rights and freedoms, and to play a full and equal part in the political, economic, and social life of their communities and nations. Yet they are frequently discriminated against on grounds of age, and feminists of older and earlier generations may not offer them space to voice their perspectives and to play a role as leaders.

Researching young feminist activism

In addition to drawing on the 2016 report *Brave, Creative, Resilient: The Global State of Young Feminist Organizing* (FRIDA and AWID 2016), we analysed data and insights derived from responses given by young feminist activists who applied for funding from FRIDA over the past three years (2015, 2016, 2018). For the purposes of this chapter, we also looked at data from FRIDA grantee partners in the 2016 and 2017 grant cycles. In addition to this, we carried out in-depth interviews in July 2018 with ten young feminist organisations and activists in three of the five regions where FRIDA is working: Middle East and North Africa (MENA; three interviews); Latin America and the Caribbean (four interviews); and Central Eastern Europe, Caucasus, and Central and North Asia (three interviews). The selection process of the young feminists that were identified for the research was based on the representation of subregions that generally receive less attention, as well as guaranteeing diversity of political, cultural, and economic context and the most pressing issues that each of the activists and groups are working for. Moreover, we engaged with activists and groups that are working towards advancing girls, young women, and trans rights with innovative and creative strategies, actions, and approaches.

The methodology we used in our interviews for this chapter reflects our ongoing commitment to ensuring the acknowledgement and respect for young feminist activist contributions. We designed an interview script organised under the following sections: background (how they got into the feminist movement); overall reflections on young feminist movements in the region/ country (focusing on the strategies and on the challenges/opportunities); expectations from other actors (especially allies, donors, and international non-government organisations – INGOs); and funding, technology, holistic security, and self-care. All the direct quotations from members of feminist organisations included in the sections below come from these interviews.

The sections that follow draw on the findings of the 2016 research, and our recent interviews with activists; also, where useful and possible, we present data from applications and grantee partner reports.

About 'us' and FRIDA

The idea for a young feminist fund originated a decade ago in 2008, at a feminist gathering in Morocco where the emergence of young feminist activism and the lack of access to resources was identified as a significant barrier for young feminist organising. Two years later, an intergenerational group of feminist activists met to bring the fund to life.[5] Today, FRIDA is anchored by a staff of 20 young feminists, with 58 advisors across five regions globally, who support and amplify FRIDA's work and outreach. FRIDA currently has over 180 grantee partners; young feminist-led groups and organisations who receive small core grants as well as capacity development support. FRIDA has continued to grow, building deep regional connections amongst feminists, and increasing its philanthropic advocacy to ensure increased flexible funding for young feminist organising. FRIDA is currently a virtual organisation, in the sense that it has no 'head office', but rather has staff and advisors across the world.

The core problem identified in FRIDA's Theory of Change (2018)[6] is that while young feminist organisers offer critical new perspectives and insight that helps galvanise and sustain global and local social justice movements, too often, however, their leadership is undervalued, unrecognised, and untrusted, leaving them with less access to funding and strategy-setting roles. This reduces the power and vibrancy of movements and organisations globally, leaving us entrenched in traditional leadership styles and systems and missing out on alternative energies and talents. One of FRIDA's core beliefs is that young women, girls, and trans* youth are the experts of their own reality. We therefore believe that if young feminist activists and their organisations are provided with the resources, leadership opportunities, and capacities that they have identified as critical to mobilising progressive and political change, then radical shifts to movements' landscapes and social change trajectories occur (*ibid.*).

We are also aware of the difficult context that young feminists in the global South function within, as shared above. The greatest challenges for FRIDA in doing its work within this context has been the closing space for civil society we see today. The direct challenges to our work which emerge from this include: restrictions for foreign funding for grantee partners[7] which creates difficulties in the transfer of funds, registration restrictions for groups working on issues considered taboo[8] which affects some groups' ability to mobilise additional funds from other donors, and the surveillance of groups[9] which deters activists from carrying out their initiatives and our ability to provide additional support to them. We therefore fund young feminist groups both formally registered as non-government/non-profit organisations and those organising informally, using a participatory grantmaking model which involves advisors (mainly screening for basic funding criteria) and a voting process conducted by applicants to make decisions on who gets the grants. Furthermore, with support from advisors and local organisations, we are able to get funds to all grantee partners safely. In addition to funding, we allocate a significant portion of our budget to capacity development, linking, and learning opportunities in recognition of the support and need to connect with others from the feminist movement for emerging groups. Finally, the last major component of our work is philanthropic advocacy, ensuring that the impact of young feminist activism is recognised and that it translates to more funders providing accessible and flexible funding for young feminist organisers.

As young feminists from different regions ourselves, the authors of this chapter play complementary roles at FRIDA as advisors and staff members, where we have the space to organise as feminists cross-thematically and cross-regionally. While we all may occupy different spaces within social justice movements or the international development sector, or as part of the funding sector, we all share a deep commitment to amplify the voices and experiences of other young feminists that have been supported by FRIDA, which brought us together to write this piece.

Young feminist strategies: an overview

FRIDA uses the term 'feminist' broadly to refer to individuals and collectives working within women's movements or in other social movements to promote and work towards the safety, equality, justice, rights, and dignity of girls, women, and other marginalised groups. Based on the understanding that fundamental discrimination occurs within patriarchal systems of domination in all societies, young feminists are determined to challenge, address, and change the root causes of these existing inequalities, rights violations, and injustice. We recognise that there are multiple feminisms and foster opportunities for expressing those principles in our work. FRIDA emphasises feminist principles throughout all of its work. These principles include: non-hierarchy, collectivity, participation, diversity, and inclusion. We define young feminist activists as individuals from across the gender spectrum committed to advancing gender equality and women's rights through explicitly feminist means. FRIDA focuses on activism led by feminists under 30 years of age (FRIDA 2018).

Young feminists have made their presence felt across the globe through their sheer numbers and powers to mobilise large constituencies. The strategies that they use, and the issues that they take forward are, more often than not, those that have to do with the shifting of deeply held norms, and patriarchal beliefs and attitudes, and are not only focused on changing laws and policies.

Two of the most recent examples of the power of young feminism manifested in the Southern Cone. In Argentina, the debate about legalisation of abortion was catalysed by a wave of young women, trans* youth, and girls whose participation marked a generational divide around conservative politics in the country. They spoke truth to power: on the streets, in their schools, in intergenerational debates with health providers and older feminists, and also had the opportunity to advocate for their rights in front of Congress, despite the fact that many were underaged and not able to vote yet (Peker 2018). In Chile, a feminist movement called #EducaciónNoSexista (A Non-sexist Education) had started with strikes in universities, and spread throughout the country, defying not only sexual harassment in the education system, but also machismo culture. More than 30 universities were occupied and hundreds of Chileans protested in the streets, demanding educational spaces free of sexism, patriarchy, and sexual harassment (McGowan 2018).

Every year, FRIDA receives hundreds of proposals from young feminist-led groups and organisations across the global South, all with varying thematic areas and strategies which they use to catalyse change in their communities and beyond. What is clear from the work that these collectives carry out is that young feminists themselves are indeed experts of their own realities. They have a firm understanding of the context and current dynamics at play in their communities, and will often change or rethink strategies to function within these complexities. Since young feminist organisations are often staffed by the populations they work with, many of whom dedicate their time and energy to a cause because of their own personal experiences, the strategies they use directly engage with these populations and are responsive to their immediate needs.

What factors inform young feminist strategies?

There are several factors which shape and influence the kinds of strategies that groups use: safety and security, the capacity and skills of the team, the budget of the group, friendships, and their understanding of feminism itself. From the interviews that we conducted for the research, we saw that feminism is more a way of living and a practical answer to daily problems than a set of theories for academic discussion. We saw how the idea that feminism is the-oretical, academic, 'Western' or 'bourgeois' had alienated several participants in our research:

> I experience feminism in my daily life: when I walk in the street, when I travel in public transportation, and not through books or concepts. For me feminism was healing. Then I discovered its political dimension. Feminism saved my life, and I hope it can save other people's lives.
> (Respondent from Gordas sin Chaqueta,[10] Colombia)

> My approach to feminism was by experience and following intuitions. It was a natural, genuine, and autonomous evolution. The theoretical and conceptual framework came later.
> (No Tan Distintas,[11] Argentina)

In 2016, the *Brave, Creative, Resilient* report found that most young feminist groups consulted had a budget of under US$5,000 per year, a quarter of them having an annual budget of just US$500; which means a majority of their work is self-funded and carried out with very limited financial resources. Their budgets therefore influence the types of strategies they utilise.

While in some instances, the use of the creative and innovative strategies to be presented within this chapter suggests that they are pursuing social jus-tice in new ways, several young feminists are also taking forward key strategies that the feminist movement has used in the past and enriching them. For example, during the recent strikes and occupations against sexual harassment in Chile, young feminists have shown the scale at which they can mobilise and lead a large-scale movement to change laws and policies around violence and discrimination.

Some of the distinct features identified by young feminists between their work and that of the older generation of feminists were intersectionality and the attitudes and emotions embedded in their work. A research participant representing the organisation Fe-Male in Lebanon noted the rejection of the inclusion of LGBTQ rights and refugee rights by older feminists. In addition, a young feminist from Tunisia stated the following:

> Younger feminist groups are much more aware politically, are much more intersectional, and more radical ... I believe that young feminists adopt these new strategies because they are more aware of the needs of the younger generations, because the needs of the society have changed and making the change becomes much more urgent and sometimes needs strong, radical, interventions. But also, because they have wit-nessed the emergence of new movements and have been part of them, their intersectional understanding is broader.

Another (much less spoken-of) factor that informs the attitudes and practices of young feminists is the importance of friendships in shaping their world-views, particularly in contexts where older women are not feminists. In our research, young feminists from Las Hijas del Rap (Mexico) emphasised that they are working from a place of joy, and happiness and emotions play a significant role in their work. In a recent chapter about young feminism in Argentina, Agustina Lanza also highlights the central role of friendship in the development of the movement:

> It was their friends who pointed out [to the young feminists] that certain attitudes of their couples were violent, that encouraged them to defend themselves or to answer to street harassment. It was those friends who lent them a book about the issue [feminism] or that took them to a march. Most of the times neither their grandmothers nor their mothers were feminists. (Lanza 2018)

Awareness raising, capacity building, and advocacy and lobbying: the young feminist way

In reviewing FRIDA grantees' primary strategies over the past two years (2016 and 2017 grant cycles), as well as application data (2015, 2016, 2018), the top three strategies that emerged were: awareness raising, capacity building, and advocacy and lobbying.

Awareness raising is a vital strategy because often the lack of access to information and the impact of certain practices and beliefs are unknown or misunderstood. In fact, over the past two years, a majority of FRIDA grantee partners indicated that their work contributed to changing individual or community attitudes, practices, or consciousness, indicating the widespread need for awareness-raising strategies. In 2016, 37 per cent of grantees and in 2017, 35 per cent of grantees stated that their core strategy was awareness raising: some of the activities conducted as part of this strategy included social media campaigns against the objectification of women in the media, community sensitisation meetings on sex workers' rights, radio programmes on forced marriage, and the translation of key sexual and reproductive health rights information into indigenous languages.

Capacity building is another important strategy, with some FRIDA grantees focusing on internal strengthening of the organisation while others focus on trainings and capacity building of the communities in which they work. FRIDA awards core and capacity development grants to enable groups to allocate funding to the sustainability of the collectives through strengthening the human resources of the group and enabling them to access additional funding.

The capacity development grants currently awarded by FRIDA are used on a variety of self-identified needs, e.g. some groups use the grant to go for Monitoring, Evaluation and Learning training or to get a consultant to support them with proposal writing. Several groups focus on capacity development with their communities as particularly in the global South, socioeconomic and political contexts have left girls, women, and trans* youth with limited access to resources, services, and opportunities; capacity development has been identified as a critical strategy to address this limited access. For example, Hashtag Generation,[12] a young feminist group in Sri Lanka, conducts trainings for aspiring female politicians on running successful campaigns (including the use of social media) as part of efforts to increase women's political partici-pation and representation in the country.

Finally, advocacy and lobbying or campaigning is also a popular strategy for groups. Groups who work in this area have, for instance, lobbied local leaders to change customary laws regarding forced marriage (FRIDA 2015) or politicians to raise issues in parliament.

Innovative and creative: young feminist tools and tactics

While the above are the most commonly used strategies, in the following sec-tion we share some emerging creative and innovative ways of engaging used by young feminist groups in the global South: the use of online platforms/social media for awareness raising, mobilisation, and virtual safe spaces, art for development or change (commonly referred to as 'artivism') and, increasingly, carrying out self-care initiatives with self-care as an end in itself, but also as a strategy to sustain movements. Groups use a range of strategies alongside each other as a multi-pronged approach to contributing to positive change in their communities.

Online platforms and creating virtual 'safe spaces'

Young feminists have used social media as a tool for mobilisation and increas-ing awareness on vital issues, creating social pressure for change, as well as public and private virtual safe spaces for women to connect and share their experiences. Social media activism, sometimes referred to as 'hashtag activ-ism', is often a complementary strategy done alongside initiatives on the ground. This makes visible the various causes and issues that young people are addressing.

In reflecting on the role of online awareness-raising campaigns and calls to action, #MeToo and #NiUnaMenos are considered extremely important by young feminists. Beyond that, the campaigns were seen to visibilise issues often regarded as private, lessening the shame often associated with sexual harassment and abuse, they also opened up introspective processes, and urged survivors of sexual harassment and abuse to speak out and report cases. This is specifically because they spurred groups and organisations to analyse and rethink their strategies. Bonds and alliances were established with women's groups and collectives from other regions, in recognition of common trends and problems that women face worldwide, regardless of the particular context.

Online platforms have been critical in supporting young activists to orga-nise collective action, so much so that often during political unrest, social media platforms or the internet is shut down in several countries in the global

South. It has also enabled younger women and girls to have a direct link to audiences to hear their stories, from their perspectives.

Case study 1: Tackling objectification of women: Fe-Male, Lebanon
Fe-Male[13] was founded in 2012 by a group of young feminists in Beirut, Lebanon. It is a civil non-sectarian association that works on raising gender awareness through mass and social media, women's empowerment, elimination of stereotyping and objectification of women, and changing discriminatory laws. Fe-Male leads a campaign against the objectification of women in the media and the role this plays in contributing to gender-based violence. One of the creative activities conducted to address this has been social media campaigns, which included visuals from their offline initiatives as well. The offline activities range from street art/graffiti, screenings, panel discussions, or presenting their messages on radio. More recently, Fe-Male has conducted a study on laws in Lebanon that regulate media content, which included providing recommendations for the media and advertising industries.

Fe-Male has also sought partnerships with media departments at universities as well as some media agencies, which has strengthened the methodology of their various campaigns. Finally, Fe-Male was part of the campaign aiming to abolish Article 522 from the Lebanese penal code – which allowed rapists to marry their victims to avoid punishment and imprisonment. The campaign was launched by ABAAD organisation; Fe-Male participated through direct and online advocacy, leveraging their large following to create social pressure for its abolition. The law was then abolished in August 2017.

Case study 2: Talking sex, gender, and sexuality: HolaAfrica, South Africa
HolaAfrica[14] was founded in 2012 in Johannesburg when the original collective realised that there was very little online in terms of the African queer female experience. The group was a FRIDA grantee partner from 2016 to 2017. The original idea has evolved, and the collective focuses now on adding to the African female sex and sexuality narrative. This narrative was historically erased, and is currently under-developed, but is still extremely powerful. By publishing stories of African women on all aspects of sex and sexuality – be it political, economic, social, or sexual – the group seeks to add to the general narrative and rhetoric surrounding these issues. This is done whilst engaging in online activities and campaigns, looking to have conversations on everything from masturbation and safe sex to cyber violence.

HolaAfrica's website challenges perceptions and norms beyond and within the LGBTQI community on African queer women's experiences. They have published audio, visual, and written material such as a blog post on 'How Femme Invisibility kills sex & social interactions', as an act of knowledge production, awareness raising, and activism on African queer experiences. Their contributors are queer women from across the African continent and diaspora. The group has recently published a safe sex and pleasure manual[15] compiled after a series of workshops to collect the concerns, issues, and interests of women. The manual particularly focuses on pleasure to disrupt norms on the lack of discussion on women's sexual pleasure and the portrayal of sex between women from the male lens and for a male audience.

Art for social change: theatre and music

Art for development or 'artivism' is an approach which allows groups to use art (whether it be drawings, musical compositions, or theatre) as a form of activism. Artivism has been an approach that has been embraced by the feminist movement to document struggles, facilitate learning and sharing, and even dream 'feminist futures'.[16] The young feminists whom we spoke to through our interviews for this chapter in July 2018 pointed out the importance of art in connecting with their audiences, and challenging existing patriarchal narratives:

> Enjoyment, music, and art make feminism more powerful and has helped many women to support feminist struggles and to acknowledge that feminism is not just about suffering and pain.
>
> (Member of Las Hijas del RAP, Mexico)

Case study 3: Consensus building through theatre: Giuvlipen, Romania
Giuvlipen[17] (meaning feminism in Romani language) was founded in 2014 and is a feminist theatre group with, for, and about Roma women, with the goal of contributing to the empowerment of Roma women in their communities. The group creates theatre performances based on life stories of Roma women, about their difficulties living between a traditional patriarchal community and a demanded integration into the dominant (often racist) Romanian community.

For example, one of the issues the group has used their performances to tackle is forced marriage and its impact on girls' lives. This approach opens a unique space to build awareness of the effects of forced marriage as well as for open discussion on how to address these. Furthermore, it encourages consensus building in the community to challenge the patriarchal norms around forced marriage (FRIDA 2015).

Case study 4: Feminism through rap: Las Hijas del Rap, Mexico
Las Hijas del Rap[18] is an initiative of the hip hop women of the Yucatan Peninsula that began in late 2015. Formed by dancers, rappers, and visual artists, Las Hijas del Rap is a collective of feminist hip hop artists dedicated to using artivism for eradicating gender violence and motivating social action based on art and culture. Las Hijas del Rap translates to 'the daughters of rap'! In the past year, the group conducted urban dance, art, and rap workshops with girls in their community (specifically Mayan speakers in Yucatan). The first of the workshops is a discussion on feminism, the objective of which is to initiate reflection on identity, their rights, and to talk about the concept of friendship between women. The purpose of the workshops was to give

the girls an opportunity to share about their challenges and reinforce their identity and their ability to influence their spaces. More importantly, the workshop was a space to create community among them and develop a sense of friendship between the girls; the workshops have therefore served as both a space for self-awareness, acceptance, and celebration, as well as a space for connection and building feminist friendships and support systems through the use of rap music. One of the main outputs of the workshops was for the girls to co-write a song, and direct a music video for the song.

Self and collective care: sustaining our movements

The ongoing assault on women's and trans* youths' bodies, lives, and activism has led to the burn-out of many activists. Several are personally known to us. Self-care is a strategy to ensure that individual feminist activists do not burn out, ensuring the sustainability of our movements.

According to FRIDA's paper, 'Strengthening Communities of Resistance':

> When young women challenge their oppression and subordination they attack a carefully crafted system that does not tolerate those that challenge it. In its endeavor to self-preserve, patriarchy therefore responds in very violent ways towards anyone that steps out of its boundaries. Movement building work with young women in addition to driving resistance seeks to challenge these very structures by strategizing on how to deal with the backlash and providing solidarity and support for those that are violently attacked. Wellbeing, safety and security become central features of a movement building agenda. The wellness of individuals within a collective as well as the wellness of the collective are critical. (Chigudu 2018, 9)

Self-care is present in almost all the young feminist groups and regions we have worked with, but at different levels. While some are just being introduced to this concept, other collectives have gone through a learning and awareness-raising process, and are recognising self-care as a political issue. The prevalent approach is based on intuition and informal practices, such as fair communications, flexible hours, healthy nutrition, and creating spaces for expression of feelings.

Case study 5: Self-care of marginalised communities and WHRDs:
the BuSSy project, Egypt
BuSSy[19] is a project intended to empower women and raise awareness about women's issues through storytelling. Together with different groups of men and women, stories of Egyptian women, about their memories and experiences of womanhood, are told on stage, to expose real women's stories and provide a space for free expression on issues that society was failing to address.

The group organised storytelling workshops for marginalised communities; girls and young women who are homeless, wives and widows of fishermen in Damietta, and youth in Luxor. The storytelling workshops were designed to provide women and young girls with a safe space to share their personal stories and everyday experiences, as well as the obstacles they face as women in their communities. In addition, the group held private story-telling sessions for people (such as researchers, councillors, and activists) working on gender-related issues, including gender-based violence. This was done to create a space for them to share the challenges and joys of their work, and to exchange strategies of self-care given the emotional strain that this work can have. BuSSy's participants have expressed appreciation for the creation of a space for self-expression, the identification of self-care tools, as well as creating and linking them to support networks.

Solidarity and support for young feminist organising

In this section, we discuss some of the core expectations that young feminists have from civil society, donors, and other movements aiming to work in sup-portive ways to enable young feminists to achieve their goals. All the strategies discussed in the sections above are underpinned, according to our interviews and analysis, by the need to work in a collaborative way. Young feminists wish – and need – to work with others to achieve their goals and increase their impact. But perhaps most importantly, their own stories bring back the need to come together in solidarity to work towards gender equality, inclusion, and social justice. This includes working intergenerationally.

NGOs, aid organisations, and donors have historically been part of a more 'professionalised' architecture, aimed at creating social change through local programming, capacity building, and support to activists. Over the last decade or so, the debates around the need for these organisations to rethink their relationships with activists and movements have been crucial to reflect on the sometimes 'extractive' nature of this relationship (Sriskandarajah 2017).

In addition to the tremendous pressures and challenges young feminists face at community level, interacting at multiple levels with governments, NGOs, and donors can make it quite challenging for them to navigate these spaces in ways that can contribute to their strategic goals, and not merely as a 'tick-box' activity. Below we share some of the key learnings, thoughts, and rec-ommendations from young feminist organisations on how to improve young feminist organisations' relationships with these organisations and systems, to work better together in shifting/balancing the power which includes core 'ingredients' for the 'recipe': feminism, solidarity, connecting, and investing.

Funding – the young feminist way

As documented by the FRIDA and AWID report in 2016, funding for young feminists is one of the most serious challenges they face. The crisis of funding is juxtaposed against the need for young feminist groups to remain auton-omous. This is one of the reasons why other than funding and providing capacity development opportunities, a core part of FRIDA's work is philanthropic advocacy, so that more funders not only dedicate funding to support young feminist activism but that the funding is accessible to all types of groups (one of the most significant accessibility criteria being supporting both registered and non-registered groups) and that the funding supports the groups' sustainability and ability to remain responsive to their changing contexts and needs of the communities they serve. Some groups have fundraising experience at a local level or use strategies to be autonomous and are aware of how donors could influence in their own agendas and language.

> You have to be patient, to learn, to get to know donors. To be ready to invest a lot, to do a lot of things for free and then you are going to see results. Step by step.
>
> (Member of Her Rights,[20] Belarus)

FRIDA's grantee partners have views on what funders should avoid doing when working with young feminist organisations:

> [Donors should] ... not use difficult language, and application processes to consider that everybody speaks English. Central Asia countries have lack of resources and understanding regarding resources not only material, information, skills, knowledge, money.
>
> (Member of Teenage Youth for Justice and Equality,[21] Kyrgyzstan)

> To establish more horizontal and human bonds. To take into account our reality and not to ask for quantitative indicators. To get to know each other, promoting meetings and face-to-face interactions. To foster participatory approaches. (Member of Las Hijas del RAP, Mexico)

In addition to concerns about the donor–grantee relationship, one interviewee also pointed out the importance of increased gender awareness within donor organisations, and more women on their staff.

Some of those interviewed stated that working with FRIDA was their first experience of working with an international donor. Others said FRIDA is different from their previous experiences working with other donors, stating differences in the way they are listened to, the horizontal dialogue, and opportunities for networking and capacity development as important factors in the relationship. The flexible funding and reporting requirements have allowed them to make strategic decisions for their organisations and therefore maintain full ownership of their projects and the direction they chose to take, using intersectional feminist values, ideology, and practice.

The importance of supporting networks

Networks – local, regional, and global – have been crucial to bringing social, economic, and political justice within different contexts. Young feminists echo the demand of the wider feminist movement – to support networks and movements – thus going beyond funding projects and programmes. In recognition of this work, FRIDA allocates a part of its budget to supporting groups to travel to spaces that facilitate networking and exchange or collaboration grants to support peer learning and collective organising, in addition to holding regional and global convenings. Convening spaces are widely recognised as key to networking and movement building – creating a space for alliance building, reflection, and dialogue. They are spaces where young feminists can share organising actions, deepen their understanding of how change happens in their diverse focus areas, as well as an opportunity to network beyond their borders and harness their collective power (FRIDA 2018). In the coming year, a movement-building strategy will be developed to strengthen our efforts in supporting networks.

Recognising autonomy

While recognising that all movements have complex and multi-pronged strategies, it is important to allow young feminists the space to operate with a high degree of autonomy – to set their own agendas, and define their own visions of change and how they see themselves (and others) contributing to achieving this. The organisations and activists interviewed emphasised the need for donors to recognise the situated knowledge and to understand and adapt their requirements to local realities:

> We hope they recognise our autonomy. (Member of Gordas sin Chaqueta, Colombia)

> Other organisations try to set priorities and we don't have many expectations but we hope that they could understand that every organisation has their own context. (Member of Fe-Male, Lebanon)

> The support of international organisations is most important first for the exchange of experiences and for the learning process that we both have to undergo to be able to collaborate on projects and on expanding the feminist culture but it is also very important because these international organisations are our only financial support so far and we have to reach a more flexible and sustainable way to support us financially. (Young feminist activist, MENA)

Investing in feminist approaches

A final finding that it is important to mention here is that young feminists we interviewed for the 2016 research stated a belief that INGOs should invest in the capacity development of young feminist organisations. Some referenced FRIDA's capacity development work, which is based on providing additional resources young feminists may need to amplify their leadership including skills, spaces, and relationships-networking.

Overall, our interviews revealed that while young feminists are open and willing to establish collaborations with other actors, they need to be on an equal playing field, and be able to influence existing agendas to benefit the communities and constituencies with which they work.

Conclusion

The young feminist movement has continuously carried out its work, while applying key principles of inclusivity, participation, and intersectionality within social justice movements (Johnson and Ranganathan 2016). Most recently, at the March 2018 Commission for the Status of Women 61, young feminists from across the world came together to put out key demands to governments, one of the key messages being the importance of flexible and continued support to the development and growth of movements, and not just to specific institutions and organisations (Young Feminist Caucus 2017).

Even though the young feminist interviewees (interviewed for this chapter) all came from different regions, there were more similarities than differences in the way they embodied gender and social justice struggles, have become feminists, their histories within movements, the ways in which they conduct their work (with a more horizontal and participatory perspective) as well as their strategies, and how they find ways to generate new dialogues and interaction with other organisations and movements, including in governmental spaces.

The key findings while writing this chapter re-emphasise what we, as young feminists, are witnessing too: the power of solidarity, collective (and self-) care, networking, and bringing together creative strategies such as music, dance, poetry, writing, and technology to rethink and create new ways of resistance and resilience. But most important is how these innovative strategies are bringing more girls, young women, and trans* youth to the forefront of the 'fourth wave', where young people are the crest of the wave, pushing forward fearlessly and tirelessly, for their rights and to challenge the status quo.

While we have highlighted several innovative approaches through this chapter, we recognise that it is just a starting point, and that there is a need for much more documentation and analysis around the contribution of young feminists to challenging many of the structural and systemic challenges faced by marginalised women, girls, and trans* communities across the globe. The young feminist movement continues to push forward rights-based, inclusive narratives that have the power to inform wider social justice movements for generations to come.

Notes

1. For more information on FRIDA | The Young Feminist Fund, see https://youngfeministfund.org/ (last checked 10 September 2018).
2. For more information on AWID, see www.awid.org/ (last checked 10 September 2018).

3. The Global Gag Rule is another name for the Mexico City Policy, first implemented in 1984 by USAID. It requires NGOs that receive federal funding from the US government to neither perform nor promote abortion as a method of family planning in other countries. For more information on The Global Gag Rule, see https://foreignpolicy.com/2017/03/20/the-global-gag-rule-americas-deadly-export-trump-africa-women-reproductive-rights/ (last checked 13 September 2018).

4. For more information on the Me Too Movement, see https://metoomvmt.org (last checked 31 August 2018).

5. All information given in this section comes from the FRIDA Timeline: http://youngfeministfund.org/time/#event-this-is-our-history (last checked 13 September 2018).

6. FRIDA Theory of Change (Garden of Change), see http://youngfeministfund.org/GardenofChangeA.html (last checked 10 September 2018).

7. Funding restrictions create barriers for FRIDA in transferring grants to grantee partners in certain countries. For more information on funding restrictions, see Global NPO Coalition on FATF Foreign Funding Restrictions: http://fatfplatform.org/foreign-funding-restrictions/ (last checked 10 September 2018).

8. For example, see the 2014 ruling which allowed an LGBTQI group in Botswana (not a FRIDA grantee partner) to formally register: https://legabibo.wordpress.com/2014/11/15/register-legabibo-judge-rannowane-orders-botswana-government/ (last checked 12 September 2018).

9. For example, surveillance of activists in China; read more in the following article: Christian Shepard (2017) 'China activists fear increased surveillance with new security law', https://www.reuters.com/article/us-china-security-idUSKBN18M09U (last checked 12 September 2018).

10. For more information, see https://youngfeministfund.org/grantees/colectiva-feminista-gordas-sin-chaqueta-colombia/ (last checked 13 September 2018).

11. For more information, see https://youngfeministfund.org/grantees/no-tan-distintas/ (last checked 13 September 2018).

12. For more information, see https://youngfeministfund.org/grantees/hashtag-generation/ (last checked 13 September 2018)

13. For more information, see the Fe-Male website: http://www.fe-male.org/ (last checked 13 September 2018).

14. For more information, see the HolaAfrica website: http://holaafrica.org/ (last checked 13 September 2018).

15. To read the safe sex and pleasure manual for African women, see http://holaafrica.org/wp-content/uploads/2016/09/TIFFM1038-HOLAA-PleaseHer-Manual_V.0.4.pdf (last checked 13 September 2018).

16. For more information, see https://www.awid.org/sites/default/files/atoms/files/feminist_futures.pdf (last checked 13 September 2018).

17. For more information, see https://youngfeministfund.org/grantees/giuvlipen/ (last checked 13 September 2018).

18. For more information, see https://youngfeministfund.org/grantees/las-hijas-del-rap/ (last checked 13 September 2018).

19. For more information, see https://youngfeministfund.org/grantees/bussy/ (last checked 13 September 2018).

20. For more information, see https://youngfeministfund.org/grantees/center-promotion-womens-rights-rights/ (last checked 13 September 2018).
21. For more information, see https://youngfeministfund.org/grantees/teenagers-youth-justice-equality-ty4je/ (last checked 13 September 2018).

Acknowledgements

We would like to recognise and acknowledge the contributions of all the young feminists we interviewed for this chapter, and other FRIDA staff and advisors who shared resources, contacts, and reflections for this chapter.

Notes on contributors

Gopika Bashi was previously a campaigner for Oxfam International on its worldwide Enough campaign to end violence against women and girls. She has been an advisor with FRIDA since 2015. Gopika is based in Bangalore, India.

Lucia Martelotte is a feminist researcher and activist. She was the Deputy Executive Director at ELA – Equipo Latinoamericano de Justicia y Género, a feminist NGO based in Argentina, and Programme Management Specialist at UN Women Argentina (2019–20). From 2016 to 2019 she was an advisor on the Latin America and the Caribbean region for FRIDA.

Boikanyo Modungwa is FRIDA's Research and Knowledge Building Officer; prior to that she was Monitoring, Evaluation and Learning Program Officer. Boikanyo is from Botswana.

Maria Eugenia Olmos worked at FRIDA as the Communities and Culture Co-ordinator (2017–19). She was also an advisor with FRIDA and co-facilitator for the Latin America and the Caribbean region. She works at Prospera – International Network of Women's Funds. Euge is based in Cordoba, Argentina.

References

Al Jazeera and News Agencies (2018) 'Rohingya "Ethnic Cleansing in Myanmar Continues": UN', 6 March, https://www.aljazeera.com/news/2018/03/rohingya-ethnic-cleansing-myanmar-continues-180306062135668.html (last checked 13 September 2018)

Amnesty International (2018) *Amnesty International Report 2017/18: The State of the World's Human Rights*, https://www.amnesty.org/download/Documents/POL1067002018ENGLISH.PDF (last checked 13 September 2018)

Chigudu, Rudo (2018) *Strengthening Communities of Resistance. A Reflection Paper*, https://youngfeministfund.org/FRIDA-Strengthening-Communities.pdf (last checked 13 September 2018)

Deb, Siddhartha (2018) 'The Killing of Gauri Lankesh', https://www.cjr.org/special_report/gauri-lankesh-killing.php/ (last checked 11 September 2018)

Freijó, María Florencia (2018) 'América Latina. Una mujer en pie de lucha', in Mujeres: Crónicas de feministas en lucha, Edición Especial N°14, *Revista Sudestada*, January

FRIDA | The Young Feminist Fund (2015) *My Body. My Life. My Choice: Challenging Forced Marriage. FRIDA Special Impact Report*, http://young feministfund.org/wp-content/uploads/2015/09/Forced-Marriage-Impact-Report.pdf (last checked 13 September 2018)

FRIDA | The Young Feminist Fund (2018) *Convening Reports – A Series of Four*, https://youngfeministfund.org/ComeTogether-FRIDAConvenings.html (last checked 13 September 2018)

FRIDA | The Young Feminist Fund and the Association for Women's Rights in Development (AWID) (2016) *Brave, Creative, Resilient: The Global State Of Young Feminist Organizing*, https://youngfeministfund.org/wp-content/uploads/2017/05/Global-State-of-Young-Feminist-Organizing.pdf (last checked 13 September 2018)

Global Fund for Women (2016) *Europe and Central Asia Activist Convening 2015 Learning Memo*, https://www.globalfundforwomen.org/wp-content/uploads/2016/05/Global-Fund-for-Women-ECA-Convening-2016-Learning-Memo.pdf (last checked 13 September 2018)

Gordon, Sarah (2016) 'NiUnaMenos: How the brutal gang rape and murder of a schoolgirl united the furious women of Latin America', *The Telegraph*, 21 October, https://www.telegraph.co.uk/women/life/niunamenos-how-a-schoolgirls-brutal-gang-rape-and-murder-united/ (last checked 13 September 2018)

Johnson, Ruby and Deepa Ranganathan (2016) 'The global pulse of young feminists organising', 50:50 openDemocracy, 8 March, https://www.opendemocracy.net/ruby-johnson/pulse-of-young-feminist-organising (last checked 13 September 2018)

Lanza, Agustina (2018) 'La juventad feminista', Anfibia, http://www.revista anfibia.com/cronica/juventud-feminista/ (last checked 13 September 2018)

LATFEM (2017) 'Ni Una Menos: la cuarta ola del feminismo', LATFEM Periodismo Feminista, 22 June, http://latfem.org/ni-una-menos-la-cuarta-ola-del-feminismo/ (last checked 13 September 2018)

McGowan, Mary (2018) 'How the Feminist Movement is Defying Machismo Culture in Chile', Culture Trip, 22 June, https://theculturetrip.com/south-america/chile/articles/why-the-feminist-movement-is-amplifying-in-chile/ (last checked 13 September 2018)

Paulier, Juan (2016) '#MiPrimerAcoso, la creadora del hashtag que sacudió inter-net y la importancia de que las mujeres no callen', BBC Mundo, 25 April, https://www.bbc.com/mundo/noticias/2016/04/160425_mexico_hashtag_mi_primer_acoso_violencia_mujeres_jp (last checked 13 September 2018)

Peker, Luciana (2018) 'La revolución de las hijas brilla por derecho propio', Página 12, 14 June, https://www.pagina12.com.ar/121553-la-revolucion-de-las-hijas-brilla-por-derecho-propio (last checked 13 September 2018)

Phillips, Dom (2018) 'Marielle Franco: Brazil's favelas mourn the death of a champion', *The Guardian*, 18 March, https://www.theguardian.com/world/2018/mar/18/marielle-franco-brazil-favelas-mourn-death-champion (last checked 13 September 2018)

Sriskandarajah, Dhananjayan (2017) 'How NGOs and social movements can learn to work together better', openDemocracy, 6 December, https://www.opendemocracy.net/democraciaabierta/dhananjayan-sriskandarajah/how-ngos-and-social-movements-can-learn-to-work-togethe/feed (last checked 13 September 2018)

Trucchi, Giorgio (2016) 'Extractive Model: the dispossession of territories and the criminalization of protest in Central America', in Bulletin 226, World Rainforest Movement, https://wrm.org.uy/articles-from-the-wrm-bulletin/extractive-model-the-dispossession-of-territories-and-the-criminalization-of-protest-in-central-america/ (last checked 11 October 2018)

UN (2018) 'Urgent action needed to stop violence and discrimination against LGBT people worldwide, says UN expert', UN Office of the High Commissioner for Human Rights, 18 June, https://www.ohchr.org/SP/NewsEvents/Pages/DisplayNews.aspx?NewsID=23209&LangID=E (last checked 13 September 2018)

Young Feminist Caucus (2017) *Young Feminist Caucus Statement at the Sixty First Session of the Commission on the Status of Women*, https://youngfeminist.org/wp-content/uploads/2017/03/young-feminist-csw61.pdf (last checked 14 September 2018)

CHAPTER 5

In the land of wise old men: experiences of young women activists in Myanmar

Agatha Ma, Poe Ei Phyu and Catriona Knapman

Abstract

In a society in which leadership is still largely defined by age and gender, young women in Myanmar face social, cultural, and even administrative challenges to raising their voices and taking on leadership roles. This chapter explores the experience of young women activists in Myanmar, considering social norms and challenges to leadership, coping strategies, and solutions to the obstacles that young women face to participating in ongoing legal and political reform in Myanmar.

Keywords: Myanmar; youth; women; age; leadership; policy reform; socio-cultural norms

Introduction

Since 2010, Myanmar has undergone rapid political changes: from an authoritarian, military-led government towards democratic leadership (Gaens 2013). However, at the time of writing in mid-2018, political leadership in Myanmar remains highly gender-unequal, dominated by older men who are still seen widely as natural leaders and decision-makers at all levels from family to national government. Although there are very famous and influential women leaders in Myanmar, notably the current State Counsellor Aung San Suu Kyi, women remain largely excluded from political institutions at all levels. They are enormously under-represented in decision-making roles, in particular at village and township level, but also in state and national parliaments (Minoletti 2014). In this challenging context, young women face particularly acute social, cultural, and even administrative challenges to raising their voices and taking on formal political leadership roles. In our wide experience working on these issues since 2012, only a small number of young women are able to participate in policy-level dialogue and discussions.

In recent years, civil society voices in Myanmar have been increasingly articulating a range of agendas for social and political change (Thin Thin Aye 2015). The response to Cyclone Nargis in 2008, followed by the 2010 political reform process, created a significant opening for civil society activism. Since

2012, in particular, there has been notable progress in terms of freedom of speech and expression (*ibid.*). Political prisoners have been released, exiled human rights activists have returned, and new rights activists and movements have emerged.[1]

A range of factors are currently encouraging young women to voice their interests and take on leadership roles in civil society spaces. There is now an active civil society in Myanmar, the majority of which are faith-based or charity organisations: fewer are activist groups. In addition, there are around 67 women-focused organisations, yet few of these focus on the particular issues of young women. There are also four women's-rights networks: Women's League of Burma (WLB; http://womenofburma.org) which has 13 members largely from remote and ethnic areas; Women's Organisation of Myanmar (WON; www.facebook.com/WONMM) which has 30 members; and the Gender Equality Network (GEN; www.genmyanmar.org) which has 26 local non-government organisation (NGO) and 24 international NGO members. WON members and GEN are based in urban areas. Alliance for Gender Inclusion in Peace Building Process (AGIPP; www.agipp.org) brings together seven main networks, including GEN and WON, focusing on gender inclusivity in the peace process.

New forms of activism are emerging and new spaces appearing. Civil society activism is now facilitated by new technologies (e.g. Nyein Nyein 2018). Increased affordability and quality of mobile phone and internet services have allowed Myanmar people to access apps and social media, in particular Facebook (Hogan and Sofi 2018; Mod 2016). In addition, a free and diverse press has meant that Myanmar society is exposed to global ideas much more than it was ten years ago. The availability of the internet enables new forms of organisation and activism to develop, as individuals and groups encounter each other in virtual spaces. Indeed, being online has been identified as a critical enabling factor for global activism – including so-called 'fourth-wave feminism', and the #MeToo movement focusing on issues of sexual rights and gender-based violence, although these specific movements have not had much impact in Myanmar. There are, however, downsides to these developments as being online also creates a space for hate speech, cyber violence, and repression to exist (see e.g. Holland 2014; Mclaughlinby 2018; Stecklow 2018). This can have additional impacts for women activists, such as online harassment.

Another factor in the growth of activism is the steady and growing exposure to different ways of being and doing that comes from the increasing mobility of women and men from Myanmar and other countries. An estimated two million Myanmar people (39 per cent women and 61 per cent men) are employed as migrant workers outside the country (MIMU 2014). While most migrant workers are not activists, the increased mobility has also had a positive impact in developing learning opportunities for Burmese civil society groups through access to higher education grants and travel to conferences and exposure trips abroad.

In this rapidly evolving context, increasing numbers of young women are protesting, leading, and organising. The forms that their activism takes can range from individual actions on social media, to more 'traditional' forms of activism offline, as members of activist groups, organisations, and unions. These new and older forms are often intertwined as groups use multiple means of operating to interact with the government and private sector to influence laws, policies, and practices and to mobilise communities and provide training. These latter actions were an important facet of activism in Myanmar under dictatorship and remain a component of activist strategies.

In this chapter, we explore the specific experience of a small number of young women activists in Myanmar, identifying some specific challenges they face, and offering some potential ways forward. As age is a particularly powerful determinant of power in Myanmar (GEN 2015; Svensson 2015), young women are working at the intersection of two systems of discrimination based on gender and age. Many other dynamics are also operating to shape the experience of each individual, including race, ethnicity, class, and location in the country.

For the purposes of this chapter, we have defined the age range for 'youth' as between 18 and 35 years old. This reflects the government youth policy of 5 January 2018, which was created in consultation with youth groups in Myanmar.[2] We draw on various sources of information: key informant interviews with young women activists and other civil society activists, and a review of research reports by NGOs and donor organisations. We also write from our own extensive experience working for civil society organisations and government donors in Myanmar as employees and consultants from 2012 to the present.

Agatha Ma is a gender specialist, currently working with Phan Tee Eain NGO[3] and as a freelance consultant. She has worked for a range of international and national NGOs across Myanmar, focusing on women's participation and capacity building, as well as working on the peace process and her role as steering committee member of Women Can Do It – Myanmar (WCDI).[4]

Poe Ei Phyu is a freelance gender consultant, who has previously worked with Oxfam Myanmar as a Gender Policy Advisor. Here, we draw on her experience working nationally on gender-responsive budgeting, gender analysis, gender mainstreaming and gender-related research, and her role as steering committee member of GEN.[5]

Catriona Knapman is a freelance land and gender consultant, based in Yangon since 2012. Since 2005, she has worked in Latin America, different parts of Africa, and for UK/EU organisations on a range of social development and human rights issues. In this chapter, we draw on her experience working for donors and civil society organisations across Myanmar, leading programmes, research, and workshops on women farmers' rights and gender-equal land governance. Finally, all three of us are creators of the Gender Academy,[6] a Myanmar think-tank which provides training and develops discussion around gender.

The next section briefly examines the historical context of young women's activism and the gender- and age-related discrimination that young women face today when they attempt to voice their concerns in public fora.

Young women's political participation in Myanmar – past and present

In Myanmar, young women have been involved for many decades in political movements in the country, calling for social justice. One prominent example is the 1988 uprising (Linter 1990). The focus of activism during this time was for democratic governance and these movements did not create any specific demands for women's rights or participation, yet they were spaces in which young women were politically active and occupied leadership positions (Hedstrom 2015; Svensson 2015). Clearly, young women can choose many forms of activism, across a range of movements, only some of which may be seen as feminist (Molyneux 1998).

Much work exists to explore the reasons for women's marginalisation from formal politics and leadership worldwide (Evelyn and Adedayo 2014). In Myanmar, as elsewhere, this is rooted in social and cultural gender norms (GEN 2015). Practical barriers also exist to participation in politics, due to gender divisions of labour in the family. Division of household responsibilities dictates that women are responsible for child care, cooking, cleaning, and other household responsibilities, while men take on the role of attending meetings and other responsibilities relating to the community. It also affects women's abilities to travel to government offices for land registration or prevents them from serving as village administrators (Faxon and Knapman 2017). The male domination of politics from local to national level creates a vicious circle, with women ending up under-informed about decisions in which they were not involved that affect them, their families, and their communities.

Young women in Myanmar continue to encounter a range of gender- and age-related factors that constrain their political participation. Intersectional hierarchies of gender and age can be observed across social situations, ranging from family and household level to formal employment and governance structures, where older men tend to dominate decision-making. Social norms around power, leadership, and respect within families mean that older people are seen as having the right to question younger people (GEN 2015).

We have ourselves observed Burmese speakers reminding each other to pay respect to or listen to older colleagues or friends, and traditions reinforce this, such as serving a meal to older people first. This results in everyday awareness of the age of those around you, and constant reminders to follow the guidance of those who are older. Our perception is that the overall impact of such everyday practices and the social norms that underpin them is that older people tend not to respect or want to listen to younger people's ideas and there is a widespread belief that young people are less knowledgeable and do not have valuable ideas to contribute. For young women especially, there is a strong expectation that they listen and not raise their voices (authors' personal experiences, 2012–18).

One study of women's participation in public life at local level in Myanmar argues that participation is low because there is a lack of institutional mechanisms to promote it (Burnley *et al.* 2016). Young women activists, working with local and village-level administration, have to deal almost exclusively with men when talking to the state. In Myanmar's First Female Farmer's Forum, held in Mandalay on 21–22 July 2016 and convened by the Land Core Group, women farmers did a role-play activity, demonstrating their experiences of interacting with the local authorities. Two of the role plays showed young women dealing with local authorities, encountering discrimination and macho-style behaviour. In both cases, they needed an older woman who knew her rights to support and help her negotiate the male-dominated state system (Faxon and Knapman 2017).

In the next sections, we explore further the challenges to young women's activism through the specific experiences of five young women activists.

Researching young women's experiences of activism

Our key informants were five young women activists who discussed their experiences with us in in-depth interviews in April and May 2018 in Yangon, Taunggyi, and Kayah. All the direct quotations used in this chapter come from these interviews. We interviewed using an in-depth process covering the whole 'lifespan' of each interviewee's activism. While some of them were older at the time of interview, all of them had become active politically by their early twenties, and we focused on the experiences they had gained at that younger age and stage. While a case-study approach with a small number of interviewees can never hope to be representative, we hope that the data we were able to gather provide telling insights into the ways in which gender and age intersect in the lives of young women involved in a range of civil society struggles for change in Myanmar today.

We identified the five activists by a snowballing[7] technique – asking for suggestions from our own circle and widening out our search until we had successfully identified potential participants. Each of these activists has a wide range of experience in different areas of activism in Myanmar, and taken as a group of five, they also represent a range of ethnic nationalities and geographic experiences.

We aimed to find interviewees who were particularly interesting for the experiences they have had, their willingness to participate, and the insights that we could draw from the wide range of different experiences.

Wint War Yu is a land rights activist from Thanintharyi region in southwest Myanmar. She currently works on protecting land rights and promotes awareness of land-related laws in her local community, as well as promoting women's rights and leadership. She is 27 and began her activism aged 21 when living at home with her parents and siblings. She started as an activist as a co-ordinator with WCDI Myanmar, still helping at home with household chores. Her activism has mostly been at the community level and she is a member of Dawei Youth Organisation, involved in lobbying, awareness raising and advocacy with local government.

Kyel Sin is a 25-year-old women's rights activist of Pa-O ethnicity from Taunggyi, Shan State, the eastern part of Myanmar. She started working as an activist when she was 19 as an intern with WLB. While working with WLB she learnt about women's rights and became actively involved in working on gender-based violence and women's participation. She decided to start working for women from her own community as part of the Pa-O Women Union and she was elected as co-director due to her active engagement and commitment. Her activism is mostly at the local level.

Ei Ei Min is an activist working on indigenous and environmental rights. From Yangon, she belongs to the Karen[8] ethnic group and has a Master's degree in International Development. She started her activism as a student volunteer. After graduation, she worked as an intern with one of the organisations on the Thai–Burma border in 2006–7. She is now 37 years old, married with two children, taking responsibility for child care and household chores as well as the director position of the organisation POINT (Promoting of Indigenous and Nature Together) which she founded in 2012. Although she is of Karen ethnicity group, she works for a variety of the country's ethnic groups.

Mon Yee Kyaw is a 26-year-old educational reform activist from Mandalay. She joined the Student Union when she was 20. She was imprisoned for 13 months due to her activism on the educational reform process in 2015. Now she is working as executive director at 'Nyan Lin Thit – Ye Nyun' Library. She has completed her Master's degree in Technology but is continuing study to develop her research skills in Yangon, away from her natal family. Mon Yee Kyaw is continuing her activism work as a volunteer with a focus on creating change in policy at national level.

Mu Angela is a 27-year-old women's rights activist from Kayah State. She started her activist work aged 20 as an intern with Kayan Women Organization (KyWO). She studied development and human rights with NGOs on the Thai–Burma border. After her studies, she was appointed as Women's Centre Co-ordinator with KyWO due to her commitment and active engagement with different stakeholders. In 2013, she was elected as joint secretary of KyWO, working on women's participation and peace-related issues in Kayah State. Her activism is mostly at local level (Kayah State and southern Shan State) and she spends part of her time living in her parents' home.

We also interviewed four other civil society activists to corroborate and deepen our understanding of the attitudes of men and older women towards young women activists. Their experience, plus the authors' own, augments the accounts of our informants in the analysis below.

Routes into activism

The five young women interviewees were motivated by different experiences of injustice to become activists. Each of our participants was able to identify a particular personal experience which had such a powerful impact on her that she was motivated to become an activist despite the clear difficulties. Poverty, marginalisation, and violence (or the threat of violence) are real risks in Myanmar's sociocultural context and may seem to be strong deterrents to activism. However, in the face of injustice, political action can seem the best route to achieve change.

Wint War Yu's route into land activism began when her family land was confiscated and her father and elder sister were sent to prison as a result of activism to protect their land:

> Our family members, especially my father and elder sister, were sent several times to prison, we were threatened. Our community was encouraged (by business men) to sell our land ... Therefore, I am focusing on land rights and land-grabbing issues.
>
> (Wint War Yu, Yangon, 11 April 2018)

Ei Ei Min's motivation comes both from her experience as an ethnic Karen woman and her experiences of being ignored and dismissed as a leader working in the resource rights sector. She began working on indigenous rights activism in 2012 and within two years realised it was essential to introduce gender issues into her activism due to her own experiences of being a woman leader and her observations of the lack of awareness of gender amongst those working on resource rights.

> Both men and women rely on environment but women are often excluded from Community Forestry and Management of the Nature. Since women consume and rely more on forest than men, women's voices and experiences should be integrated. I am committing to integrate women's voices or gender into every single project in which I am involved. Whatever I have learnt, I will share back my experience to the other women and I will promote gender in environmental sectors.
>
> (Ei Ei Min, Yangon, 10 April 2018)

Ei Ei's vision of feminism focuses on creating gender equality and equity for women in what she sees as a male-dominated society. This includes taking special measures to advance women's representation and address current discrimination by gender (Ei Ei Min, Yangon, 10 April 2018).

Mon Yee Kyaw noted her interest in politics coupled with exposure to the student youth network as key factors in her activism:

> My original aim is to study about political science and history but my parents didn't allow me to study about politics and forced me to join GTU [Government Technological University], the university that fit with my exam marks. However, during my free time, I read magazines,

journal and other political related books to fuel my vision. Due to my original interest in politics, I decided to join immediately when the youth committee mobilised in 2012.

(Mon Yee Kyaw, Yangon, 10 May 2018)

Kyel Sin stated that initially she was scared to become involved in politics and scared of the concept of women's rights. This is because they are still sensitive issues in rural Myanmar culture and related to issues which many feel they cannot question things such as local traditions and customs. However, once she had done women's rights and political training with WLB she began to realise how important it was for people in her community to understand their rights and she wanted to help them learn about these issues (Kyel Sin, Taunggyi, 8 April 2018).

Mu Angela studied with an activist group on the Thai–Burma border in 2005. In the process of studying she read many Myanmar laws and policies and noticed that many of these documents were discriminating against women and that women's voices were excluded in law and policy development. Even in her own study group she noticed only a few women were interested in politics. She realised that if this continued, women's voices would not be included ever and so she decided she wanted to become an advocate to influence Myanmar law, policy, and the peace process to include women's needs and ideas (Mu Angela, Loikaw, 1 May 2018).

Challenges facing young women activists

Young women report facing a range of different challenges to their activism, which are discussed in this section.

Embodied activism: harassment relating to young women's appearance and behaviour

All interviewees detailed the backlash and harassment they face regularly based on their bodies and behaviour. For women, and young women in particular, their physical bodies become objects which patriarchal societies seek to control. Moving around in public and taking on the roles of activist and leader increases women's vulnerability to criticism, objectification, and harassment, much of which is focused on the female body and female behaviour. Ei Ei Min stated:

> Being judged on their personality, the clothes they wear, their hairstyle and the length of hair are all very common challenges faced by young feminists.

(Ei Ei Min, Yangon, 10 April 2018)

These experiences are not just related to men's opposition to young women whose activist agendas run contrary to their own agendas. In activist spaces where young women are working alongside young men on shared goals, young women encounter similar behaviour. Mon Yee Kyaw noted that female student activists are talked about a lot more than their male colleagues (Mon Yee Kyaw, Yangon, 10 May 2018). Criticism was focused on their appearance or personality, and did not engage with the issues they were seeking to raise as activists. To us and to the young women we interviewed, we experience this as an attempt to try to make young women question their knowledge and worth as activists. In some instances, this criticism and harassment is so strong that the women involved decided to leave activism. As Mon Yee Kyaw noted:

> Again we, women, were the subject of gossip and many people made comments about the shape of our bodies. Because of this strong negative feedback many women stop participating in political reforms and student movement.
>
> (Mon Yee Kyaw, Yangon, 10 May 2018)

It seems from our participants' experience that strategies to derail young women's activism via comments about appearance were especially common when dealing with government officials. This was the case in dealing with village-level as well as national-level government. Ei Ei shared an experience of an event where she was appointed Master of Ceremony, during which some government officials told her that she had to dress and wear her hair in traditional Burmese style if she wanted to be appointed again in the future (Ei Ei Min, Yangon, 10 April 2018). This reflects the experience of the authors in a range of forums. It seems that it is much easier for young women activists to make their arguments heard if they wear modest and traditional clothes, in line with the expectations of wider society.

Women interviewed also discussed their own reflections and ideas regarding their body. One activist, Mu Angela, discussed how her own perception of weight, and her feeling that young age undermined her credibility with men in meetings, undermined her confidence in stressful encounters. She stated:

> When I was younger, I felt insecure because of my body, as I was very thin. Now I put on weight, I feel it is easier in meetings, especially with armed groups, as I feel more like a mature woman.
>
> (Mu Angela, Loikaw, 1 May 2018)

These comments reflect social norms discussed above regarding expectations of women's roles and behaviour, and wider social pressure to ensure women conform to these.

Experiences of dealing with male colleagues

A common theme from our interviews was the difficulties of dealing with male colleagues, especially when they are older or more senior.

Kyel Sin stated:

> Sometimes I don't want to attend the meetings or meeting with other male counterparts. I have faced discrimination because of my age and gender. As I am young, they don't want to listen my voice. If they have to accept my idea, then they try to make a statement to show that they are teaching me.
>
> (Kyel Sin, Loikaw, 8 April 2018)

Many young women activists reported being belittled, treated as if they were in traditionally female roles that support men – e.g. secretaries – and not being given the opportunity to put forward their ideas, often to the extent that they no longer wanted to attend meetings or conferences when they were going with male colleagues. Three of our key informants, including Wint War Yu and Mon Yee Kyaw, noted that while male colleagues would encourage them as their junior, they were not supportive when they were attempting to operate at the same level as them, and would often try to prevent them from doing so.

> Sometimes, I feel like I don't want to attend the conferences or meetings together with elderly men and my male colleagues. They look down on me and criticise me when we are together in the events, particularly when we are doing group work. They tease me and say I have to write down whatever they discuss and they don't invite me to join the discussion in the group work. Once after group work, they forced me to do the group presentation, saying they are giving me the chance to claim my rights as a woman by presenting their ideas. I often experience this kind of behaviour from male colleagues. I hate their ways of perceiving gender equality.
>
> (Wint War Yu, Yangon, 11 Apr 2018)

On the same issue, Ei Ei Min noted that Myanmar men sometimes looked down on women in leadership positions, highlighting that they had to try double to influence male colleagues when sharing her ideas at events or meetings (Ei Ei Min, Yangon, 10 April 2018). Kyel Sin suggested that while there seems to be a tendency for younger men to be more supportive and more flexible than older men, this support can be limited in nature (Kyel Sin, Taunggyi, 8 April 2018).

In student activism, similar dynamics played out, as noted by Mon Yee Kyaw. She reported that in her experience young men and young women would initially sit in a meeting and discuss issues together, yet differences would start to occur when the agenda had been agreed and activities began to be implemented. At that point, she had seen men taking on extra work and developing new networks without telling the female groups and members, to enable them to join in (Mon Yee Kyaw, Yangon, 10 May 2018).

Young women's experience of activism with other women

Age-related difference between women was very clear from the accounts of the key informants. Intersecting identities including age create difference among women, which can have implications for programming and policies assuming women's shared interests will always lead to mutual support (Cornwall 2000).

The support and patronage of older women – in the family, in the wider community, and beyond – is critically important for younger women, and it is a very difficult decision to risk this through offending older women's sense of what younger women should be or do.

While there are many women activists who collaborate, there is a feeling that women's groups do not respect and support each other, and these problems are also felt by individuals within the same group.

There are age-related dynamics here. Our key informants reported that older women leaders had not always been supportive of their efforts as activists. While there were some examples of support from older women, there were many stories of women acting as obstacles for younger colleagues. Some influential women in the country often come from rich or political families, and do not necessarily know – or give space to – the experience of other women outside a small elite circle. There seems to be a sense of limited space which is reserved for certain older elite women, which they themselves expect to occupy. Key informants confirmed similar views from their own experiences. Ei Ei Min noted that in everyday situations, there may be jealousy and criticism from women activists when a young woman became a leader, took on a public speaking role, got a promotion, or received an award.

Wint War Yu stated:

> There are some minor cases where I received support and encouragement from elderly women but I was left out when we had to present in front of the public. I felt that I was not allowed to take such role and incapable to represent our activities to the public. In relation to working with other older women or women of the same age as me, I have received many comments or been discriminated against because of my age.
>
> (Wint War Yu, Yangon, 11 April 2018)

Key informants noted that when working with older women, they often genuinely felt their capacity was not equal, so they might limit their participation to just listening, without sharing their opinions. This lack of self-confidence could be understood by older women if they were committed to working in solidarity with their younger colleagues, to ensure they are able to contribute equally and fully.

Our participation in feminist networks from 2012 to the present date suggests to us that if these dynamics go unaddressed, young women can feel discouraged or not heard in meetings, and consequently do not continue to participate in certain groups. The overall consequence of this can lead to lack of integration between groups and silos in civil society movements, especially as this issue affects women of all ages, not only young women.

Mu Angela noted that while both women and men from her surrounding community elected her for her role in the peace process, she received criticism from older women through social media. Also, when she was nominated for an additional role, representing civil society organisations at national level, she heard that rumours were spread about her on social media. Her story also highlights the differences between women activists from before and after the political transition. She notes that there are women who feel that they suffered a very hard time during the dictatorship and she, as a younger woman, should not be representing the community in the peace process because she is too young and did not experience the difficulties of the dictatorship in the same way. She remembers feeling that her voice was not valid because she began her career during the transition period (2012–15), a time when speaking out on issues no longer involved high personal risk, like it did during the dictatorship (Mu Angela, Loikaw, 1 May 2018).

This reflects a wider division of cultures in Myanmar between civil society activists during the dictatorship, and emergent leaders since the 2010 transition. One older activist, Noble Aye, was part of the student movements during the 1990s and early 2000s. In an interview with her in May 2018, she noted that she sees many young people are active and trying to participate in political reform, but she did not think that they get support from older activists. The two groups have had different life experiences, and as such have different priorities for political change.

Noble Aye also noted a wider culture gap between the groups, highlighting that, while she and other activists were in prison for their activism over the last 20 years, many changes happened relating to the explosion of ICTs and online activism mentioned at the start of this chapter. She now feels that she lacks the computer and IT skills to be able to participate in the workplace and in campaigns, whereas young activists have experience and knowledge of these (Noble Aye, Yangon, 8 May 2018).

The risks of activism for young women

Activism can carry significant social – and economic – costs for young women. The interviews detailed the interviewees' experience of these costs.

There is a vicious circle for the young women who want to become activists to participate in public life, advocate for reforms and progress, and campaign for change. Women human rights defenders face huge risks in contexts across the world (Stockholm Forum on Gender Equality 2018). Two of our five key interviewees mentioned that due to a lack of laws and policies on the protection of women, it is very difficult for them to work – in particular, on certain issues. For example, while there is a law against harassment, there are no specific laws to tackle issues such as workplace harassment or domestic violence. The fact of being an activist places young women at risk of these abuses.

Even where there is a law to protect victims of violence and abuse, such as for rape cases, the legal definitions are outdated and weak, and the law and judicial systems make it difficult for them to claim justice. Kyel Sin described feeling as if the system is against those who try to claim justice. Below, we discuss some of the different themes that emerge out of this broad theme of risks (Kyel Sin, Taunggyi, 8 April 2018).

Family resistance to young women's activism

The notion that women are safer at home and the knowledge of the social disapproval that young women will face in political participation and leadership can motivate parents to try to prevent daughters from joining movements. As imprisonment has been a consequence in the past for activism in Myanmar, it is considered a very risky activity, and for the most part parents do not want their children, especially their daughters, to participate. Currently, right-wing movements around the world are creating new waves of risks for activists who take part in actions to support and further human rights. Mon Yee Kyaw noted, 'because I was a woman, my parents stopped me joining the student movement'. She stated that despite an interest in politics from an early age, her parents forced her to study another subject. When student unions at her university began to mobilise, her interest in politics led her to become an active member. However, she had to keep these activities secret from her parents:

> I secretly joined at day time and went back home at night and joined the campaign again the next day. I had to go back and forth from home and pretend I was studying. However, I could not pretend anymore when we worked on higher-profile cases.
>
> (Mon Yee Kyaw, Yangon, 10 May 2018)

Ei Ei Min noted that she felt 'too protected' by her parents, when in 2006–7 her parents tried to prevent her doing a media interview because they were concerned about her security and that she would put herself at risk (Ei Ei Min, Yangon, 10 April 2018).

Raising a family and balancing this with activism

The need to provide unpaid care and balance this with productive work is a reality for almost all women in Myanmar. For poorer women, as noted earlier, activism can often appear impossible as lack of funds prevents either paying for support at home or travel enabling them to juggle activism with life at home.

Ei Ei Min, the only one of our interviewees who is married and a mother, remembered how social stigma affected her when she gave birth:

> Mothers were assumed to be staying at home and doing household chores. Society blames and stigmatises me whether I leave my baby at

home or take my baby to my work place. People criticised me, comment-
ing on how a mother could never leave a child or bring a little baby on a
trip, saying that for doing these things, I was not a real mother.

(Ei Ei Min, Yangon, 10 April 2018)

Women who travel regularly are seen as trouble makers, compared to those
who stay at home. Ei Ei Min pointed out that if she travelled with male colleagues she faced teasing, as it was widely assumed that there was a sexual
relationship between her and her colleague:

When I travelled abroad with my senior male colleague, other men gos-
siped about it. They thought about women as a sexual object of men or
we were having a sexual relationship.

(Ei Ei Min, Yangon, 10 April 2018)

Exclusion from friendship groups

Wint War Yu noted the risk of social exclusion, and gave an example from her
personal experience:

When I got involve in land rights campaigns as well as the activities
of student union, some of my friends excluded me as their friends.
Their parents and teachers also told not to spend time with me. I think
Myanmar ways of thinking on politics makes the younger generation
afraid of becoming interested in politics and other state development
activities.

(Wint War Yu, Yangon, 11 April 2018)

Young women activists' strategies and solutions

Given these challenges, this next section shares some of the strategies and solutions young female activists have sought to support them in their activities.

Support from family

As discussed above, natal and marital families can seek to protect young
women from the risks of becoming politically active. On the opposite side,
however, many of the women interviewed mentioned that having strong
family support – especially from husbands and parents – was important in
their work. The idea that close relationships, including partner relationships,
can be an essential facilitating factor for women to organise and take collective action is familiar from studies elsewhere (e.g. Rowlands 1995), as well as
resonating with women everywhere! For married women, this was essential,
especially after having children. Ei Ei Min told us:

I would say that the most important was my husband. He always assists
and supports me when I face difficulties. He even allows me to pursue

my further study. I have seen cases where a husband feels insecure when his wife becomes a leader and I think the support of family members is very important for [a young woman activist] to grow.

(Ei Ei Min, Yangon, 10 April 2018)

This also is key for activists who are taking risks in their work, as the moral support from the family is vital. Wint War Yu reported:

Whenever I face challenges I discuss with my family and we have dialogue and solve together. The more challenges we face, the stronger we are … These are our ways of reducing our suffering.

(Wint War Yu, Yangon, 11 April 2018)

Working to build trust, credibility, and networks

Our five key interviewees highlighted the importance for them of working to build trust, enhance credibility, and develop networks and alliances. They work at a number of levels typically, in activities intended to create change in many different ways. Activists provide role models to other young women, but also consciously discuss and challenge popular patriarchal views in their community, seeing this as critical work alongside the work of influencing policy reform processes. Ei Ei Min mentioned the value of building trust with key officials and developing a strong fact-based knowledge, in order to be able to gain credibility (Ei Ei Min, Yangon, 10 April 2018). This demonstrates a clear injustice in the current reality as young women activists have to work harder than their male counterparts to be effective.

The interviewees also mentioned that working with other alliances and feminist groups motivates them. Some mentioned that getting support from influential women is a good entry point for them to influence other stakeholders and policymakers. Being part of larger alliances also allows them the opportunity to influence national-level processes and link to national networks. As mentioned earlier, older men are reluctant to accept young women activists to work alongside them, however, it is easier for young women to form alliances with male youth groups. Kyel Sin pointed out that influencing these groups can create significant change in attitudes ultimately and even promote the idea of women's leadership, networking with policymakers, and influencing other stakeholders (Kyel Sin, Taunggyi, 8 April 2018).

Support from international and national actors

A number of activists highlighted that government, international and national NGOs can play an important role in supporting activism. Government and civil society donor organisations have an ability to create space and value particular groups in their work.

Our research participants stated that NGOs working in Myanmar and in the border areas have played an important role in supporting young women to become activists in movements where they are fighting alongside men on shared goals – e.g. land rights – and in feminist movements and women's rights work. A key activity often offered as support is training sessions and courses which aim to build capacities and skills associated with leadership. As women have specific needs related to child-bearing and child-care roles, as well as needs relating to criticism and socialisation, flexible and understanding donors can make a difference to valuing the needs of young women and helping them to operate effectively. Ei Ei Min stated that one donor which supported her work over the long term was effective in increasing her confidence and voice, and in overcoming obstacles or criticism (Ei Ei Min, Yangon, 10 April 2018).

Conclusion

This chapter has aimed to share the experience of young women activists in Myanmar, notably the challenges facing them, and the ways in which they seek support and encouragement to continue their work in a fairly hostile environment. While social norms do not change overnight, we recommend that government, donors, and NGOs consider systematically how to counter the sociocultural norms which exclude those who are not traditional leaders in Myanmar, so that diverse voices are contributing to political reform processes. This would enable a process of change which values younger female voices alongside those who have traditionally played a leadership role.

Currently, women's voices and especially young women's voices are largely absent from key national fora, including parliament, the peace process, and law reform processes. As noted above, there is a sense of limited space for participation and only certain people are allowed to the table. There needs to be more awareness of discrimination in Burma relating to age and sex, which would allow for inbuilt strategies to value the voices of women and especially younger women.

Various national and international organisations are currently playing important roles in supporting the idea that young women can and should participate and lead. However, more needs to be done, beyond workshops and training sessions, to help young women build trust, credibility, and networks. Some of the interviewees suggested that policymakers and other senior officials tend to judge young women and, as such, they need to work harder to provide evidence and facts in support of their case.

Government, donors, and civil society organisations have an awareness of the difficulties faced by younger women activists, yet they have done little to actively support them to overcome the difficulties. It seems important, considering that social norms and practice are not supportive of young women activists, that government, donors, and civil society actively champion their voices and contributions. This can be through specific policy and quotas, but also through championing their work, and developing space within their own organisations for young women to be supported and heard.

Notes

1. A full account of current political processes in Myanmar cannot be given here but brief details on the key facts include the following. Since 2011, a peace process has been taking place in Myanmar, which aims to bring to an end the long-standing civil wars between the government and ethnic armed groups (Burke *et al.* 2017). In March 2016, an elected National League for Democracy (NLD) government took power, although the military still retains control of some ministries up to the time of writing (June 2018). In addition, the peace process is not fully realised and is currently under strain: not all ethnic armed groups have signed the National Ceasefire Agreement, and conflict is ongoing in parts of the country (Mark 2018). There has also been no disarmament or demobilisation (Strasser 2016).
2. For more details on the government draft youth policy, see www.moi.gov. mm/moi:eng/?q=news/6/01/2018/id-12475.
3. For information on Phan Tee Eain, see www.phanteeeain-myanmar.org.
4. For information on the WCDI, see www.wcdimm.org.
5. For information on GEN, see www.genmyanmar.org.
6. For information on the Gender Academy Myanmar, https://www.face book.com/Gender-Academy--110976366168183/ (last checked 4 October 2018).
7. For information on the snowballing research method, see Kitchenham and Pfleeger (2002) and Acharya *et al.* (2013).
8. The Karen people, also known as Kayin people, are an ethnic group who live in the south-east of Myanmar. It is estimated that there are 6–7 million Karen people in Myanmar with most of them living in Mon State, Kayin State, the Ayeyarwaddy region, the Yangon region, and the Thanintharyi region. They speak Karen language. For more research on the specific situation of the Karen people, see Karen Human Rights Group (http://khrg.org) and The Asia Foundation (https://asiafoundation.org/ where-we-work/myanmar).

Notes on contributors

Agatha Ma works for Gender Academy Myanmar as trainer and managing director.
   Poe Ei Phyu is a freelance gender consultant.
   Catriona Knapman is a freelance gender consultant.

References

Acharya, Anita S., A. Prakash, P. Saxena and A. Nigam (2013) 'Sampling: why and how of it?', *Indian Journal of Medical Specialties* 4(2): 330–3, https:// www.researchgate.net/profile/Anita_Acharya/publication/256446902_ Sampling_Why_and_How_of_it_Anita_S_Acharya_Anupam_Prakash_ Pikee_Saxena_Aruna_Nigam/links/0c960527c82d449788000000.pdf (last checked 11 August 2018)

Burke, Adam, Nicola Wiliams, Patrick Barron, Kim Jolliffe and Thomas Carr (2017) *The Contested Area of Myanmar: Subnational Conflict, Aid, and Development*, Yangon: The Asia Foundation

Burnley, Jasmine, Melanie Hilton, Poe Ei Phyu and Nilar Tun (2016) *A Case for Gender-Responsive Budgeting in Myanmar*, Oxford: Oxfam, https://policy-practice.oxfam.org.uk/publications/a-case-for-gender-responsive-budgeting-in-myanmar-603484 (last checked 4 October 2018)

Cornwall, Andrea (2000) 'Making a Difference? Gender and Participatory Development', IDS Discussion paper 378, http://www.participatorymethods.org/sites/participatorymethods.org/files/Dp378.pdf (last checked 11 August 2018)

Evelyn, Yusuf Hauwa'u and Yusufu Adefarakam Adedayo (2014) 'Entrenched patriarchy, women social movement and women participation in politics', *American International Journal of Contemporary Research* 4(7): 149–62

Faxon, Hilary and Catriona Knapman (2017) *Myanmar's First Female Farmers Forum: Reflections and Findings for Women's Land Governance*, Yangon: Land Core Group

Gaens, Bart (2013) 'Political Change in Myanmar: Filtering the Murky Waters of "Disciplined Democracy"', Helsinki: The Finnish Institute of International Affairs

Gender Equality Network (GEN) (2015) *Raising the Curtain: Cultural Norms, Social Practices and Gender Equality in Myanmar*, Yangon: GEN

Hedström, Jenny (2015) 'We did not realize about the gender issues. So, we thought it was a good idea, gender roles in burmese oppositional struggles', *International Feminist Journal of Politics* 18(1): 61–79

Hogan, Libby and Michael Sofi (2018) 'Revealed: Facebook hate speech exploded in Myanmar during Rohingya crisis', *The Guardian*, 3 April, https://www.theguardian.com/world/2018/apr/03/revealed-facebook-hate-speech-exploded-in-myanmar-during-rohingya-crisis (last checked 30 August 2018)

Holland, Hereward (2014) 'Facebook in Myanmar: Amplifying hate speech?', *Al Jazeera*, 14 June, https://www.aljazeera.com/indepth/features/2014/06/facebook-myanmar-rohingya-amplifying-hate-speech-2014612112834290144.html (last checked 30 August 2018)

Kitchenham, Barbara and Shari Lawrence Pfleeger (2002) 'Principles of survey research, part 5: populations and samples', *Software Engineering Notes* 27(5): 17–20, http://www.idi.ntnu.no/grupper/su/publ/ese/kitchenham-survey5.pdf (last checked 11 August 2018)

Linter, Bertil (1990) *Outrage: Burma's Struggle for Democracy*, 2nd ed., Gartmore, Scotland: Kiscadale Publications

Mark, Eugine (2018) 'Myanmar's Challenging Path to Peace', The Diplomat, https://thediplomat.com/2018/02/myanmars-challenging-path-to-peace/ (last checked 11 August 2018)

Mclaughlinby, Timothy (2018) 'How Facebook's Rise Fuelled Chaos and Confusion in Myanmar', Wired, 7 June, https://www.wired.com/story/how-facebooks-rise-fueled-chaos-and-confusion-in-myanmar/ (last checked by the author 30 August 2018)

MIMU (Myanmar Information Management Unit) (2014) 'The Myanmar Population and Housing Census', http://themimu.info/census-data (last checked 4 October 2018)

Minoletti, Paul (2014) *Women's Participation in the Subnational Governance of Myanmar*, Yangon: MDRI, CESD and TAF

Mod, Craig (2016) 'The Facebook Loving Farmers of Myanmar', *The Atlantic*, 21 January, https://www.theatlantic.com/technology/archive/2016/01/the-facebook-loving-farmers-of-myanmar/424812/ (last checked 23 May 2018)

Molyneux, Maxine (1998) 'Analysing women's movements', *Development and Change* 29(2): 219–45

Nyein Nyein (2018) 'Activists Launch Campaigns Ahead of International Women's Rights Day', The Irrawaddy, 6 March, https://www.irrawaddy.com/news/burma/activists-launch-campaigns-ahead-international-womens-rights-day.html (last checked 29 August 2018)

Rowlands, Jo (1995) 'Empowerment examined', *Development in Practice* 5(2): 101–107, https://www.tandfonline.com/doi/abs/10.1080/0961452951000 157074 (last checked 4 October 2018)

Stecklow, Steve (2018) 'Hatebook: Inside Facebook's Myanmar Operation', Reuters, 15 August, https://www.reuters.com/investigates/special-report/myanmar-facebook-hate/ (last checked 30 August 2018) The Stockholm Forum on Gender Equality (2018) 'Countering the Shrinking Space for Women

Human Rights Defenders: A Global Call To Action By The Bravest Women in The World', Sunday 15 Apr 2018, Session Report 1A, http://genderequalworld.com/app/uploads/2018/06/gender_eqality_-sunday-1a.pdf (last checked 11 August 2018)

Strasser, Fred (2016) 'Myanmar Peace Process: Slow Progress, Delicate Steps', USIP, 10 November, http://www.usip.org/publications/2016/11/10/myanmar-peace-process-slow-progress-delicate-steps (last checked 23 May 2018)

Svensson, Emelie (2015) 'Women's Particiation in the Burmese Ethnic and Student Oppositional Movement', Master's Thesis, Lund University, Sweden, http://lup.lub.lu.se/luur/download?func=downloadFile&recordOId=5410045&fileOId=5470666 (last checked 9 October 2018)

Thin Thin Aye (2015) 'The Role of Civil Society in Myanmar's Democratization', International Conference on Burma/Myanmar Studies, Chiang Mai University, Thailand, 24–25 July 2015

CHAPTER 6

Reading girls' participation in Girl Up as feminist: club members' activism in the UK, USA and Malawi

Rosie Walters

Abstract

The United Nations Foundation's Girl Up campaign has been criticised by many feminists for perpetuating patronising discourses that see girls and women in the Global North as the saviours of their counterparts in the South, while doing little to challenge underlying global inequalities. This chapter draws on focus group data with Girl Up club members in the UK, USA and Malawi, and explores how they are adapting the aims of the campaign to better fit their own vision of empowerment. From girls in New York attending women's marches together to girls in a township of Lilongwe marching to their friends' parents' houses to demand that they send their daughters to school, the girls have shown courage and creativity, their actions rejecting discourses of empowered Northern saviours and passive Southern girls in need of rescue. This chapter explores the agency with which girls negotiate discourses emerging from powerful international institutions, and puts forward the argument that these girls deserve recognition as feminist activists who are adapting campaigns, such as Girl Up, in order to challenge the many and complex injustices that they face in their own communities and globally.

Keywords: Girls; United Nations; girl power; activism; feminism

Introduction

Girl Up is one of many schemes that has emerged in recent years with the aim of empowering girls in the Global South through formal schooling. Launched by the United Nations (UN) Foundation in 2010, Girl Up encourages girls in the Global North to set up clubs and fundraise for the education of the world's 'hardest to reach girls' in the Global South (Girl Up n.d. a). As then UN Foundation Executive Director Elizabeth McKee Gore explained at its launch, the purpose of the campaign is to 'give girls in America an opportunity to become global leaders themselves, and then in the meantime be supporting their sisters overseas' (Biddle 2010). The campaign only allowed girls in the

USA to register clubs, although membership has since been opened to girls anywhere in the world with access to the internet. The resources on the website, however, remain targeted towards girls in the Global North, encouraging them to become the 'sisters, saviours, and "BFFs"'[1] of their Southern counterparts (Koffman *et al.* 2015, 161). Girl Up is typical of the many girl power campaigns that have emerged in recent years, in what Ofra Koffman and Rosalind Gill label the 'girl-powering of international development' (2013, 86). There is a wealth of literature on this subject, although, to date, it has largely focused on analysing girl power discourses and has had little to say on the possibility that girls might be subverting or resisting them.

The Girl Up campaign has been criticised by feminist scholars and activists for perpetuating patronising discourses that see women and girls in the Global South as awaiting rescue by the North. Criticisms include the following key points. The campaign encourages girls in the North to see gender inequality as something that only happens elsewhere, and that can be solved through fundraising. It encourages girls to take individual responsibility for solving issues such as universal access to education and ending child marriage, which the international community itself has so far failed to solve. Finally, with their claims that girls work harder, take on greater domestic responsibilities, and invest more of their income in their families and communities, campaigns such as Girl Up advocate investing in girls in the Global South not because they have an equal right to such investment as boys, but because of the promise that they will help to achieve other development outcomes. These criticisms are discussed and referenced in the next section.

Despite this evidence of intense interest in Girl Up and similar initiatives, much of which is critical, one element has not been researched. This is girls' own participation in Girl Up clubs, and the extent to which participation may be experienced by girls as empowering, enabling them to challenge constraints on their agency and further their own goals. In this chapter, I draw on my recent fieldwork with club members in the UK, USA and Malawi to argue that girls' participation in the campaign constitutes a form of feminist activism.

Girls' participation in politics has frequently been overlooked by campaigning organisations, the media, academia, and girls themselves, despite research showing that girls are 'equally (if not more) civically minded and politically oriented than their male counterparts' (Bent 2013, 174). Jessica Taft, drawing on her work with girl activists, argues that if feminist scholars are to embrace fully the mantra that 'the personal is political', then those studying girls' activism need to acknowledge all forms of girls' political participation. These include, for example:

> Online blogging that challenges the sexualisation of girls, resisting and confronting a domineering boyfriend, father, or brother, everyday practices of interaction across differences in a public park, mentoring other girls, media-making, participation in human rights organisations, and social movement activism. (Taft 2014, 263)

In this chapter I show that the girls in my research were engaged in activities of this kind in every setting I visited, even when they did not match official Girl Up activities. Members adapted the campaign with creativity and agency, fitting it to their own vision of what is empowering for girls.

In the following sections, I review the current literature on girl power campaigns in international development, before introducing Girl Up, its position within the UN Foundation, and the construction of Northern and Southern girlhood in its promotional materials. I then outline my research design for this study. In the second half of the chapter, I discuss my findings, showing how girls frequently rejected or ignored the official purpose of Girl Up, and instead engaged in a range of activities that would come under Jessica Taft's broader interpretation of girls' activism. Many of these activities also rejected Girl Up's model of Northern girl-saviour and Southern passive victim. Finally, I note that, in every setting, girls experienced and resisted stigma, and even bullying, for participating in Girl Up clubs and for championing girls' rights and feminism. I conclude that these girls are feminist activists, whose work in challenging discrimination in their own communities and more broadly deserves recognition both from feminist scholars and from organisations such as Girl Up.

The 'girl-powering' of international development

Since the Nike Foundation launched its campaign, The Girl Effect, in the mid-2000s, with the aim of persuading key decision-makers in international development of the benefits of investing in adolescent girls, a process has followed that Ofra Koffman and Rosalind Gill have labelled the 'girl-powering of international development' (2013, 86). Campaigns such as The Girl Effect and Girl Up have created 'feel-good' advertisements and viral videos, claiming that when a girl in the Global South receives an education she marries later, has fewer, healthier children, earns more income, and invests more of that income in her family and community than a boy would do. It is a logic that is epitomised by the tagline to one of The Girl Effect's first promotional videos: 'Invest in a girl and she will do the rest' (Girl Effect, n.d.). This logic has been embraced by transnational corporations, international institutions, and celebrities alike. At its core is a targeting of girls, both as Northern donors and as Southern recipients of international aid.

Feminists' critiques of this logic can be grouped around two main themes, the first of which is the simplistic and individualistic solution to complex problems that it advocates. For many it is a continuation of previous instrumentalist approaches to gender in development, which see the rights of women and girls in the Global South not as a goal in and of themselves, but rather as a means to achieving other development outcomes. As Janet Momsen (2004, 14) argues, these are approaches that question 'what women could do for development rather than what development could do for women'. Investing in women and girls becomes a way of facilitating 'development on the cheap'

(Chant and Sweetman 2012, 521). Campaigns such as these resonate strongly with neoliberal discourses that have taken the feminist concept of empowerment and 'economised' it (Shain 2013, 5), reducing calls for gender justice to campaigns focused almost entirely on providing education as a means to gaining work-based skills (Khoja-Moolji 2015). Where alternatives to girls' education are proposed, they are criticised for being based on an individualistic, neoliberal view that all that is needed to achieve gender equality is to provide a girl in the Global South with a loan to buy a cow (as in Girl Effect n.d.) or a sewing machine (as in Girl Up 2010), thus placing the responsibility to lift herself out of poverty firmly on the shoulders of an adolescent girl (Hickel 2014, 1356).

Such solutions do seem very simplistic and reductive. It is difficult to imagine any organisation advocating the provision of a sewing machine as a solution to a girl's struggle with poverty, lack of education, and/or risk of sexual exploitation in the Global North. Furthermore, the assertion that a school education or a loan to buy a cow is enough to unleash the incredible potential of the Southern girl ignores the complexity of the injustices faced by girls everywhere and the socioeconomic factors that mean they might not overcome them.

The second criticism of campaigns such as The Girl Effect and Girl Up focuses on the way these construct the Global North as a well-meaning benefactor of the Global South. In Girl Up, Northern girls are encouraged to see themselves as always already empowered, with nothing holding them back. In contrast, the Southern girl is seen as constrained by outdated gender norms that only intervention from the Global North will help to break down. The construction of the Northern girl as an individual with agency is dependent on the construction of the Southern girl as victim. It is typical of a representational trend in development campaigns, in which, as the author Uzodinma Iweala argues, 'Africans are the props in the West's fantasy of itself' (cited in Cameron and Haanstra 2008, 1482). This depiction leaves no space for girls in the Global South to claim agency in their own lives, nor for girls in the Global North to be the victims of patriarchal norms. The construction of benevolent Northern saviours also serves to mask the inequalities within the global economy that disadvantage Southern economies. This is perhaps most evident in the sponsorship of such campaigns by transnational corporations whose business activities in the Global South are at times extractive or harmful. Examples include the Nike Foundation's central role in The Girl Effect, despite previous claims of child labour at sweatshops producing Nike clothes in the Global South (Calkin 2015, 664), and the partnership between Girl Up and Caterpillar, whose selling of military construction equipment to the Israeli Defence Forces in the occupied Palestinian territories was criticised in 2012 by the UN Special Rapporteur on human rights as violating international human rights and humanitarian law (United Nations 2012). It is deeply problematic that corporations such as these use partnerships in girls' education projects in the Global South to position themselves as benevolent investors in Southern girls and their communities. In summary, then, campaigns such as The Girl Effect and Girl Up are criticised for being based on a logic that 'works to explicitly racialise, depoliticise, ahistoricise, and naturalise global structural inequities and legitimise neoliberal interventions in the name of girls' empowerment' (Switzer 2013, 347).

Girl Up and the construction of 'oppositional girlhoods'

The UN Foundation was launched in 1997 with a billion-dollar donation by CNN founder Robert Edward 'Ted' Turner. The donation came at a time when the UN was grappling with a budgetary deficit of US$272 million, exacerbated by the USA's refusal to pay its membership dues (Williams 1999, 430). Ted Turner's donation was intended to send a clear message to President Bill Clinton in support of the work of the UN. Its priority from the outset was to raise money towards, and build public support for, the work of UN agencies. The Foundation's first President, Tim Wirth, described a crucial part of its work as being 'telling the [UN] story to Americans' (*ibid.*, 428).

From the outset, one of the policy areas central to the work of the Foundation has been adolescent girls' access to education and reproductive health services, both of which are particular passions of Ted Turner and his then wife, Jane Fonda (Toepler and Mard 2007). It is within this context that the Foundation launched Girl Up in 2010, which encouraged girls in the USA to raise money for UN agencies' girls' education projects in the Global South. Girl Up now claims to be a 'community' of 'more than 1,900 clubs registered in 48 US states and territories and 98 countries' (Girl Up n.d. b). However, a brief survey of the map of Girl Up clubs on the website reveals that they are still heavily concentrated in North America (Girl Up n.d. c) and to date, none of the website's resources appear to have been translated into any language other than English.

This North American focus is especially evident in the promotional materials available on the Girl Up website, some of which have not been updated since 2010 and are thus aimed at girls in the USA. One promotional video, entitled 'Connecting the Dots' (Girl Up 2010), is exemplary of the discourse that Emily Bent and Heather Switzer (2016, 123) identify as 'oppositional girlhoods', in which 'global girlpower discourses reduce the intersectional complexity of girls' lives into opposing representations that reinforce artificial, neo-colonial divides between and among girlhoods'. As suggested earlier, this is a discourse that positions Northern and Southern girlhoods as completely opposed to one another: girlhood in the North is characterised by supposed gender equality and opportunity, while girlhood in the Global South is characterised by oppression and constraint.

In 'Connecting the Dots', a black and white animation shows a girl in jeans and a t-shirt, with her hair tied back, while a voiceover actor with a US accent asks the viewer to imagine that she is 12 again. We are told that her life will play out as follows: getting 'decent grades', making 'good decisions about boys', studying at college and finding work, buying shoes, falling in love, and planning for the future (Girl Up 2010). As the girl gets a job, a pile of bank notes increases in size and then morphs into a sparkling pair of shoes. Her future love holds the hand of her adult self, while thought bubbles from them both are united in an image of a swaddled baby.

The narrator then asks us to rewind. A globe spins around the girl, and the viewer is asked to imagine that, instead, she is 'one of the eighty-five percent of all the world's adolescent girls with a lot fewer options' (Girl Up 2010). Her jeans become a full-length skirt, her long hair falls loosely and, as she sweeps the floor, a school building in the bottom corner of the screen disappears from view. We are told that the Southern girl will be forced to marry at 13, will contract HIV from her unfaithful husband (who appears to be much older than her), and will have four children by the age of 20. The girl is left alone in darkness.

As the video zooms out, we see that she is one black dot on a map in which the Global South has been covered in black dots, and the narrator asks us to 'multiply' that story 'by the six hundred million adolescent girls in developing countries' (Girl Up 2010). As a coin spins in the air, the video tells the viewer, 'when you connect the dots, you start to improve the options for girls around the world' (*ibid.*). It rewinds once more to see that, as a result of that coin, the girl attends a school with a UN flag flying, she has access to health care, a loan to start a business (represented by a sewing machine), and she therefore creates 'a better future for herself, her family, her community and her world' (*ibid.*). The video tells the viewer that she can make this change happen by clicking on the Girl Up website, and demands to know, 'what are you waiting for?' (*ibid.*).

In just under two minutes, 'Connecting the Dots' establishes girlhood in the Global North as characterised by success, opportunity, delayed childrearing, and consumption, while it establishes girlhood in the Global South as characterised by poverty, disease, and early marriage. It makes a sweeping claim about hundreds of millions of girls, reducing a map of the world to countries covered in black dots and those left white: countries where girls wear jeans and buy shoes, go to school and have careers; and those where girls wear long skirts and live in poverty, are married and in poor health. It proposes a solution to poverty and abuse – a sewing machine representing self-sufficiency – that would never be deemed appropriate for a young girl in the Global North. And it sets up the supposedly empowered Northern girl as the saviour-in-waiting of her passive, victimised Southern counterpart.

However, while this video may be exemplary of neoliberal, individualistic discourses of girls' empowerment and patronising assumptions about North–South relations, what it cannot tell us is whether Girl Up members themselves subscribe to this logic and reproduce these patronising discourses. Alternatively, are they able to use their membership in ways that enable personal goals to be met and do they therefore experience their participation as positive, maybe even empowering? This is something that has yet to be explored in the literature on this topic, and to which the rest of this chapter is dedicated.

Research design and methodology

The findings in this chapter are drawn from a wider study analysing girls' participation in Girl Up. My theoretical approach is poststructuralist, feminist, and postcolonial, an approach that 'recognises that global inequalities that are gendered and racialised remain entrenched' (Koffman and Gill 2013, 85). As discussed above, while much has been written about girl power discourses in international development, little has been done to analyse how girls themselves negotiate these discourses. With this aim, I conducted fieldwork in 2016 and 2017 with Girl Up club members in schools in the UK, USA and Malawi. The schools were as follows: a state-funded secondary school and sixth-form centre in North Wales; a state-funded, selective high school in New Jersey; a Catholic, fee-paying (approximately US$15,000 per year) school in New York; a fee-paying (approximately US$40,000 per year) high school in New York; a fee-paying (between US$13,000 and 20,000 per year depending on parents' tax status) international school in Lilongwe; and a fee-paying school (approximately US$20 per term) in Lilongwe. The latter school, while fee-paying, was being run at cost price by the two directors in order to give as many children as possible from the surrounding townships an education, and was cheaper than the local government-run secondary school.

The fieldwork sites were chosen to include girls on both sides of the discursive divide between the Global North and South established in Girl Up resources. The UN Development Programme (UNDP) currently ranks Malawi as 170th in the world in its Human Development Index and estimates that a girl in Malawi will spend an average of just 3.8 years in school (compared to 5 years for a boy) (UNDP n.d. a). This, coupled with the fact that Malawi is one of six countries that funds raised for Girl Up go towards, places it firmly within the Global South in this divide. By contrast, the UK ranks 16th in the world on the same index, and the USA 10th, and in both countries girls can expect a slightly higher number of years of education on average than boys (16.7 compared to 15.9 in the UK, and 17.3 compared to 15.8 in the USA) (UNDP n.d. b; UNDP n.d. c). This places both countries firmly in the Global North in this discursive divide, both in terms of development and of girls' educational opportunities.

I conducted focus groups with each Girl Up club. The focus group method is well suited to poststructuralist research because it opens a 'window into the formation, contestation, and negotiation of ideas, understandings, and claims' (Jowett and O'Toole 2006, 464). It is an excellent way to generate public discourses about a topic. The focus on participants' identity as relational and constructed within a group setting, rather than as an isolated individual, and the ability of the group to steer the conversation towards topics that are of interest and importance to them also make the focus group method well suited to feminist research (Wilkinson 1999, 70; 1998, 112).

In total, 95 girls participated in 29 focus groups across the six schools. Focus groups typically lasted between 45 minutes and an hour, and groups ranged from two to eight in size, with most groups consisting of around five girls. The focus groups were arranged by contacting teachers at schools with a Girl Up club, and they then took place within the school. In three of the schools (in the UK, New Jersey and the township school in Lilongwe), I worked with each group twice, but in the other three schools I only met with each group once. The participating girls were all of secondary school age, ranging from 11 to 18 years old, except in the school in a township of Lilongwe, where a small number of participants were adult women in their early 20s, who had returned to complete their education after having children.

I sorted the transcripts using the qualitative data analysis software NVivo, coding to various tropes identified from the literature on girl power campaigns in international development. I then identified concepts emerging from the data, in the girls' own words, and conducted a second round of coding according to these. Once this was complete, I began an in-depth analysis of the extracts within each conceptual code, to assess whether they reproduced, adapted, or rejected outright the dominant discourses about girlhood in international development. Over the next four sections, I analyse the girls' participation in Girl Up, describing the many activities they engaged in that meet Jessica Taft's broader definition of girls' political activism.

Girls' rejection of the primary purpose of Girl Up as a fundraising campaign

Although the main purpose of Girl Up is to fundraise for UN agency projects with girls in the Global South, very few Girl Up members I spoke to were doing activities of this kind. The Girl Up 'Club Starter Guide' states that clubs' activities must be 'aligned with Girl Up's mission and directly benefit the UN programs Girl Up supports' (Girl Up n.d. d, 3). According to the guide, girls registering clubs commit to the following responsibilities: hosting at least five Girl Up activities each year; reporting on their activity each term; recruiting new members; participating in the 'community' section of the Girl Up website; and undertaking fundraising activities (*ibid.*, 4). Of the six schools I visited during my fieldwork, just two – the UK school and one of the schools in New York – had held fundraising events with the intention of sending the money raised to Girl Up.

In the school in New Jersey, the girls agreed with the idea of running fundraising events; however, they had been unable to host any so far because of school policies. As Madison, one of the girls, explained:

> We come up with ideas but to actually get them approved is a really difficult process ... our administration is just very, very strict. (Focus group, New Jersey, 28 March 2017)

Two rules that the girls felt had been of particular nuisance were the rule that prevented them from organising a charity cake sale, because that was deemed to be competing with the private catering company that ran the high school canteen, and the rule that to hold any event in the evening they would need to hire a security guard, which was beyond the club's budget. Instead, they focused on hosting awareness-raising events and on events linked to women's charities in their own community, as discussed below.

In two schools, the girls overtly ignored the Girl Up fundraising commitment. In the Catholic school in New York, the girls had previously had a women's empowerment club that met regularly to hold discussions about gender inequality in the USA and around the world. They decided to register it with Girl Up because they felt this would give more structure to their club; however, they had not changed their activities in any way. They felt that being part of Girl Up gave them access to resources on the website, ideas and topics for their discussions, and the ability to recruit more members by offering them the opportunity to be involved in an international movement. When I asked them what the main purpose of their club was, Nicola, one of the girls, replied, 'just talking about certain issues that we may not have known about or going into deeper understanding of what's going on in the world around us' (focus group, New York, 10 April 2017).

Similarly, in the international school in Lilongwe, where two girls had just decided to start a club, the girls did not feel that fundraising was the primary focus of Girl Up. They told me that the campaign appealed to them precisely because they felt it was different to the other extracurricular clubs on offer in their school. As one girl, Ahadi, explained, 'I want something that's like more personal, 'cos with the clubs here it's like fundraise [and] donate' (focus group, Lilongwe, 27 February 2017). These girls eventually made contact with the other Girl Up club in Lilongwe, at the school in a township, and established a long-term partnership with the girls there. They had interpreted the campaign to be about connecting girls in different settings and saw it as a welcome change from all the other fundraising clubs on offer in their school.

Finally, although the girls in the township of Lilongwe were hosting fundraising events, they used the money to fund scholarships for girls in their school. This was the decision of the school director who had registered the club. He explained that if they sent that money to the UN Foundation they would never see it again, yet girls at the school were dropping out every term because their parents could not afford fees or wanted them to marry. During a focus group with some of the girls, including the club president, Olivia, I asked them if they thought it was a good decision. A section of the transcript is shown below.

> Olivia: Mm, somehow no, somehow yes, no because when we register our Girl Up club, we register to United Nation Foundation that mean every decision that United Nations made we, we should do that decision with they want, they say half million per year,[2] we are supposed to give that money because we are on that foundation.
> RW: Mm mm.

> Olivia: So I feel like, somehow it's good to donate our fundraising money to the United Nation, but, no because here in Malawi we have a lot of challenges.
>
> RW: Mm.
>
> Olivia: Because Malawi it's a, a poverty country, so, (laughs) so, ah, it's difficult to take money from here and deliver to the United Nation but we support just to give those girls who are not able to go to school because of school fees maybe school (inaudible) uniforms, school bag, boots, so it's better just to put those things to build those who are in need here.
>
> Aisha: Ah.
>
> Olivia: I know. (Focus group, Lilongwe, 1 March 2017)[3]

For Olivia, my question posed a moral dilemma, clearly one that she had reflected on long and hard. She hesitated frequently and laughed nervously during this conversation, interrupting her own stream of thought with 'ah it's difficult', suggesting a real dislike of disregarding the rules of Girl Up. Yet she eventually concluded that this course of action is 'better'. Although it is unclear what Aisha meant by 'ah', which she said with a shake of her head, I interpreted it to mean that she too was struggling with the ethics of the situation. Perhaps Olivia's response of 'I know' was intended to reassure her that as club president, she was not taking this decision lightly. Rebelling against the UN Foundation's campaign was not something these girls enjoyed; however, the official purpose of the campaign did not allow space for activism by girls like them.

For girls living in the townships of Lilongwe, who are struggling to find the money to attend school, accepting Girl Up discourses would mean not having a club at all, but rather waiting around for the UN to use the funds raised by girls in the Global North to start funding girls' education in their area. Instead, they took action themselves, and in doing so had to deviate from the official purpose of Girl Up. Interestingly, when I told the girls in the other schools what this group were doing, they expressed nothing but admiration and awe for them, and wholeheartedly supported this decision.

While the Girl Up materials for clubs make it clear that fundraising for the UN Foundation is an essential part of Girl Up membership, for the girls participating in this study this was interpreted as a negotiable or optional part of the campaign. As the following section outlines, they came up with many other creative and interesting activities, many of which had a distinctly feminist and political orientation.

Girl Up clubs' engagement with feminist issues

For most of the girls, the main purpose of a Girl Up club seemed to be about giving each other support and encouragement, discussing the challenges they were facing, and debating issues relating to women's rights. At the Catholic school in New York, the girls organised discussion events about issues such as the gender pay gap, sexual harassment, and intersectional feminism. Their most recent meeting had included a discussion on the stereotypes faced by Muslim women in the USA. One of the girls, Gabriella, explained that Girl Up was a place to 'vent' with like-minded people:

> Here like people can kind of understand you 'cos they were like fighting for the same thing or they understood the same thing. (Focus group, New York, 10 April 2017)

Similarly, Chloe, the club president in the UK, felt strongly that she wanted Girl Up club to be a place where girls could support each other:

> I know that this goes like outside of what the UN want us to do but I kind of wanna make it like a … I guess safe space, like anyone can come from like lower school if they need help with anything, 'cos I know being like a kid in high school is really scary. (Focus group, North Wales, 27 September 2016)

For her, this is an important focus of the club, even though she knows full well that it is not a priority of the campaign.

In New Jersey, as well as hosting awareness-raising events, the girls also organised a collection of sanitary products for a local women's shelter. They placed posters in school lavatories to inform their peers that these items were not included in food stamps and were still taxed as luxuries. They collected donations of hundreds of products and delivered them to the shelter. In both the USA and the UK, the girls spoke of the many gender inequalities they had experienced themselves or that they were aware of in their communities. Contrary to the depiction of the Northern girl as always already empowered in Girl Up materials, these club members made it an explicit aim of their clubs to tackle gender inequality in the Global North.

In the township in Lilongwe, the girls were helping each other in practical ways that did not match the Girl Up depiction of the Southern girl either. As well as holding meetings for debates and discussion, they performed songs, dances, and role-plays exploring how girls could stand up for themselves if, for example, their parents or husband should threaten to take them out of school. The support did not stop there though. If a girl should stand up to her parents or husband to no avail, the club members would go to their house and try to persuade them themselves:

> Mayamiko: And we will teach the person we will teach the husband you.
> Chikondi: Husband.
> Mayamiko: Have not do good thing, have married a young girl and can you see there are so many problems here, this one must go to school.
> Fatsani: For the future. (Focus group, Lilongwe, 9 February 2017)

While the depiction of the Southern girl in Girl Up resources such as 'Connecting the Dots' is of a victim, alone and awaiting rescue, these girls' depiction of Southern girlhood is of girls uniting to challenge domineering husbands or parents. They also helped each other to overcome cultural taboos and to be informed about important issues for girls, such as caring for the body during menstruation. One of the girls, Janet, explained that 'sometimes we miss school as girls ... we feel some pain', but this was changing because 'now in this girl club we teach each other that yeah, you need to do that, do this and you have painkiller' (focus group, Lilongwe, 2 March 2017).

The girls' school had no access to running water, with only four pit latrines for 200 staff and students, only two of which had closing doors. Research suggests that a lack of access to running water, along with the physical symptoms of menstruation, including pain and diarrhoea, and a lack of information about menstruation all contribute to girls' absenteeism in Malawi (Grant *et al.* 2013, 263–4). While many of these factors were out of their control, the girls used their Girl Up club as an opportunity to change the one element they could control: how informed they were about managing their symptoms and taking care of their bodies. Once again, they used initiative and creativity to help themselves and support other girls, and to challenge gender inequalities in their own communities.

Girl Up members' political activism

Some of the Girl Up clubs took more overt political action, even though few of the groups said they would describe Girl Up as a political movement. Chloe, the UK club president, complained that women's participation in politics was still treated as a 'joke' in her school, and said that one of her aims for the club was to 'make the school sort of like more used to like girls doing stuff in politics' (focus group, North Wales, 27 September 2017). As well as writing to their congressman's office about why they felt that tampons should not be taxed as a luxury item, the girls in New Jersey also hosted a 'forum' for anyone from the school who wanted to come and discuss the results of the 2016 US presidential election. The girls in the township of Lilongwe told me of their plans to speak to village chiefs about the need to enforce the recently introduced law making it illegal for girls to marry below the age of 18 in Malawi, and they talked of wanting to 'reach the government with our manifestos' (focus group, Lilongwe, 6 March 2017).

Some of the girls in New York participated in the women's marches that followed Donald Trump's election as US president. This was something they wanted to do together as a club, but like the girls in New Jersey, they had found that school rules about trips, as well as a limited budget, had restricted their activities.

> Nicola: Well I was gonna go anyway and then in Girl Up we started talking about trying to get like a bus down or something like that, but

it kind our plans kind of fell through, so I went kinda separately like, with all the things I've learned in Girl Up just in the back of my head.

Gabriella: Yeah.

Nicola: It was amazing.

Lucia: It was awesome.

Gabriella: It was like such a great experience 'cos like I'd never like done something like that before, like I'd never been as, I think like Girl Up really gave me an opportunity to be educated about this. (Focus group, New York, 10 April 2017)

Here, Nicola and Gabriella both implied that they might not have attended a march if it were not for 'all the things I've learned in Girl Up', or the 'opportunity' that Girl Up gave them to become educated about feminism. Nicola and Lucia's proclamations of 'it was amazing' and 'it was awesome' suggest that this was an extremely positive experience and one they might repeat in future. The girls in the UK were similarly inspired by participating in Girl Up to attend feminist demonstrations, although they had been unable to organise travelling to any of the women's marches. They told me, however, that they were resolved to find a way to get to the next one.

Girls resisting hostility to Girl Up

It is worth noting that in every fieldwork setting the girls experienced stigma and even bullying for their decision to attend their Girl Up club. In the UK, the girls talked about family members who did not understand the need for a women's rights club in 2017 and who mocked them for attending. When these girls gave an assembly to younger students about girls' rights, speaking to an audience of over 100 of their peers, some of the male teachers at the school did not support their efforts. One of the girls, Rhiannon, explained:

I think also male teachers are also the issue ... if they're on the sides and sat there just like ... sniggering and not taking it seriously then they're just, all the kids are gonna think it's OK to laugh at it. (Focus group, North Wales, 24 January 2017)

Despite the feeling that they were not being supported by their own teachers, the girls continued with their awareness-raising efforts, eventually speaking to every single member of their school through talks and assemblies.

In every school participating in the research, girls talked about negative attitudes from their peers towards Girl Up. This mostly came from boys, although the girls also spoke of their disappointment that it sometimes came from girls too. The most common complaint was that there was no 'boy up' club, or that the money raised was only going to girls' education projects, which the boys claimed was discriminatory. Some boys did not even draw on the language of equality and discrimination to express their negative views about Girl Up; some were more overtly misogynistic. For example, the girls in the township of Lilongwe told me that boys mocked them for attending a club that encouraged them to dream of achieving their goals. One of the girls, Ethel, explained that

> ... sometimes boys always saying that you are just wasting your time because in future you will be a wife. (Focus group, Lilongwe, 16 February 2017)

When I asked how they felt about this, Aisha, another of the girls, told me, 'we don't care 'cos we're empowered'.

In this climate of hostility towards feminism and girls' rights activism, Hailey, one of the girls in New Jersey, even hinted that the decision to register with Girl Up was a strategic one:

> Being affiliated with the UN and like, helping like girls in other countries like makes it kind of like, appear less like radical like, I like I don't think like a simply like women's empowerment or feminist club like would've been as popular. (Focus group, New Jersey, 18 April 2017)

While she was keen to stress that this was not why the girls had registered the club, Hailey's comments show a critical assessment of girls' rights discourses. While they were not actually engaged in fundraising, and were instead hosting politically themed events and organising collections for local women's charities, Hailey is aware that being affiliated with a fundraising campaign for girls' education in countries in Africa appears less 'radical' than tackling inequality in the USA. This shows an awareness that discourses of rescuing the Southern girl would resonate more strongly with their Northern peers than claims of enduring inequalities in their own context. Whilst their decision to register as a Girl Up club reproduces these discourses of rescue, the girls also subvert them by using them strategically in order to facilitate their activism within their own community. Participation in Girl Up, then, for one club, represented a way of dealing with stigma and hostility, and enabling members to carry out the local activism they were so passionate about.

Conclusions and final thoughts

The girls participating in this research are feminist activists, whose activism aims not only to challenge sexism in their own schools and communities, but also to take their demands for girls' rights to political fora. They encouraged their classmates to be more engaged in politics and feminism, and they continued to do so despite experiencing mockery and stigma from schoolmates, families, and even teachers. Their activities included political debates, confronting domineering boys, parents and teachers, mentoring younger girls, and participating in political demonstrations. They were engaged in almost all of the formal and informal activities identified by Jessica Taft, which deserve to be recognised as activism (2014, 263). Although they were limited by restrictions imposed upon them because of their age, including school rules and financial constraints, these girls should not be seen as activists 'in progress' (Taft 2017, 29). Rather, they are activists now, and their clubs have reached thousands of members of their communities with information about girls' rights, with support to girls experiencing discrimination and with calls to action.

Furthermore, my findings suggest that girls negotiate affiliation with a powerful international institution with creativity and agency. They rarely reproduced powerful discourses about girl power in international development uncritically, frequently adapted them to their own contexts and experiences, and sometimes rejected them outright. The girls in the Global North did not see themselves as living in gender-equal societies, while those in the South were not waiting for anyone to rescue them. They all rejected an individualistic model of empowerment, instead using their clubs to support one another and act together to overcome oppression.

Returning to Heather Switzer's argument, the logic of campaigns such as The Girl Effect and Girl Up 'works to explicitly racialise, depoliticise, ahistoricise, and naturalise global structural inequities and legitimise neoliberal interventions in the, name of girls' empowerment' (Switzer 2013, 347). However, the Girl Up members in this study organised discussions on intersectional feminism, attended political rallies, and showed an awareness of global power structures that mean that a club purporting to send girls in Africa to school comes across as less 'radical' than one demanding, for example, the scrapping of luxury tax status on tampons in the USA. The findings suggest a need for research to explore further how girls and women demonstrate agency in relation to neoliberal and instrumentalist discourses in international development. To identify that such discourses exist is to tell only half of the story.

These findings can also tell us a great deal about the kinds of activism in which girls would like to participate. The girls told me that they joined Girl Up because they wanted the structure and resources that a UN Foundation initiative could provide, because they felt the UN Foundation name would make their feminism more palatable to their peers in school, because they wanted to set up meaningful connections with girls in different contexts to their own, or because they wanted to feel part of an international movement and, as Chloe, the UK club president, said, 'I don't think we'd have the opportunity otherwise'. Girls under 18 may be excluded from voting or from meaningful participation in formal political structures in all three of these countries; however, these girls longed for ways to undertake their own forms of activism. They saw Girl Up as one way to do so, even if they did not always undertake the kinds of activities advocated by the campaign. If international organisations want to mobilise a 'community' of girls to make change, then the findings of this study suggest they could start by consulting girls in different contexts about what they see as empowering for girls and taking them and their political views seriously. In doing so, they will not only fill a gap left by girls' marginalisation from formal political structures, they will also be able to harness the huge amount of creativity, passion, and courage these girls show in tackling sexism. They are already making changes in their own communities and as part of global initiatives and protests, yet they face many challenges because of their age, the restrictions placed on them by institutions such as schools, and hostility and stigma. They are eager to be part of a feminist community that supports them to overcome these challenges and to take their activism further.

Notes

1. 'Best Friends Forever'.
2. Half a million Malawian Kwacha, approximately US$700.
3. All names used are pseudonyms.

Acknowledgements

I am grateful to Jutta Weldes and Karen Tucker for their feedback on a draft of this chapter. I would also like to thank the editor and reviewers for their insightful comments. This research was supported by ESRC studentship number 1488667.

Notes on contributor

Rosie Walters is a postgraduate researcher at the University of Bristol's School of Sociology, Politics and International Studies.

References

Bent, Emily (2013) 'The boundaries of girls' political participation: a critical exploration of girls' experiences as delegates to the United Nations Commission on the Status of Women (CSW)', *Global Studies of Childhood* 3(2): 173–82

Bent, Emily and Heather Switzer (2016) 'Oppositional girlhoods and the challenge of relational politics', *Gender Issues* 33(2): 122–47

Biddle, Tabby (2010) 'Girl Up Kicks off its "United for Girls Tour"', *Huffington Post*, 8 November, https://www.huffingtonpost.com/tabby-biddle/girl-up-kicks-off-its-uni_b_780187.html (last checked 30 November 2017)

Calkin, Sydney (2015) 'Post-feminist spectatorship and the girl effect: "go ahead, really imagine her"', *Third World Quarterly* 36(4): 654–69

Cameron, John and Anna Haanstra (2008) 'Development made sexy: how it happened and what it means', *Third World Quarterly* 29(8): 1475–89

Chant, Sylvia and Caroline Sweetman (2012) 'Fixing women or fixing the world? "Smart economics", efficiency approaches, and gender equality in development', *Gender & Development* 20(3): 517–29 Girl Effect (n.d.) 'The Girl Effect', https://www.youtube.com/watch?v=WIvmE4_KMNw (last checked 19 March 2018)

Girl Up (2010) 'Girl Up: Connecting the Dots', https://www.youtube.com/watch?v=XgVwm8sl4os (last checked 14 February 2018)

Girl Up (n.d. a) 'About', https://girlup.org/about/ (last checked 14 February 2018)

Girl Up (n.d. b) 'Girl Up Clubs', https://girlup.org/take-action/be-a-leader/girl-up-clubs/ (last checked 30 November 2017)

Girl Up (n.d. c) 'Map of Girl Up Clubs', http://clubs.girlup.org/map (last checked January 2017)

Girl Up (n.d. d) 'Club Starter Guide', https://girlup.org/wp-content/uploads/2016/02/Club-Starter-Guide-Final.pdf (last checked 30 November 2017)

Grant, Monica, Cynthia Lloyd and Barbara Mensch (2013) 'Menstruation and school absenteeism: evidence from rural Malawi', *Comparative Education Review* 57(2): 260–84

Hickel, Jason (2014) 'The "girl effect": liberalism, empowerment, and the contradictions of development', *Third World Quarterly* 35(8): 1355–73

Jowett, Madeleine and Gill O'Toole (2006) 'Focusing researchers' minds: contrasting experiences of using focus groups in feminist qualitative research', *Qualitative Research* 6(4): 453–72

Khoja-Moolji, Shenila (2015) 'Suturing together girls and education: an investigation in the social (re)production of girls' education as a hegemonic ideology', *Diaspora, Indigenous, and Minority Education* 9(2): 87–107

Koffman, Ofra and Rosalind Gill (2013) '"The revolution will be led by a 12-year-old girl": girl power and global biopolitics', *Feminist Review* 105: 83–102

Koffman, Ofra, Shani Orgad and Rosalind Gill (2015) 'Girl power and "selfie humanitarianism"', *Continuum: Journal of Media and Cultural Studies* 29(2): 157–68

Momsen, Janet H. (2004) *Gender and Development*, Abingdon and New York: Routledge

Shain, Farzana (2013) '"The girl effect": exploring narratives of gendered impacts and opportunities in neoliberal development', *Sociological Research Online* 18(2)

Switzer, Heather (2013) '(Post)Feminist development fables: the girl effect and the production of sexual subjects', *Feminist Theory* 14(3): 345–60

Taft, Jessica K. (2014) 'The political lives of girls', *Sociology Compass* 8(3): 259–67

Taft, Jessica K. (2017) 'Teenage girls' narratives of becoming activists', *Contemporary Social Science* 12 (1-2): 27–39

Toepler, Stefan and Natascha Mard (2007) 'The Role of Philanthropy within the United Nations System: The Case of the United Nations Foundation', in Helmut K. Anheier, Adele Simmons and David Winder (eds.) *Innovation in Strategic Philanthropy*, Boston, MA: Springer, 167–82

United Nations (2012) 'UN Independent Expert Calls for Boycott of Businesses Profiting from Israeli Settlements', 25 October, http://www.un.org/apps/news/story.asp?NewsID=43376#.Wh7OMIVI-Uk (last checked 30 November 2017)

United Nations Development Programme (n.d. a) 'Country Profiles: Malawi', http://hdr.undp.org/en/countries/profiles/MWI (last checked 12 April 2018)

United Nations Development Programme (n.d. b) 'Country Profiles: United Kingdom', http://hdr.undp.org/en/countries/profiles/GBR (last checked 26 April 2018)

United Nations Development Programme (n.d. c) 'Country Profiles: United States,' http://hdr.undp.org/en/countries/profiles/USA (last checked 26 April 2018)

Wilkinson, Sue (1998) 'Focus Groups in Feminist Research: Power, Interaction, and the Construction of Meaning', *Women's Studies International Forum* 21(1): 111–125

Wilkinson, Sue (1999) 'How Useful Are Focus Groups in Feminist Research?', in Jenny Kitzinger and Rosaline Barber (eds.) *Developing Focus Group Research: Politics, Theory, and Practice*, London: Sage, 64–78

Williams, Stacy (1999) 'A billion dollar donation: should the United Nations look a gift horse in the mouth?', *Georgia Journal of International and Comparative Law* 27: 425–55

CHAPTER 7

Young feminists working globally to end violence against women and girls: key challenges and ways forward

Christine Homan, Divya Chandran and Rita Lo

Abstract

Drawing from our experience as young feminists working with an emerging feminist advocacy collective focused on addressing violence against women and girls (VAWG), our chapter focuses on some of the key challenges young feminists face while advocating for feminist-informed programming in efforts to address VAWG in humanitarian and development settings. Drawing on our own experience as young feminists to prevent and address VAWG in a patriarchal world, we see ourselves as walking a tightrope. On one hand, our radical activism is instrumental in achieving a world where no one is left behind. Yet we are often told, in direct and indirect ways, to dial down the feminism, to be 'inclusive' and 'intersectional' with limited meaningful accountability to women and girls. We conclude by offering a set of recommendations aimed at advancing young feminist activism in VAWG work and retaining a feminist space that is political, while working in partnership with other movements and actors.

Keywords: Feminist activism; violence against women and girls; VAWG; gender-based violence; GBV; humanitarian; international development; intersectional analysis

Introduction

As young feminists working to end violence against all women and girls (VAWG), we are aware that we are standing on the shoulders of other feminist activists who have fought tirelessly to secure global recognition for women's rights as human rights. This chapter focuses on the continuing struggle to end VAWG, and the need to ensure that all involved in humanitarian and international development play their part in this struggle. Feminists are operating inside and outside humanitarian and development organisations of all sizes and types to advocate for the changes we need to see to humanitarian and development policies and practices.

A focus on young feminist work on ending VAWG is a critical contribution to this issue of *Gender & Development* focusing on Young Feminisms. VAWG is a key focus for all feminists; against the backdrop of the #MeToo movement, we are witnessing a surge in global conversations around the dynamics of patriarchal power and abuse. 'Fourth-wave' feminism is attracting millions of young women, often becoming involved initially through new forms of social media organisation, as well as traditional movement building and organising. Today's young women who begin activism in response to personal experiences of VAWG and abuse are part of a wider social justice movement across the world that is mobilising against growing violence and crises in the world.

Economic inequalities are increasing in many contexts globally (Ukhova 2015). Increasing numbers and proportions of the world's people live in fragile and conflict-affected contexts (OECD 2018). There is also a growing and escalating backlash against women's equal rights from right-wing and fundamentalist forces, and activism – both progressive and reactionary – is finding new power through opportunities for organising and collective action offered by digital technologies. Patriarchy is morphing into new forms of extreme intensity and virulence, showing its power to continue and evolve, demanding constant struggle from feminists (Enloe 2017). Young women are critical actors in this struggle, not least because of the focus of patriarchy on their bodies, sexualities, and reproductive rights.

In humanitarian and international development organisations, feminists have worked since the 1970s to ensure policies and programming responds to the reality of VAWG. But despite progress in the humanitarian and development sectors to integrate gender and women's issues since the 1970s, there is still a long way to go, and – as we argue in this chapter – the depoliticisation of women's rights issues when they come into contact with humanitarian and international development sectors has been widely remarked on by feminists working in the sector. Since our organisations are shaped by the social norms of wider society, advocacy and activism are important to ensure they are part of the solution to VAWG, rather than part of the problem.

The authors of this chapter are all members of the Coalition of Feminists for Social Change (COFEM).[1] COFEM is an advocacy collective working globally to end VAWG, which was formed in 2016 by a group of feminist colleagues from humanitarian and development settings around the globe, who came together to discuss shared concerns and to strategise around how to respond to mounting challenges and shrinking space, in their work to address VAWG in the humanitarian and development spheres (COFEM 2016).[2] COFEM's guiding objectives are twofold. First, it provides a forum for connection, discussion, problem solving, mutual support, and activism to advance feminist, women-centred strategies for ending VAWG and promoting the rights of women and girls. COFEM's second aim is to identify and implement strategies and actions collectively to overcome the challenges facing feminist-informed efforts to address VAWG, and make sure that women and girls remain at the centre of all efforts to end VAWG.

We started this work in order to address the widespread lack of sociopolitical analysis of gender inequality in VAWG work, which has increasingly led to the promotion of discourse, policies, and interventions that do not address the lived experiences of women and girls. We believe that the failure to link acts of sexual and physical violence to the broader context of intersecting oppressions of gender, race, class, age, patriarchy, and post-colonial power undermine and even close space for initiatives that are women-centred, women-led, and rights-driven.

COFEM is a space for both younger and older feminists working in humanitarian and international development. COFEM empowers younger feminists to be unapologetic in their push for transformative change to humanitarian and development policies and practice. COFEM is committed to ensuring young women's voices are central to debates and decisions in the humanitarian and development sectors. As we discuss later in this chapter, a key aspect of current feminist practice is to undertake intersectional power analysis – that is, to analyse how multiple identities, including race, gender, and age, intersect to shape the realities of individual women and girls. Only by understanding how race, gender, and age work together, simultaneously, and challenging the particular effects this has on young women, can we understand the complex strands of young feminist activism. This also holds true for VAWG work.

In this chapter, we focus on the challenges we currently face in our work. In COFEM and in our own activism as young feminists, we draw on core feminist foundational thinking in our understanding of what VAWG is, its purpose in patriarchies, and why it persists. We welcome the strides taken in humanitarian and international development work to engage with some of this thinking, but we are currently concerned that there are contemporary threats to such work. We fear that the needs of women and girls are being ignored in favour of an apolitical, broad protection agenda, which ultimately fails to address their needs and reconfigure the existing power base. The chapter focuses on the range of key challenges we see in our work, including the rise of gender-neutral language in humanitarian and development practice that has led to the depoliticising of VAWG work; misinterpretation of intersectionality; increased focus on engaging men and boys with limited meaningful accountability to women and girls; and shrinking space for feminist activism and limited funding for the women and girls agenda. The chapter concludes with recommendations aimed at advancing young feminist activism in VAWG work that retains its political and transformative nature, while also working in partnership with other movements and actors.

Our primary sources of information are the first-hand experience we have as young feminists working for COFEM, and the many discussions and conversations we have with fellow activists. The chapter also uses other sources of evidence, including interviews undertaken specifically for it, and a review of literature including published and unpublished chapters, case studies, policy documents, speeches, and a film. While we aim to focus on particular factors of concern for feminists working on VAWG, the challenges we write about here are not unique to young feminists involved in VAWG work, nor are they representative of the breadth of challenges young feminists face in their day-to-day activism.

Feminist foundations: VAWG, its causes, and its purpose in patriarchies

In the not-too-distant past, human rights law discourse failed to situate VAWG on a continuum from the private to public realm, and feminists have challenged this (examples are Charlesworth and Chinkin 1994; Kelly 1988). Feminist activism and analysis was instrumental in challenging the public–private dichotomy – that is, the idea that there is a firm distinction between public and private life and the state should only intervene in the public sphere. Feminists have called out state inaction with regard to crimes of VAWG, and pushed the issue of VAWG into the public domain. They have articulated a theory of violence that is grounded in a socio-political analysis of gender inequality. This recognises VAWG as both an outcome of, and means to maintain, women and girls' subordinate status (COFEM 2016).

Over the past four decades, feminists from the second wave of the 1970s onwards have made a collective push and sustained efforts to end VAWG. They have done this at multiple levels: local, national, and global. Through the United Nations (UN) Decade for Women from 1975 and through the series of UN Conferences on Women to the final Fourth Conference on Women in Beijing in 1995, women's rights and gender inequality came to the fore in the media throughout the world, as never before. 'Gender' became a buzzword in policy circles struggling to understand the social basis of the subordination of women (Baden and Goetz 1997). A series of UN Declarations and policy statements came out of this process. Human rights law was influenced by second-wave feminist activism during this period and of particular relevance to our discussion is the landmark Declaration on the Elimination of Violence Against Women (DEVAW), adopted by the UN General Assembly in 1993, because it was the first international human rights instrument to focus specifically on the issue of violence against women. In its preamble, the DEVAW underscored the structural inequality that underpins VAWG:

> Violence against women is a manifestation of historically unequal power relations between men and women, which have led to domination over and discrimination against women by men and to the prevention of the full advancement of women, and … violence against women is one of the crucial social mechanisms by which women are forced into a subordinate position compared with men. (UN 1993, paragraph 6)

The DEVAW defined violence against women as:

> Any act of gender-based violence that results in, or is likely to result in, physical, sexual or psychological harm or suffering to women, including threats of such acts, coercion or arbitrary deprivation of liberty, whether occurring in public or in private life. (*ibid.*, Article 1)

While the DEVAW was not legally binding on governments, it established international norms that could be used in the struggle to end all forms of VAWG, and these have been very important in ensuring further change in the years since (Ward 2016). It also underscored the issue of patriarchy and inequality between women and men, leading to the conclusion that efforts to eliminate all forms of VAWG must be informed by transformative approaches to dismantle the gender hierarchy which exists in societies throughout the world.

Feminists working in humanitarian and international development have used DEVAW and other international legal agreements to provide a framing for their efforts. States, and a range of other important actors at international, national, and local levels, all play a role in perpetuating or challenging VAWG, increasing or reducing gendered vulnerability to violence and abuse. Humanitarian and development programming plays an important part in enabling people to gain access to basic resources and security, and it is critical to integrate women's rights and gender equality into policies and programming. The prioritisation of women and girls in humanitarian and international development policy and practice over recent decades is a positive and welcoming change; however, it does not necessarily translate into programming that is fully informed about women's perspectives, interests, and needs.

As young feminists working across the humanitarian–development nexus today, we build on the knowledge of earlier feminists, and evolve knowledge of our own based on our experiences of the current context and the challenges that we encounter. We know that the interventions that aim to end VAWG need to be rooted in an analysis of unequal power, centred on women and girls, and be led by women and girl-led movements. We also know that to actively challenge patriarchy and gender inequality, women's and girls' voices, agency, and leadership must be supported and amplified. Yet we find huge resistance to efforts to reconfigure the existing power base and to centre women and girls in efforts to end VAWG, despite apparent progress in the humanitarian and development sectors to integrate 'gender' into their work. It seems that despite policy statements and commitments, gender training, the development and roll-out of gender tools and frameworks, and other initiatives associated with 'gender mainstreaming' (Jahan 1995), progress is painfully slow at best, and stalled at worst. A feminist approach to VAWG is crucial so that donors, governments, and agencies are able to comprehend why different approaches to service provision and distinct prevention strategies are required.

In the next section, we start to consider some of the key challenges to progress as we perceive them.

Key challenges

The depoliticised language of 'gender' and the challenges this presents to feminist work

> And we all know that, where there's no name for a problem, you can't see a problem, and when you can't see a problem, you pretty much can't solve it. (Crenshaw 2016)

In the wake of the Beijing Conference in 1995, a transformative agenda of gender mainstreaming was developed to integrate principles of gender equality into policies, projects, and programmes from design to implementation. The Women in Development (WID) approach of the 1980s became the Gender and Development (GAD) approach of the 1990s and beyond (Moser 1989). While this was intended to problematise gender power relations to serve the agenda of women's rights and gender equality, in practice the outcome has been very different. Feminist critiques have argued that the key analytical concepts of gender roles, gender relations, and gender equality have been delinked from analyses of patriarchal power relations, co-opted, and neutralised (Mukhopadhyay 2004; Pillay 2015).

As young feminists, these critiques resonate with us. While still in higher education, we experienced the way that use of gender as a concept depoliticises discussions about power and inequality. All three authors attended Columbia University's School of International and Public Affairs (SIPA), and two participated in the Gender and Public Policy specialisation. While there was variance between classes, many of the gender courses steered away from an explicit discussion of the power and politics of gender hierarchy, patriarchal violence, and anti-racist scholarship. Added to this was a sense that gender work need not be transformative, as long as it is seen to be 'inclusive': during one of the Gender Policy Practicum seminars, a senior director and gender advisor from a multilateral development institution insisted that such 'theories of gender do not matter, they are too complex and mean nothing' – claiming that it is preferable to hire someone who has specific technical expertise, with gender expertise 'added on'. For the many emerging gender specialists in the room, to hear an influential person (also a potential employer) dismiss a rigorous body of research, policy, and practice was demoralising. And yet, with greater and greater frequency, young feminists are having to navigate this conundrum: do we need to dial down the feminism in order to be employed by the very institutions/entities mandated to promote gender equality in humanitarian and development work?

In our working lives, the feminist critiques of 'gender' being a depoliticised concept resonate even more powerfully. Our reality is that we work in a world where 'gender' means many things to different actors. Our reality today, nearly 25 years after the Beijing Conference, is that the language of gender and gender mainstreaming is used widely across humanitarian and development organisations, and it masks widely varying commitments to real, transformative change. It is normal for us to need to question and probe beneath gender language to uncover the varying commitments to change that are concealed behind it. For those who lack a strong understanding of feminist theory and praxis, gender-neutral language and gender-inclusive approaches may be perceived as more inclusive than the language of women's rights. However, they can also reinforce gender inequality by leaving unequal power equations and structures intact (Mukhopadhyay 2004).

In gender training 30 years ago, at the start of the push to integrate gender inequality and women's rights issues into development and humanitarian work, participants were encouraged to use binary distinctions between two sexes – male and female – and two corresponding sets of gender roles and relations, which varied according to context (Mwau *et al.* 1994). Today, we are working in a world where these binary distinctions are questioned (Oosterhoff and Sweetman 2018, 1). However, while moving away from a simplistic binary distinction is welcomed by LGBTQI+ rights activists and others, feminists have pointed out how the language of gender inclusivity often overlooks the gender hierarchy, which in turn deflects attention from women and girls and the need to end patriarchal power relations. A gender-equality advisor with an international development and humanitarian organisation that focuses on girls' rights shared one example with us:

> As part of my orientation, I asked a fellow gender advisor about an apparent dichotomy in the marketing – which is very girl-focused exter-nally, but which internally takes a much more technocratic approach to analysing the conditions of girls, boys, women, men. This is also in the context of a new policy on gender and inclusion. I was told that this was part of campaigns, and that in the future she expected they would be altering the messaging to be, in her words, 'less binary'. I took this to mean that they plan to shift attention away from a girl-centred focus in the coming years. (E-mail interview, 25 July 2018)

The terms 'feminist' and 'feminism' are often unwelcome in humanitarian and development organisations, once more showing the depoliticisation that has occurred since the early days of gender mainstreaming. Another senior gender advisor at an international organisation told us she was forewarned by a friend in the same organisation before interviewing for her current position, to avoid mentioning the word 'feminism' – or discussing women at all – if she wanted to be hired.[3] Despite her shock, she took the advice because she needed the job (Skype interview, 19 July 2018).

It is deeply problematic that powerful concepts of feminism and women's rights are not welcome in so many humanitarian and development organ-isations that state a commitment to ending VAWG. In her 2014 report on violence against women, its causes and consequences, Rashida Manjoo, the former UN Special Rapporteur, described the implications of using the neutral language and concept of 'gender' for efforts to address VAWG:

> violence against men does not occur as a result of pervasive inequality and discrimination, and ... it is neither systemic nor pandemic in the way that violence against women indisputably is ... The shift to neu-trality favours a more pragmatic and politically palatable understanding of gender, that is, as simply a euphemism for 'men and women', rather than as a system of domination of men over women. Violence against women cannot be analysed on a case-by-case basis in isolation of the individual, institutional and structural factors that govern and shape the lives of women. Such factors demand gender-specific approaches to ensure an equality of outcomes for women. Attempts to combine

or synthesize all forms of violence into a 'gender neutral' framework tend to result in a depoliticized or diluted discourse, which abandons the transformative agenda. A different set of normative and practical measures is required to respond to and prevent violence against women and, equally importantly, to achieve the international law obligation of substantive equality, as opposed to formal equality. (UN Human Rights Council 2014, 17)

This 'pragmatic' and 'politically palatable understanding' of gender both reflects and reinforces the power imbalance between men and women, further eclipsing the different and specific needs of all women and girls. It should go without saying that every group subjected to violence deserves specialised services. However, challenges arise with gender-neutral framings of violence, or with efforts to try to frame a variety of different forms of violence under the same umbrella. In particular, such an approach ignores the root causes and drivers of VAWG. Feminist research has long shown that gender inequality is the root cause of VAWG (Namy *et al.* 2017). Evidence also shows VAWG can be reduced in low- and middle-income countries through initiatives that tackle gender inequality and imbalances of power (Michau *et al.* 2015).

Our final point in this section concerns the dangers of using the language of 'gender' in relation to men and boys. While gender *inequality* is the root of VAWG and wider gendered oppression, 'gender' used on its own is simply a description of difference between women and men. It has become common for discussions on gender to begin with the claim, 'gender is not about women and girls' – often intending to include men in discussions and recruit them as supporters of gender equality and women's rights. In our experience, these discussions often limit themselves to a recitation of the challenges men face, while at the same time failing to discuss explicitly power differentials, structural discrimination, and intersecting oppressions. In an interview with a feminist practitioner currently developing the Uganda Country Programme for the UN/EU Spotlight Initiative,[4] she described the constant challenge of ensuring women and girls remain at the centre of discussions and interventions on VAWG:

> When the discussion turned to a focus on gender equality, it veered toward 'what are we doing for the men' and this in a program where the focus is on ending violence against women. If there aren't feminists in the room who can guide the discussion back – or where we are outnumbered or have a particularly hostile group – a program/project/initiative/ policy that was intended to be in service of women and promoting gender equality can become all about men's issues. It is extremely time-consuming, demoralizing and risky. Decisions can be made so quickly and it means we always have to be present and ready. (E-mail interview, 24 July 2018)

Increased focus on engaging men and boys with limited meaningful accountability to women and girls

It is not uncommon for those of us working in VAWG programming to hear the recurring refrain: what about men and boys? (Goetz and Dore-Weeks 2018). This section follows our previous observation about the language of gender and the danger that using this term as a noun shifts the focus away from women and gender inequality.

The feminist community does not refute the importance of supporting male victims of violence. We also recognise that it is critical to challenge and change gender inequality and patriarchy by working with men and boys. However, this work has to be grounded in a feminist analysis of gender inequality and the role of men and boys in challenging inequality and promoting the rights of women and girls. Yet it is very problematic when we see groups and individuals in humanitarian and international development work discuss violence against men and boys in ways that result in VAWG being sidelined or minimised.

Our current work as young feminists continues the work of earlier feminist activists, who have engaged men for decades and at multiple levels in efforts to prevent and respond to VAWG (Alemu 2015). These efforts are aimed at dismantling patriarchal structures and include work in changing and transforming social norms as well as notions of masculinity built on the subjugation of women and girls. At the same time, feminists and women's rights activists have stressed that accountability to women and girls should be at the heart of male involvement efforts to prevent and respond to VAWG (Pino 2017).

In this context, accountability to women and girls means working at both the individual and structural levels to change personal behaviour while transforming patriarchal systems – this requires a recognition of the existing gender hierarchy and a true commitment to transform a system of inequality from which men have benefited and continue to benefit (COFEM 2017a). As young feminists navigating VAWG programming in humanitarian and development contexts, we feel a heightened sense of backlash when we raise concerns about the practices that are not accountable to women and girls because key stakeholders in the humanitarian and development community are prioritising the engagement of men and boys in their policy agendas, while at the same time depoliticising VAWG work.

As Shamim Meer brilliantly points out:

> Gender, stripped of ideas of male privilege and female subordination, came to mean that women and men suffered equally the costs of the existing gender order. Women's organisations were increasingly asked 'if you are working on gender, then where are the men?' and they were increasingly pressurized (particularly by donors) to include men. On the heels of this pressure, a new development actor came into focus – men's organisations. (Meer 2012, 4)

We have seen that women-led initiatives are often subjected to higher degrees of scrutiny and everyone from donors to governments insists on 'a strong evidence base' to measure the effectiveness of gender justice programming. In contrast, studies have highlighted that the evidence base of the effectiveness of interventions solely with boys and men is limited, and while most of it describes some measured attitudinal changes, it does not necessarily capture change in violence perpetration or social norms (Jewkes *et al.* 2014). This observation echoes findings of a 2014 systematic review of VAWG prevention programming where male engagement models were described as demonstrating some potential in shifting attitudes although behavioural impact on male perpetration of VAWG was limited (Ellsberg *et al.* 2015).

The amount of attention and resources that have been channelled into 'male engagement' efforts with limited meaningful accountability to women shows how hard gender discrimination is to root out. Furthermore, it is worth noting that the emphasis on transforming masculinities in the literature on engaging men and boys in violence prevention, while enriching and useful, translates into programming that is often limited to community education, workshops, and 'awareness-raising' activities targeted at the individual level, without a commitment to address misogyny which requires interventions that also change and challenge larger social systems and structures that perpetuate and reinforce the gender hierarchy.

Feminists and women's rights activists have built reservoirs of expert knowledge on VAWG over decades, in a range of contexts, grounding their practice-based evidence in a multi-layered understanding of the complexity of women and girls' lives that is informed by an analysis of the ways patriarchal dynamics manifest in that context (COFEM 2017b). However, their knowledge and their position as 'knowers' are often overlooked, devalued, and positioned as non-credible. The value of women's knowledge is sidelined in patriarchies and this is no different in humanitarian and development organisations. This means each new generation of feminists in these organisations is forced to try, once more, to push forward in a context where progress is constantly rolled back.

This partly explains why actors in the male engagement space have leap-frogged over well-established women's rights organisations, activists, and scholars – in the process, undermining the knowledge and leadership of these groups instead of drawing greater attention to their vast body of work, and often unwilling to take on board the concerns, demands, and advice of diverse women and girls regarding programming on men and boys.

Ending VAWG requires the knowledge, leadership, and voices of women and girls. In a comprehensive guidance paper published by White Ribbon on the principles and practices for promoting accountability for men as allies in violence prevention, a pertinent point was made in relation to men's position in violence prevention work:

> [I]t is inappropriate for men to take on leadership roles in violence pre-
> vention. Being an ally means having a supporting role in relation to

campaigns under women's leadership rather than as leaders or equal partners. This is because of men's dominance and privilege and the structural gender inequalities within which men's violence takes place. (Pease 2017, 1)

As young feminists, we are concerned about the prevalence of discussions and programmes that seek to address this issue, but disregard the voices of women and girls. In light of this lack of feminist analysis and research, and poor accountability to women and girls, COFEM was invited by the Sexual Violence Research Institute (SVRI) to conduct a pre-conference workshop on achievements and challenges facing feminist efforts to end VAWG in humanitarian and development settings and facilitate a panel at the 5th SVRI 2017 forum in Rio de Janeiro. At the special panel session, COFEM launched the Feminist Perspectives on Addressing Violence Against Women and Girls Series, comprised of five papers and co-authored by 15 members. The series identified four practices that reduce accountability to women and girls: (1) investment in male involvement programming without demand or evidence; (2) male-dominated efforts that do not support women's leadership; (3) shifts towards men's priorities and needs; and (4) failure to transform patriarchy.

(Mis)interpreting intersectionality

Another challenge for us as young feminists is the increasing use of 'intersectionality' in humanitarian and international development organisations. Our problem with this is that it is used as a frame to speak about difference, instead of power and oppression. Jenny Enarsson (2015, 5) points out, 'much like gender mainstreaming, intersectionality has been turned into a technical tool rather than the practical application of a radical political position'.

As young feminists, we feel it is important to resist the erasure of the radical roots of intersectionality, to assert it as a critique of power and privilege, and to recognise the knowledge and thinking of social movements such as the Combahee River Collective[5] as well as Black feminists, women of colour,[6] and antiracist scholars. Intersectionality is a concept with its roots in the political movements of Black women, Chicana and Latina women, and other women of colour (Carastathis 2014). Most of the early intersectionality movements were also lesbian-identified (*ibid.*).

Similar analysis of intersecting systems of power and privilege also appeared in critiques of WID approaches to development, from Southern feminists envisioning a new model of development (Sen and Grown 1989). Feminists from post-colonial contexts argued that international development was itself exploitative of the Third World (Mohanty 1991). They argued that the experiences of poor women in the global South were shaped by gender, race, and class intersecting (Tinker 1990).

These two different literatures offer complementary critiques which challenge all feminists – but we think young feminists, especially – to think and act intersectionally. This means resisting using 'intersectionality' as a catch-all buzzword, and to question actively how an 'intersectional' approach, analysis or programming is genuinely analysing and addressing interlocking systems of oppression. This means complex and difficult analysis and nuanced planning to ensure particular groups are able to benefit from programming. We are not being 'intersectional' when we call for a broad protection agenda in place of specialised services for groups that suffer from specific forms of violence and discrimination.

Intersectionality is being co-opted, diluted, and depoliticised by various stakeholders, especially in the context of the Leave No-one Behind agenda of the UN's Sustainable Development Goals (UN 2016). It is being co-opted into policy documents and practice in ways that ignore the structural nature of patriarchy, racism, and other systems of oppression (GADN 2017). Jenny Enarsson outlines the importance of re-politicising intersectionality in the work of international NGOs (INGOs):

> INGOs should use an intersectional perspective not just to 'quantify' the structural discrimination that different groups are subjected to but to understand how that discrimination shapes their political action – and ultimately, how INGOs can support such action. Political intersectionality can also help cenwwtre development programming around the agency of women and their organisations. Rather than being seen primarily as people who are subjected to structural oppression, it helps INGOs recognise them as people who make active decisions about how to fight discrimination that they face. When applied in this way, an intersectional perspective can help INGOs become better allies to women's rights movements as they challenge power. (Enarsson 2015, 11)

The future for young feminists: shrinking space and limited funding

Feminist thinking and knowledge, skills in organisation, and movement building including grassroots mobilisation have contributed to the advancements of women's rights and the prioritisation of addressing VAWG across the globe over the past few decades. As noted earlier, currently fourth-wave feminism is evolving new ways of working using digital space, often to combat new forms of VAWG which are also evolving in response to online possibilities. Despite the positive gains, many women's organisations that work to end VAWG and promote gender equality are facing new challenges. These challenges in the current political climate are further aggravated by the unfavourable funding landscape for women's organisations and protection work, restricting the already limited space in which they operate.

Across the globe, we are witnessing ongoing and growing political repression and shrinking democratic spaces characterised by restrictions on the rights of freedom of expression, association, and peaceful assembly, attack of media and journalists, oppression of political dissents, and restrictions on foreign funding for NGOs in both democratic and non-democratic states. The rise of religious fundamentalism, xenophobia, conservative political forces, and nationalism further contribute to a shrinking space in which civil society operates.

However, it is crucial to note that not all civil society actors are suffering equally (or at all) under restrictive laws and political repression (Hayes *et al.* 2017). This shrinking space is a gendered phenomenon, with a disproportionately negative effect on women's organising and movements as the restriction of civil society often coincides with the reinforcement of patriarchal values (Bishop 2017).

Aiming to upend existing social and political structures shaped by systems of patriarchy and to dismantle gender hierarchy, women's organisations and activists find their voices silenced and their safety and security compromised. Nevertheless, not all women's rights work receives a similar level of backlash or challenge. For instance, women's economic empowerment and health issues have mostly been accepted as 'mainstream' human rights work – which do not challenge too much of the existing social norms (Bishop 2017). On the other hand, issues such as VAWG, sexual and reproductive rights, feminist organising, and advocacy around sexual orientation and gender identity often challenge rather than reinforce the established gender roles, male privilege, and male domination in most places – thus receiving greater pushbacks (Htun and Weldon 2012).

Young feminists also represent their peers and share their experience of patriarchal backlash that is meted out in particular ways, shaped by the intersection of gender and age, with other factors including race and class. Patriarchies control women's bodies and their reproductive potential, police young women's behaviour and freedom to move and act, deny them their reproductive and sexual rights, and block choices beyond inevitable marriage and motherhood by curtailing their freedom to receive education and gain employment. VAWG is used as a means of control and intimidation. In such an environment, young feminist human rights defenders face appalling risks daily.

Older feminists are also deeply affected by the hostile environment for activism, and the resilience and renewal of women's movements cannot be assumed in the face of this hostile political, social, and funding environment. As one of our interviewees said:

> Feminists from my generation have been working in the gender sector for decades and have been through a lot of conflicts just to get the space to open up, but most of them have gone underground or in hiding now due to the hostility and backlash they face … the young feminists are negatively impacted because it's so difficult to find good mentors. (Skype interview, 19 July 2018)

It is this increasingly difficult funding landscape and closing space in which young feminist activists and organisations (especially those from the global South) working on the most pressing issues find themselves. According to findings from a 2013 AWID report (Arutyunova and Clark 2013) and a 2017 COFEM policy paper on funding for gender-based violence/VAWG work (COFEM 2017c), four major trends are shaping or reflective of the current funding landscape in development and humanitarian initiatives, which have significant impact on financing women's organising and VAWG work: recognition of 'women and girls' as a priority; emergence of new actors, primarily the private sector, in development financing; corporatisation on development agendas and financing; and underfunding of protection work, particularly in humanitarian emergencies.[7]

Many women's activists have reported that due to the backlash and sensitive issues on which they focus, donors are withdrawing funding to protect their own aspects of work and avoid negative association and state scrutiny (FRIDA and AWID 2016). This is of great concern because women's organising has historically been important in delivering positive changes to the ending violence against women (EVAW) work across the globe. A 2012 report on the global comparative analysis of policies on violence against women and women's mobilisation in 70 countries from 1975 to 2000 found that strong autonomous feminist movements in civil society are a critical factor (more important than women's representation inside the legislature or political parties or other economic factors) for influencing progressive policy change, especially those concerning violence against women (Htun and Weldon 2012).[8]

It is crucial that we understand how resources are distributed as 'the control and distribution of resources is inherently political' (Arutyunova and Clark 2013, 31). Priorities and agendas of donors, the extent to which and what organisations or movements are marginalised, speak greatly about whom the current structure is benefiting and who is oppressed. The growing influence of private actors, corporatisation on development agendas, and 'marketization of NGO activism' could lead to the shrinking influence and space for civil society actors (Hayes *et al.* 2017, 9). This is especially true when NGOs are engulfed in corruption or sexual misconduct scandals, further discrediting the effectiveness of the NGO sector (Dearden 2018).

Ways forward and conclusion

In this chapter, we have set out to highlight some key challenges that we are trying to address through our work at COFEM: the rise of gender-neutral language in humanitarian and development practice; misinterpretation of intersectionality; increased focus on engaging men and boys with limited meaningful accountability to women and girls; shrinking space for feminist activism; and limited funding for the women and girls agenda.

We emphasise that the content and analysis presented in this chapter are informed by our unique backgrounds, locations, and positions within COFEM and beyond. We are acutely aware of our privilege as young feminists working for an emerging feminist collective that is not formally registered or incorporated within an institution. We have access to a digital safe space and a community of feminist activists, practitioners, and scholars who empower us with tools, skills, and knowledge to navigate spaces that are hostile to feminist approaches to VAWG work. We recognise that many young feminists might not have access to such feminist sanctuaries, and that they are often working in challenging environments. We want to reiterate that the issues highlighted in this chapter are specific to our experiences working in research, advocacy, and strategy positions within the wider COFEM community and do not capture the breadth and depth of the diverse lived realities, dangers, and risks faced by young feminists who organise in different ways in different contexts.

We believe that reasserting a feminist lens in VAWG work is necessary to transform patriarchal structures and to reconfigure the existing power base. We propose the following ways forward to advance young feminist activism in VAWG work and retain a feminist space that is political, while working in partnerships with other movements and actors:

- Confidently claim the politically transformative language of gender and intersectionality, and ground VAWG theory and practice in feminist scholarship.
- Engage in continuous reflection and be critically aware of our own power and privilege as an activist, practitioner, researcher, donor, and policy-maker *vis-à-vis* women and girls in the communities where we work.
- Actively take steps to amplify the voice, agency, and leadership of all women and girls, and promote their meaningful participation in decision-making within community, organisational, and government spaces on issues affecting their safety, well-being, and rights.
- Document, critique, and unpack practices, approaches, and strategies that claim to promote 'meaningful participation of youth', 'young feminist activism', 'gender equality', 'feminist principles', and 'intersectional analysis'.
- Recognise, acknowledge, draw attention to, and cite the contributions and work of feminist networks, women's movements, and women's rights activists, especially those who are often erased from mainstream discourse and efforts to end VAWG.
- Advocate for transformational social change around gender as a strategy to end VAWG, and reflect this in VAWG initiatives, programmes, and research.
- Promote female-centric and female-led framing of the issue, discourse, strategies, and resources on VAWG.
- Call on donors to invest in programmes that have strong accountability measures and ensure funding frameworks prioritise initiatives that are explicit in how they intend to be accountable to women and girls.
- Ensure any male engagement work supported has practical, measurable accountability mechanisms to local women's movements/organisations.
- Advocate for synchronising work with other groups, and do not subsume women and men's experiences and needs under a single umbrella.

- Be intentional in strengthening the ecosystem of resources available to end VAWG – this means engaging proactively with the donor community and promoting the work of women's rights, feminists organisations, groups, and networks that have a proven and significant potential in ending VAWG.
- Work in partnership with other movements and actors, situate the struggle to end VAWG within wider social movements to end racial injustice and all forms of discrimination.
- Accept and recognise the diversity of women and girls without eclipsing the needs of any specific group – all women and girls deserve to live a life free of violence.
- When working in hostile and patriarchal structures, seek out feminist allies and feminist safe spaces – self-care is important.

Our radical activism is instrumental in achieving a world where no one is left behind. Therefore, despite the resistance we face and the challenges that lie ahead, we must always remember that reasserting a feminist lens in VAWG work is fundamental and non-negotiable. All women and girls around the world deserve a life free of violence; and a feminist political project is what will get us there.

Notes

1. We wrote this chapter in our personal capacity. The views expressed are our own and do not necessarily represent the views of COFEM.
2. For more information on COFEM, see www.cofemsocialchange.org.
3. Unfortunately, we cannot name the institution because there are feminists still working in the institution who are at risk of exposure. Paradoxically, this institution is specifically mandated to address gender issues within the international aid system.
4. For more information on the UN/EU Spotlight Initiative, see www.un.org/en/spotlight-initiative/index.shtml (last checked 3 October 2018).
5. The Combahee River Collective, a Boston-based organisation active from 1974 to 1980, was a collective of Black feminists, including lesbians. Their statement, widely known as the Combahee River Collective statement, laid out key tenets of intersectionality and examined the interlocking systems of oppressions experienced by Black women. To read the Combahee River Collective statement, see https://americanstudies.yale.edu/sites/default/files/files/Keyword%20Coalition_Readings.pdf (last checked 3 October 2018).
6. Professor Kimberlé Crenshaw's seminal work in 1989 introduced the metaphor of intersectionality (in a legal academic context in the USA) to theorise what had been the practice, discourse, and scholarship of Black feminists and other women of colour for centuries. In this section, we are referring specifically to the Black feminist movement in the USA that grew out of the Black Liberation Movement and emphasised that the struggle for women's rights cannot be delinked from the struggle for civil and

human rights. We use the term 'women of colour' to articulate a political definition of solidarity for all women experiencing multiple layers of discrimination and marginalisation based on race and ethnicity and other shared global experiences textured by colonialism, displacement, stolen legacy, loss of autonomy, and racism.

7. For further analysis on funding trends, see Arutyunova and Clark (2013) and COFEM (2017d).
8. Interviewee preferred to remain anonymous.

Notes on contributors

Divya Chandran is a feminist activist, researcher, and independent consultant specialising in protection against sexual exploitation and abuse (PSEA), gender-based violence/VAWG work, migrant workers' rights, and gender mainstreaming.

Rita Lo is a project consultant for the Coalition of Feminists for Social Change (COFEM), with a particular interest in protection and education in emergencies.

Christine Homan is a consultant for the Coalition of Feminists for Social Change (COFEM).

References

Alemu, Beza Seyoum (2015) 'Working with men and boys to end violence against women and girls', United States Agency for International Development

Arutyunova, Angelika and Cindy Clark (2013) *Watering the Leaves and Starving the Roots: The Status of Financing for Women's Rights Organizing and Gender Equality*, Toronto: AWID, https://www.awid.org/publications/watering-leaves-starving-roots (last checked 3 October 2018)

Baden, Sally and Anne Marie Goetz (1997) 'Who needs [sex] when you can have [gender]? Conflicting discourses on gender at Beijing', *Feminist Review* 56(1): 3–25

Bishop, Kate (2017) *Standing Firm: Women- and Trans-led Organizations Respond to Closing Space for Civil Society*, Amsterdam: Mama Cash and Urgent Action Fund with Levi Strauss Foundation, https://www.mamacash.org/media/publications/mc_closing_space_report_def.pdf (last checked 3 October 2018)

Carastathis, Anna (2014) 'The concept of intersectionality in feminist theory', *Philosophy Compass* 9(5): 304–14

Charlesworth, Hilary and Christine Chinkin (1994) 'Violence against women: a global issue', in Julie Stubbs (ed.) *Women, Male Violence and the Law*, Sydney, Australia: Institute of Criminology, 13–33

Crenshaw, Kimberlé (1989) 'Demarginalizing the Intersection of race and sex: a black feminist critique of antidiscrimination doctrine, feminist theory and antiracist politics', *University of Chicago Legal Forum* 8(1): 139–67

Crenshaw, Kimberlé (2016) 'Kimberlé Crenshaw: the urgency of intersection-ality' [Video file], https://en.tiny.ted.com/talks/kimberle_crenshaw_the_urgency_of_intersectionality (last checked 4 October)

COFEM (2016) *Patriarchy, Power and Keeping Women and Girls Centered in Addressing VAWG in Humanitarian and Development Settings A Critical Conversation Between Feminist Academics, Activists, and Practitioners*, Coalition of Feminists for Social Change, http://raisingvoices.org/wp-content/uploads/2013/03/COFEM-Final-Report-March-2016-Convening-181028.pdf (last checked 4 October)

COFEM (2017a) 'How a lack of accountability undermines work to address vio-lence against women and girls', *Feminist Perspectives on Addressing Violence Against Women and Girls Series, Paper No. 1*, Coalition of Feminists for Social Change

COFEM (2017b) 'Finding the balance between scientific and social change goals, approaches and methods', *Feminist Perspectives on Addressing Violence Against Women and Girls Series, Paper No. 3*, Coalition of Feminists for Social Change

COFEM (2017c) 'Funding: whose priorities?', *Feminist Perspectives on Addressing Violence Against Women and Girls Series, Paper No. 4*, Coalition of Feminists for Social Change

COFEM (2017d) 'Eclipsed: when a broad protection agenda obscures the needs of women and girls', *Feminist Perspectives on Addressing Violence Against Women and Girls Series, Paper No. 5*, Coalition of Feminists for Social Change

Dearden, Lizzie (2018) 'Oxfam prostitution scandal: charities report over 1,000 sexual abuse incidents every year, says regulator', *The Independent*, 12 February, https://www.independent.co.uk/news/uk/home-news/oxfam-crisis-latest-sexual-abuse-vulnerable-people-ngos-report-charity-commission-haiti-prostitutes-a8206431.html (last checked 12 September 2018)

Ellsberg, Mary, Diana J. Arango, Matthew Morton, Floriza Gennari, Sveinung Kiplesund, Manuel Contreras and Charlotte Watts (2015) 'Prevention of violence against women and girls: what does the evidence say?', *The Lancet* 385(9977): 1555–66

Enarsson, Jenny (2015) 'Re-politicising intersectionality: how an intersec-tional perspective can help INGOs be better allies to women's rights move-ments', Boston, MA: Oxfam America, https://policy-practice.oxfam.org.uk/publications/re-politicising-intersectionality-how-an-intersectional-perspective-can-help-in-594583 (last checked 4 October 2018)

Enloe, Cynthia (2017) *The Big Push: Exposing and Challenging the Persistence of Patriarchy*, Oakland, CA: University of California Press

FRIDA | The Young Feminist Fund and the Association for Women's Rights in Development (AWID) (2016) *Brave, Creative and Resilient: The State of Young Feminist Organizing*, https://www.awid.org/sites/default/files/atoms/files/frida-awid_field-report_final_web_issuu.pdf (last checked 12 September 2018)

Gender & Development Network (GADN) (2017) 'Intersectionality: Reflections from the Gender & Development Network', Gender and Development Network, http://gadnetwork.org/gadn-resources/2017/11/20/

intersectionality-reflections-from-the-gender-development-network   (last checked 4 October 2018)

Goetz, Anne Marie and Rachel Dore-Weeks (2018) 'What about the men? Frankly, it depends why you're asking', *The Guardian*, 8 March, https://www.theguardian.com/global-development/2018/mar/08/what-about-the-men-depends-why-youre-asking (last checked 12 September 2018)

Hayes, Ben, Frank Barat, Isabelle Geuskens, Nick Buxton, Fiona Dove, Francesco Martone, Hannah Twomey and Semanur Karaman (2017) 'On "shrinking space": a framing paper', Amsterdam: Transnational Institute, https://www.tni.org/files/publication-downloads/on_shrinking_space_2.pdf (last checked 12 September 2018)

Htun, Mala and S. Laurel Weldon (2012) 'The civic origins of progressive policy change: combating violence against women in global perspective, 1975–2005', *American Political Science Review* 106 (3): 548–69

Jahan, Rounaq (1995) *The Elusive Agenda: Mainstreaming Women in Development*, London: Zed Books

Jewkes, Rachel, Michael Flood and James Lang (2014) 'From work with men and boys to changes of social norms and reduction of inequities in gender relations: a conceptual shift in prevention of violence against women and girls', *The Lancet* 385(9977): 1580–89

Kelly, Liz (1988) *Surviving Sexual Violence*, Cambridge, UK: Polity Press

Meer, Shamim (2012) 'Struggles for gender equality: reflections on the place of men and men's organisations', Johannesburg: Open Society Initiative for Southern Africa

Michau, Lori, Jessica Horn, Amy Bank, Mallika Dutt and Cathy Zimmerman (2015) 'Prevention of violence against women and girls: lessons from practice', *The Lancet* 385(9978): 1672–84

Mohanty, Chandra (1991) 'Under Western Eyes: Feminist Scholarship and Colonial Discourses', in Chandra Talpade Mohanty, Anne Russo and Lourdes M. Torres (eds.) *Third World Women and the Politics of Feminism*, Bloomington, IN: Indiana University Press, 51–80

Moser, Caroline, (1989) 'Gender planning in the third world: meeting practical and strategic gender needs', *World Development* 17(11): 1799–825

Mukhopadhyay, Maitrayee (2004) 'Mainstreaming gender or "streaming" gender away: feminists marooned in the development business', *IDS Bulletin* 35(4): 95–103

Mwau, Adelina, Janet Seed, and Suzanne Williams (1994) *The Oxfam Gender Training Manual*, Oxford: Oxfam

Namy, Sophie, Catherine Carlsonb, Kathleen O'Harac, Janet Nakutia, Paul Bukulukid, Julius Lwanyaagae, Sylvia Namakulae, Barbrah Nanyunjaa, Milton L. Wainbergc, Dipak Nakera, and Lori Michau (2017) 'Towards a feminist understanding of intersecting violence against women and children in the family', *Social Science & Medicine* 184: 40–48

OECD (2018) *States of Fragility 2018*, Paris: OECD Publishing, https://doi.org/10.1787/9789264302075-en (last checked 12 September 2018)

Oosterhoff, Pauline, and Caroline Sweetman (2018), 'Introduction: Sexualities', *Gender & Development* 26(1): 1–14, https://policy-practice.oxfam.org.uk/publications/introduction-sexualities-620445 (last checked 3 October 2018)

Pease, Bob (2017) *Men as Allies in Preventing Men's Violence Against Women: Principles and Practices for Promoting Accountability*, Sydney: White Ribbon Australia

Pillay, Anu (2015) 'Gender Praxis in Emergencies: 20 Years after Beijing', United Nations Research Institute for Social Development (UNRISD), 2 April, http://www.unrisd.org/beijing+20-pillay (last checked 4 October 2018)

Pino, Angelica (2017) 'Engaging men and boys for gender equality ... what do women have to do with it?', *GREAT Insights Magazine* 6(2): 26–29

Sen, Gita, and Caren Grown (1989) *Development Crises and Alternative Visions: Third World Women's Perspectives*, New York: DAWN/Monthly Review Press

Tinker, Irene (1990) *Persistent Inequalities: Women and World Development*, New York: Oxford University Press

Ukhova, Daria (2015) 'Gender inequality and inter-household economic inequality in emerging economies: exploring the relationship', *Gender & Development* 23(2): 241–59, https://policy-practice.oxfam.org.uk/publications/gender-inequality-and-inter-household-economic-inequality-in-emerging-economies-561198 (last checked 3 October 2018)

United Nations (1993) *Declaration on the Elimination of Violence against Women*, A/RES/48/104, 20 December, http://www.un.org/documents/ga/res/48/a48r104.htm (last checked 12 September 2018)

UN (2016) 'The Sustainable Development Goals Report 2016', https://unstats.un.org/sdgs/report/2016/leaving-no-one-behind (last checked 4 October 2018)

UN Human Rights Council (2014) *Report of the special rapporteur on violence against women, its causes and consequences*, 28 May, A/HRC/26/38, https://documents-dds-ny.un.org/doc/UNDOC/GEN/G14/037/00/PDF/G1403700.pdf?OpenElement (last checked 12 September 2018)

Ward, Jeanne (2016) 'It's not about the gender binary, it's about the gender hierarchy: a reply to "letting go of the gender binary"', *International Review of the Red Cross* 98(901): 275–98

CHAPTER 8

Reclaiming culture, resisting co-optation: young feminists confronting the rising right

*Isabel Marler, Daniela Marin Platero
and Felogene Anumo*

Abstract

This chapter presents two case studies of young feminist resistance to the rising phenomena of fascisms and fundamentalisms. The first shows young feminists organising in Kenya, and focuses on the battle to repeal a colonial Penal Code criminalising homosexuality. The second, from Brazil, highlights how young Afro-Brazilian feminists are resisting attacks against their religions in a context of racism, rising evangelical fundamentalism, and a political shift to the right. The authors draw on the experience, analysis, and perspectives gained as three young feminists who work at the Association for Women's Rights in Development (AWID), an international feminist organisation which, among other areas, puts emphasis on young feminist activism and feminist responses to religious fundamentalisms and fascisms.

Keywords: Fascism; fundamentalism; colonialism; young feminism; Brazil; Kenya

Introduction

The current global political moment represents a threat to young women, girls, and gender non-conforming people. Rising fascist and fundamentalist movements and anti-rights sentiment are not the preserve of any one part of the world, but are interconnected phenomena, part of a global trend. From Brazil (Wood 2018) to India (Menon 2016; Norton and Wilson 2018), Turkey (Taspinar 2018), Hungary (Osborne 2018), and the United States (Egan 2018; Tumulty 2017), to name just some contexts, we have seen governments become home to authoritarian, anti-rights figures and agendas, which seek to stifle dissent, play to the most reactionary forces within society, and roll back existing rights protections taken for granted by previous generations (Mishra 2017). These movements may explicitly identify as fascist and/or fundamentalist movements, or may seek to define and present themselves in other lights.[1] While they frequently represent themselves as a break from 'the establishment', they are often in fact tied to big business and corporate power.

In this chapter, we draw on our experience, analysis, and perspectives gained as three young feminists who work at the Association for Women's Rights in Development (AWID), who are also involved in struggles in our own contexts and transnationally.[2] Across the world, the right is mobilising young people (including young women) like never before, recruiting them through spaces like 'churches, college campuses, and local-level initiatives' (Shameem 2017, 101). Yet these movements have a huge and damaging impact on women and girls. They perpetuate patriarchal power dynamics, appropriating the language of women's rights and social justice, while enforcing gender norms and policing the gender binary,[3] and threatening young feminist organising (FRIDA and AWID 2016).

It is a logical move for AWID to focus on the response of young feminists to the rise of the right. Over the last decade, one of our priority areas of focus has been feminist analysis of and resistance to religious fundamentalisms. From 2010 to 2017, we also ran the Young Feminist Activism (YFA) programme, with the purpose of building and strengthening young feminist voices within broader feminist movements, and counteracting the lack of spaces for young feminists to organise and strategise collectively. In 2016, we published our report, *Brave, Creative, Resilient: The Global State of Young Feminist Organizing* with FRIDA (The Young Feminist Fund) (FRIDA and AWID 2016). The enormity of the threat of the far-right was clear in this study, which drew on the perspectives and experiences of 694 young feminist respondents from 118 different countries. Just over half (54 per cent) said they felt unsafe or threatened because of the work they were doing, either some of the time or all of the time (*ibid.*, 50).

At the start of 2018, AWID embarked upon its new Strategic Plan for the period 2018–2022 under the title *Co-creating Feminist Realities*. Collectively, we decided this was the moment to broaden and deepen our approach to regressive identity-based movements to encompass fundamentalisms *and* fascisms as interconnected phenomena posing a global threat to universal rights and social justice. Furthermore, with the main reasons for the YFA programme fulfilled, we have also shifted to integrating young feminist movements as a priority constituency across all of AWID's initiatives.[4]

In this chapter, we explore young intersectional[5] feminist responses to the threat presented to women by the rising right. In *Brave, Creative, Resilient* (FRIDA and AWID 2016), young feminist organisers from a range of countries in both the global South and North were surveyed on the forces they perceived as a threat to their organising. More than half reported regularly feeling unsafe or threatened because of the work they do, with about one in eight saying they feel this way all the time. The organisations surveyed felt challenged by backlash, threats to safety and security, and political instability, as well as shrinking democratic spaces. They perceived threats from a wide range of perpetrators, comprising both state and non-state actors, and religious fundamentalism was reported across all regions (*ibid.*, 5).

To explore these issues further, this chapter features two case studies in particular. The first, from Kenya, shows young feminists organising in Kenya, and focuses on the battle to repeal a colonial Penal Code criminalising homosexuality. The second, from Brazil, highlights how young Afro-Brazilian feminists are resisting attacks against their religions in a context of racism, rising evangelical fundamentalism, and a political shift to the right.

In addition to the research undertaken into young feminisms for *Brave, Creative, Resilient* over almost two years (2014–2016),[6] other sources drawn on here include information from interviews undertaken especially for this chapter, with four key informants during April and May 2018, as well as informal discussions and communications with many others in our work and activism.

Case study 1: Kenya

We open this case study with two vignettes. On the morning of 2 April 2015, a group of armed young men walked into Garissa University, in Northern Kenya, and proceeded to claim the lives of 147 students. This act of terror would shatter the lives of family and friends and shake the nation at its core, as can be seen from reports in the news media (Al Jazeera 2015). The strength of feeling about the attack was related to the fact that it had happened at an institution of higher learning, which is supposed to foster values such as diversity, co-existence, and unity. This attack was, in fact, part of a broader trend of attacks in learning institutions in Kenya, pointing to the fact that they serve both as an easy target and fertile ground for the radicalisation of young people (Njeri Thuo n.d.).

Our second vignette comes from February 2016, when Art Attack, a collective of Nairobi-based artists, launched a music video titled *Same Love*,[7] whose lyrics and content focused on same-sex rights. Before the song even reached the airwaves, the Kenya Film Classification Board (KFCB) banned the video on the basis of moral standing and supported this claim by arguing that homosexuality is illegal in Kenya (Murumba 2016). Not only did the KFCB ban the video in Kenya, but it followed up with an attempt to do the same on YouTube. While YouTube did not completely ban the video at the behest of KFCB, it did flag the video as being 'potentially inappropriate'.[8]

The context

Kenya, like most of Africa, is currently grappling with many permutations of fundamentalisms, under broad categories of religious, traditionalist, and ethnic fundamentalisms. Each of these forms of fundamentalism has its roots in various types of patriarchy – the first being pre-colonial patriarchy; indigenous patriarchy, the second patriarchy that thrives in religions, and the third type of patriarchy was brought by the colonisers (Imam 2006).

In Kenya, a major threat to reproductive rights – and in particular to abortion rights – comes from religious groups, key among them being the Catholic Church, the Anglican Church of Kenya, the Presbyterian Church of East Africa, the Deliverance Church of Kenya, the Supreme Council of Kenya Muslims, and a host of contemporary Evangelical Christianities, often linked to and/ or driven by right-wing groups from the United States (Bhavnani *et al.* 2003, 112–13). These religious groups often work with youth-led organisations such as World Youth Alliance,[9] Human Life International,[10] and Africa Youth Life Foundation,[11] which have year-round youth-focused programmes.

Religious fundamentalist actors have fortified and institutionalised their opposition to progressive policies on abortion by stalling their implementation. For example, the circumstances leading to the withdrawal of *The Standard and Guidelines for Reduction of Morbidity and Mortality from Unsafe Abortion in Kenya* (Ministry of Medical Services 2012) – a document providing guidance to medical professionals on provision of abortion services in line with the 2010 Constitution of Kenya – are linked to powerful religious groups with connections to political leaders (Bhavnani *et al.* 2003, 112–13). Following these events, in February 2014, the Director of Medical Services in the Ministry of Health issued a memo to all health-care providers stating that 'abortion on demand is illegal' and further declaring it illegal for health workers to participate in trainings focusing on comprehensive abortion care (KNCHR 2016, 74).

The religious right also opposes the sexual – and wider – rights of the LGBTQI+ community in Kenya (Finerty 2012). Currently, a group of feminist organisations is in court in Kenya to interrupt the use of archaic and colonial laws to empower and fuel fundamentalisms in the country (Gikandi and Brown 2018). Attitudes, norms, and laws around same-sex relations in Kenya are deeply rooted in colonial history and imperialism. In 1930, the British introduced the Colonial Office Model Code which replaced the Indian Penal Code. This Colonial Office Model Code was based on the Queensland Code of 1899 which still exists in Kenya today and is known as the Penal Code (Finerty 2012, 437).

The Kenya Penal Code today reflects this history, and is the main legislation criminalising homosexuality in Kenya through its Sections 162 and 165. Sections 162 (a) and (c) of the Kenya Penal Code say that any person who has 'carnal knowledge against the order of nature'[12] or permits a person to have 'carnal knowledge against the order of nature' against them has committed a crime (*ibid.*). A person found guilty of this crime receives a sentence of up to 14 years in prison. Furthermore, Section 165 of the Penal Code states that any person who commits an act of 'gross indecency with another male person' has committed a crime (*ibid.*). 'Gross indecency' is defined as any sexual activity between two men that does not involve penetration, whether committed in public or in private (GALCK 2016).

The rights of LGBTQI+ people are also violated by homophobia in society shaped by conservative and fundamentalist versions of global religions including Christianity, and a rejection of Western domination of cultural space which for some includes the notion that homosexuality itself is Western, and 'unAfrican'. In an interview with Reuters, the current deputy president spokesperson categorically stated the government position on the issue: 'The government believes that homosexual relations are unnatural and unAfrican' (Reuters 2015).

The rise of violent extremism in Kenya from groups such as Al-Shabaab[13] is also catalysing the Kenyan government to mount a militarised response. The militarised response by the government has led to Kenya registering the highest numbers of extrajudicial killings in Africa (Amnesty International 2017). Critics of this militarised response have stated that this response has justified the profiling and extrajudicial killing of 'young, poor, black, Somali, Muslim, "Others"' in order to control and protect property (Blessol 2017, 6). According to a report, 'Who is Next?' from the Mathare Social Justice Center (MSJC 2017, 13), the average age of those executed is 20 years and the youngest victim was 13 years of age.

Resisting fundamentalisms, growing resistance: young feminist responses in Kenya

In this section, we examine some of the strategies that Kenya's young feminist community have used to challenge this grim situation.

In 2016, members of the LGBTQI+ community in Kenya, the National Gay and Lesbian Human Rights Commission (NGLHRC), the Gay and Lesbian Coalition of Kenya (GALCK), and the Nyanza, Rift Valley and Western Kenya Network (NYARWEK) together with their partners filed Constitutional Petitions 150 of 2016 and 234 of 2016 at the Kenyan High Court (KELIN 2018). This landmark case provides an opportunity to reflect on the history and politics of young feminist organising in Kenya, the challenges posed by key opposition actors and the power of young feminist resistance.

Young feminists in Kenya are opposing challenges to reproductive rights in Kenya at a policy level, but also at a practical level of provision of services for young women in need of support. Unsafe abortions in Kenya account for about one-third of maternal deaths (APHRC *et al.* 2013, 27). Young women, girls, and gender non-conforming youth in particular face great obstacles in accessing safe abortion care, because of misinformation and lack of resources. Ensuring access to sexual and reproductive health information and services could help millions of young women avoid unintended pregnancies and ensure they have the right to safe options. An example is 'Aunty Jane',[14] a hotline launched by Kenyan activists to provide much-needed, safe, and reliable sexual and reproductive health information, including how women can safely procure abortions. The hotline is monitored by young feminists who undergo training on potential safety and security risks, as highlighted by Jedidah Maina, Executive Director of TiCAH (Trust for Indigenous Culture and Health), which hosts the hotline.

Another key example of activism around LGBTQI+ rights comes from Warembo Ni Yes, a movement of young and diverse women mounting and supporting challenges to the homophobic laws in the current Constitution of Kenya. Warembo Ni Yes, loosely translated from Swahili, means 'Young ladies say yes'. Warembo Ni Yes has been revolutionary in Kenyan feminist organising, as it was one of the first groups with representation from different economic backgrounds, ethnicities, religious beliefs, sexual orientations, gender identities, races, and abilities (Malek 2010).

Debates fuelled by religious actors on access to safe and legal abortion and same-sex marriages dominated the constitutional reform process. In August 2010, Kenyans adopted the Constitution of Kenya, which guarantees the rights and freedoms for all citizens. Specifically, the Constitution's Bill of Rights in Chapter Four addresses the rights of Kenyan citizens to 'privacy, dignity, health, equality and non-discrimination and freedom and security of the person' (Kenya Law n.d.).

It is with this constitutional mandate that members of the LGBTQ community came together to challenge the constitutionality of Sections 162 (a) and (c) and 165 of the Penal Code of Kenya. In a landmark case, they filed Constitutional Petitions 150 of 2016 and 234 of 2016 at the Kenyan High Court. The petitions ask the court to declare these sections of the Penal Code unconstitutional and in gross violation of rights of persons as guaranteed by the supreme law of the land. Moreover, the petitions argue these sections on the Penal Code continue to enable an environment that validates stigmatisation, discrimination, and violence towards persons who do not conform to societal expectations on gender identity, gender expression, or sexual orientation (Ghai and Ghai 2018).

This ongoing court case builds on legal precedents against sexuality and gender identity discrimination that have been set in Kenya. The first of these legal precedents was a High Court decision overriding the NGOs Coordination Board decision refusing to register the National Gay and Lesbian Human Rights Commission under Coordination Board Act in March 2013. The stated and filed reason was that the name of the organisation was 'unacceptable', on the basis of Kenya's Penal Code which 'criminalizes gay and lesbian acts' (NGLHRC 2017, 2).

Second were the two landmark rulings where the courts ordered the Kenya national education authorities to amend a transgender person's name on a school certificate, and to register the Transgender Education and Advocacy lobby group (Agoya 2014). Furthermore, in November 2017, the High Court awarded approximately $300,000 to five transgender persons – Audrey Mbugua Ithibu, Maurine Muya, Alesandra Awino Ogeto, Maria Marius Mbugua, and Dalziel Leone Wafula – for denying them a name change (Anami 2017). These steps take Kenya away from the shadow of colonial oppression and ensure that the rights of sexual minorities are upheld, in progress that challenges the influence of right-wing politicians and religious groups.

Young feminists in Kenya are using new and innovative means of movement-building and organising, including ways of enhancing resilience through arts and creative expression. The NEST Collective,[15] a group of young artivists (artists and activists) uses literature, film, visual arts, music, and fashion to amplify the realities of the LGBTQ community in Kenya and advance dialogue among Kenyans. For example, their film, *Stories of Our Lives*, is based on the lives and stories of Kenyans, and aims to paint a true picture of the situation of the LGBTQ community. It was banned from circulation in Kenya by the KFCB and the film producer, George Gachara, was arrested and eventually released on bail for filming it without a licence (NEST Collective 2014). While the film is yet to be screened in Kenya, it has been shown in over 80 countries, and it has been nominated for and won several awards.

Even as fundamentalist actors allied with the state make every attempt to curtail legitimate artistic expression, Kenya's creative feminist resistance continues undeterred. In fact, most recently, the KFCB banned the Cannes-nominated lesbian-themed film *Rafiki* (Mbenywe 2018). The CEO, Ezekiel Mutua, said, 'Any attempt to normalize homosexuality in Kenya flies in the face of the law and the constitution and must be resisted'. He further posits that the film is 'too hopeful'. Dr Wanuri Kahiu, the film producer, responded: 'My philosophy is to make hopeful, joyful films about Africa' (Moore 2018).

Young feminist groups have been able to use ICTs as a political tool to imagine and create new, stronger, and more powerful types of political discourses that increase voice and citizen mobilisation. Online offers increased access to wider and more diverse knowledge, new ways of networking, and increased speeds of communication. In Kenya, the internet is full of niche communities, all with slightly different views and opinions on gender, feminism, and representation. And with this freedom comes the freedom to oppose (Gateru 2017). This was particularly evident following the ban of the video *Same Love*. Not only was there robust public debate and thus sensitisation on the laws of Kenya, but what followed was mass online distribution of the film (Langat 2016).

Another example of such powerful mobilisation was the campaign #MyDressMyChoice (Thatiah 2017). This was the case in 2014, when a video of a woman being stripped by *matatu* (public transport) touts went viral. Almost instantaneously, young feminists mobilised and Kenyans took to the streets to protest against sexual harassment and violent attacks on women for being 'inappropriately dressed' (Njagi 2015). Offline action was reinforced by online efforts through the hashtag #MyDressMyChoice. Soon the hashtag generated global outcry and backlash in equal measure. A group of men came up with a hashtag #NudityIsNotMyChoice. The culprits of the stripping act were prosecuted in court and sentenced to death (Okumu 2017) and an amendment introduced to the Security law that recommends a jail term of up to 20 years for those found guilty of privacy invasion and forcible stripping (Kenya Gazette Supplement 2014, 19).

Young feminist organisers in Kenya continue to occupy a central role in political performance in the public and political realm. For example, Yvonne Oduor from the Gay and Lesbian Coalition of Kenya was one of the organisers of the Kenyan Chapter of the Women's March in January 2017. The March

faced some criticism in that Kenyan feminists were having a hard time resonating with it as it felt quite 'US-centric'. Yvonne had this to say in response:

> I marched because I am a feminist and I believe our struggles as a people
> are connected. I marched in solidarity with women of the world, against
> patriarchy and discrimination of any kind that people in positions of
> power use to violate my body and those of people like me. If asked, I
> would do it again. In Kenya, the public space to resist and protest for
> issues like these, that are very close to my heart, are very few and far
> between. When I get the chance to come out in defiance, against the
> status quo and against everything that is wrong with the world, waving
> my rainbow flag, I will take it without fear. (Interview, 7 May 2018)

Case study 2: Brazil

A vignette to start our Brazilian case study:

> Carmen Flores, a Candomblé priestess, was leaving her house when seven
> armed men confronted her. They demanded that she destroy the sacred
> contents of her house, a spiritual home for more than 125 followers of
> Candomblé. Fearing for her life, Flores followed their directions while
> they yelled expletives at her: 'Burn everything! Break everything! The
> blood of Jesus has power!'. She destroyed porcelain bowls that she and
> her followers used during special ceremonies. She knocked over images
> of the orishas that guided her and her followers. She knocked over clay
> jugs used to store water for special ceremonies. Within twenty minutes,
> Flores had destroyed the sacred objects that had given her strength, love
> and security for the last 35 years. (Freelon 2017)

The context

Race, gender, and religion are all factors in determining who is targeted for violence in Brazil. There was a significant surge in the number of religious attacks
recorded across Brazil in 2017, and black women who are part of Afro-Brazilian
religions are particularly targeted. During September 2017, more than 30 *terreiros* were destroyed and reports of religious discrimination have increased
119 per cent since 2015 (Muggah 2017). Between January 2016 and May 2017,
1,828 cases of racial injustice were recorded in the state of Rio de Janeiro; black
women were the targets in 60 per cent of those cases (Strobl 2017). Data from the
Comissão de Combate à Intolerância Religiosa do Rio de Janeiro (CCIR; Commission
for the Fight against Religious Intolerance of Rio de Janeiro) revealed that over
70 per cent of the registered offences, abuses, and violent acts related to religion
that were reported in the state of Rio de Janeiro between 2012 and 2015 were
against believers of Afro-Brazilian religions (CCIR *et al.* 2015, 3).

The stigmatisation of Afro-Brazilian religions is a legacy of the condition
of enslavement to which its believers were submitted and the Christian

colonial history of the country. Gang members in favelas across Río have justified attacks on Candomblé temples and leaders with the rhetoric of holy war reflecting a binary spiritual view wherein 'good' Christians must wage holy war against 'evil' practitioners of Candomblé and Umbanda[16] (Muggah 2017). This narrative is characteristic of the fundamentalisms upheld by many right-wing Christian preachers and churches like the Universal Church of the Kingdom of God (IURD).

Until 1934, Afro-Brazilian cults were expressly banned and associated with illegal magic, and as such defined out of the concept of 'real' religion (Hernández 2012, 65). Some 80 years later, in 2014, a federal judge ruled that Candomblé and Umbanda were not religions, suggesting that their events lacked the necessary traits of a religion, defining these traits as a basic text such as the Quran or the Bible, a hierarchical structure, and a God to be worshipped (Greene 2014). Clearly, the assessment made by the judge was based on the characteristics of Judeo-Christian religions, just as the assessment prior to 1934 was. Although this ruling was repealed shortly after it became public, it demonstrates the ways in which Afro-Brazilian religions continue to be discriminated against structurally.

The religious right has strength in national politics. The Christian Evangelical bloc in Congress includes representatives from every party and is one of the biggest in the national parliament, holding 198 members of the 513-seat lower house. Most of the bloc's members come from the three main Pentecostal sects – the IURD, the Assemblies of God, and Four-square Gospel. The majority are pastors or bishops of their respective denominations (Encarnación 2017). The more conservative members of the bloc regularly lobby against abortion and homosexuality (Schipani and Leahy 2017), and on behalf of the 'traditional family' (Cunha 2017).

The power and alliances that the bloc holds became evident during the impeachment process of former Brazilian president Dilma Rousseff. The impeachment was instigated by Eduardo Cunha, an Evangelical former Lower House speaker. During the impeachment process, the bloc joined up with other conservative blocs, namely the 'law and order' lobby and the agricultural bloc that have lobbied for liberalisation of Brazil gun laws and the concession of indigenous territory to industry, accordingly (Douglas 2015). This triad is widely known as the 'bullet, beef, and Bible' caucus, and collectively accounts for about 60 per cent of the seats in the Chamber of Deputies (Encarnación 2017). The undeniable growing influence of the Brazilian right and its collusion with Christian fundamentalisms, corporate power, and militarism is not coincidental. These oppressive systems reinforce each other.

The resistance of young Afro-Brazilian feminists in Brazil

In Brazil, young feminists are increasingly using public space to oppose the continued intentional erasure of the legacy – and present-day practice – of Afro-Brazilian religions. Using their bodies, they are shaping narratives and imaginaries about their identities as young, black women members of Afro-Brazilian religions. They are actively embodying resistance by taking up the symbolic *turbante* (turban), which has historically had negative associations with witchcraft. When worn by young black female members of Afro-Brazilian religions it 'acquires another significance, it becomes a political symbol of resistance and empowerment' (Fortes 2016). Carol Damiá, an Afro-Brazilian activist and entrepreneur, has pointed out:

> The turbante emerges to the black movement rescued from the aesthetics and culture of our ancestors, which symbolizes the cultural resistance of the descendants of Africans enslaved in Brazil, the turban plays a strong role in religions of African matrix, as a way to protect the ori [head]. (quoted in Delalibera 2015)

By using these strategies around traditional religious garb, and other objects with religious significance outside their places of worship, young women are resisting the demonisation of their religion and its beliefs and reclaiming their right to profess their faith safely. Many campaigns against religious intolerance like *Visto Branco pelo fim da intolerância religiosa* (I wear white for the end of religious intolerance)[17] have also used the symbolism and significance of the white garb associated with Candomblé and Umbanda to mobilise civil society.

Young feminists are also increasingly re-asserting the place that their religions hold in what is considered Brazilian culture via a second and complementary strategy of reclaiming the religious significance of street music and dances such as afoxé, samba, and capoeira. Afoxé is directly linked to Candomblé. The colours used for the clothes, the dance moves, and the chants are the same as those used in Brazilian *terreiros* (the meeting places for Afro-Brazilian religions). Commonly, afoxé – like samba and capoeira – are separated from their religious significance and history of criminalisation (Fraga 2013; Nkowane 2004; Pavão 2004).

The online world is a site of resistance widely used by young feminists to demystify, denounce, raise awareness, and demand guarantees for their right to profess their religion freely. The *turbante* has also been taken online as a symbol of resistance and empowerment via hashtag campaigns like #meu-turbanteminhaacoroa (#myturbanmycrown). Young feminists are making the discrimination, persecution, and violence that they experience because of their religion visible online. They are doing this by sharing their own experiences of violence and amplifying the voices of others using social media and other ICTs. Via these digital communication channels, young women are broadening the reach of their actions and building a sense of solidarity within and beyond their online work. In Brazil, as elsewhere, the internet has become a political space where young women are disseminating their discourses, critiques, problems, and priorities using their own voices.

Networks of young cyber activists like the *Rede da Ciberativistas Negras* (Network of Black Cyber Activists)[18] exemplify the solidarity and political campaigns that young women across Brazil are building online. Projects like the *Marcha do Empoderamento Crespo* (March of Crespo Empowerment) are the result of online organising led by young women (Machado 2015). Crespo means curled hair, and as such the march takes this symbol to reclaim the beauty and resistance of the black body and its aesthetics. The theme for the 2017 March was religious racism, and over 10,000 individuals were mobilised in the streets of Salvador (Malia 2017). The March stands as an example of the intersectional ways in which these young women are connecting their struggles and politicising different aspects of their identities.

Young feminists are building alliances with other youth and movements. Youth activism is building pace in Brazil. The opportunity to meet with other youth and recognise their shared struggle has been key in the building of alliances and agendas of action. Young feminists have been working, for example, with the *Encontro de Juventude de Terreiro da RMC*.[19] This activism began in 2013, with a conversation between two young people who recognised that there were several gatherings for Catholic and Evangelical youth, but that they did not know of any gatherings for youth like them (Moraes n.d.).

Three months later, in January 2014, 80 youths from three different states gathered to celebrate the *Encontro de Juventude de Terreiro da RMC (Região Metropolitana de Campinas)*: a three-day gathering at which they established the *Coletivo da Juventude de Terreiro da RMC* (Collective of Youth from the Terreiros). Since then, the collective has joined different local and federal movements, working with local and national bodies and other youth, to defend their collective religious, cultural, and civil rights, and the guarantees for these. The group has met five times at the time of writing this chapter.

In their activism in this space, youth (both women and men) from the *terreiros* are building their collective identity and voice both locally and nationally, in gatherings where they discuss public policies, building collective agendas, and co-ordinating advocacy efforts. André Moraes, one of the initial organisers, wrote an account that stated:

> This gathering reminded us that we are many, yet our problems are very similar. It was a moment to recognize ourselves and understand that we are not alone. (Moraes n.d.)

Young feminists are also working in and with multi-faith networks, such as the *Rede Ecumênica da Juventude* (REJU; Ecumenical Youth Network).[20] This network has a presence in 13 Brazilian states and focuses on advocacy efforts aimed at shaping public policies related to youth both at the federal and state level. The network works with other social movements such as the Movement of Landless Workers, Global March of Women and *Forma do Eixo* (Axis Shape). REJU has campaigns that focus on the criminalisation and extermination of Black youth, sexuality and feminist struggles, development and socio-environmental justice, and democratisation of communications. Their analysis and framework for actions are linked to the agendas of other movements, and as such are rooted in cross-movement work.

Artivism is another political tool used by young feminists to challenge the religious persecution and racism they experience, to defend and reclaim the professed secularism of the Brazilian state and to visibilise their resistance. In the lyrics of her song *'Falsa Abolição'* (False Abolition),[21] the rapper Preta Rara speaks about the historical 'whitening' of Brazil during colonialism, and the legacy of enslavement of her ancestors, and the demonisation of their beliefs, that emerged from a Christian, colonial system. She links present state and civil violence faced by Black youth to its historical and structural roots. Speaking of a false abolition, she denounces the present inequities of current Brazilian society.

A second example of artivism as a strategy comes from Ellen de Souza, who begins her song *'Notícias do Brasil'* (News from Brazil)[22] by stating that her singing is a response to the denial of her right to faith given the growing intolerance 'viralised, reproduced and institutionalised'. She narrates scenarios of religious intolerance, denounces the growing influence of the church over the state, and reminds listeners that Brazil is a lay (secular) state – 'Brazil has no official religion'. A third example is the work of spoken-word artist Anamari Souza, who uses her poetry to speak about the religious diversity in Brazil and the racism implicit in the religious intolerance characteristic of Brazil.[23]

The voices of young feminists are central in denouncing, naming, and challenging the racist religious bigotry that today permeates Brazil. They are challenging not only the current reality that faces them, but building upon and reclaiming the historical struggles of their ancestors to ensure their religions survived colonisation, criminalisation, and demonisation. Grounded in their identities, ancestry, and religions, their resistance reclaims the public space and the national imaginary of Brazilian society. Their voices of resistance are embedded in the physical and symbolic realm. Resistance is expressed through their bodies, in the streets, through artistic expressions, and online.

Conclusion

Right-wing political and religious actors, including self-avowed fascist and fundamentalist actors, are active across the world today. They are adopting ever-inventive strategies, cross-issue alliances, and discourses to mobilise support, recruit young people, and push regressive agendas.

Nevertheless, young feminists are at the forefront of transnational resistance to the right. Young feminists recognise that the current global shift to the right exists on the same continuum as colonial and imperial histories. As the two case studies featured here show, their activism builds on existing legacies of struggle. Grounded in multiple identities, young feminists are practising resistance that is intersectional and rooted in the specificities of their respective contexts.

In the face of the criminalisation and co-optation of their struggles, young feminists are steering clear of single-issue approaches. Rather, they are striving to build solidarity across movements, and strategically targeting loci of power within and beyond the state in order to influence laws and occupy public and cultural spaces (both online and offline).

This is not mainstream feminism. What young feminists bring to the table are fresh and hopeful alternatives to divisive and reactionary ideologies that might otherwise circulate undisputed. Their visions of a just world are reflected in their very organising, and affirm that there are other ways of being and relating to each other – that feminist realities are emerging right here and now.

Notes

1. Definitions of 'fascism' vary and are contested, but common ideological and organisational themes can be identified. Robert Paxton's (2004, 218) definition provides a good starting point. Paxton defines fascisms as: 'A form of political behaviour marked by obsessive preoccupation with community decline, humiliation or victimhood and by compensatory cults of unity, energy and purity, in which a mass-based party of committed nationalist militants, working in uneasy but effective collaboration with traditional elites, abandons democratic liberties and pursues with redemptive violence and without ethical or legal restraints goals of internal cleansing and external expansion'. John Weiss' (1967, xi) listing of fascist ideological traits is also helpful: 'organicist conceptions of community, philosophical idealism, idealization of "manly" (usually peasant or village) virtues, resentment of mass democracy, elitist conceptions of political and social leadership, racism (and usually anti-Semitism), militarism and Imperialism'. Marxists have articulated fascism in relation to capital and class, outlining that fascism gains political power through the assistance of the ruling class and with funding from big business. The *Encyclopedia of Marxism* (www.marxists.org) defines fascism as 'right-wing, fiercely nationalist, subjectivist in philosophy, and totalitarian in practice', and as 'an extreme reactionary form of capitalist government'. For feminists, the characteristics of militarism and militarised masculinity, chauvinism, machismo, emphasis on male dominance, and patriarchal power relations are of particular concern, even while it must be recognised that women have played and continue to play active roles in fascist movements.
2. In El Salvador and Canada; the UK; Kenya and across the African Continent (for Daniela Marin Platero, Isabel Marler, and Felogene Anumo, respectively) as well as all being part of transnational coalitions and networks working for gender justice.
3. The term 'gender binary' refers to the classification of gender into two distinct and opposite forms of masculine and feminine, and a correlating social system which splits people into one of two sets of gender identities, roles, and attributes (potentially including sexual orientation), based on the sex assigned to someone at birth (based on the appearance of their genitalia).
4. For more information on AWID's intiatives, see www.awid.org.
5. 'Intersectionality' is a concept coined by Black feminist and legal scholar Kimberlé Crenshaw in 1989, which has roots in Black feminist responses

to the historical exclusion of Black women from the feminist movement, and from feminist theory. The concept shows how interlocking systems of power work together to oppress those who are most marginalised in society, and illustrates that experiences of gender cannot be separated from experiences of race, and other forms of oppression, such as class, sexual orientation, and disability.

6. The research was conducted using a combination of quantitative and qualitative analysis of two major data-sets. The first phase of data collection and analysis took place between August and December 2014 and entailed coding and analysis of applications from three separate FRIDA grant-making cycles between 2012 and 2014 – 1,360 applications representing over 100 countries (FRIDA and AWID 2016, 17). The second phase was a global survey of young feminist organisations, consisting of a questionnaire in three languages (English, French, and Spanish) which was completed by 694 respondents from 118 different countries.

7. See www.youtube.com/watch?v=8EataOQvPII) (last checked 5 September 2018).

8. See https://thisisafrica.me/18578-2/ (last checked 5 September 2018).

9. See www.wya.net/ (last checked 5 September 2018).

10. See www.hli.org (last checked 5 September 2018).

11. See www.facebook.com/Africa-Life-Youth-Foundation-166495786720484/) (last checked 5 September 2018).

12. The GALCK website defines this as follows: 'Carnal knowledge against the order of nature' is defined as any sexual activity between two or more persons that does not involve the penis penetrating the vagina (see www.galck.org/know-your-rights/, last checked 5 September 2018).

13. Al-Shabaab (official name Harakat al-Shabaab al-Mujahideen) is a militant Muslim fundamentalist group active in East Africa. 'Al-Shabaab' literally translates from Arabic as 'The Youth'. It is banned as a terrorist group by both the United States and the UK and is believed to have between 7,000 and 9,000 fighters. Al-Shabaab advocates the Saudi-inspired Wahhabi version of Islam, while most Somalis are Sufis. The group has imposed an oppressive interpretation of religious law in areas under its control, including the stoning to death of women accused of adultery. For more information, see www.bbc.co.uk/news/world-africa-15336689 (last checked 5 September 2018).

14. See https://auntyjanehotline.weebly.com/about-us.html (last checked 5 September 2018).

15. See www.thisisthenest.com/ (last checked 5 September 2018).

16. An Afro-American religious tradition, practised mainly in Brazil. Candomblé officially originated in Salvador, Bahia at the beginning of the 19th century, when the first temple was founded. Umbanda is a syncretic Afro-Brazilian religion that blends African traditions with Roman Catholicism, Spiritism, and Indigenous American beliefs.

17. See https://fld.com.br/blog/reju-promove-a-campanha-visto-branco-pelo-fim-da-i/ (last checked by editor 6 September 2018).

18. See www.facebook.com/ciberativistasnegrasma/ (last checked by editor 6 September 2018).

19. https://juventudedeterreirormc.wordpress.com/.

20. See http://reju.org.br (last checked by editor 6 September 2018).
21. See www.youtube.com/watch?v=9977Wwnl_H8 (last checked by editor 6 September 2018).
22. See www.youtube.com/watch?v=lHhqb3j1UpI (last checked by editor 6 September 2018).
23. See www.youtube.com/channel/UC8stIDEXrKootUAqz09AmUw (last checked by editor 6 September 2018).

Acknowledgements

The authors would like to sincerely thank Valérie Bah for her editorial support.

Notes on contributors

Isabel Marler is the Communications Coordinator of the Advancing Universal Rights and Justice Program at the Association for Women's Rights in Development (AWID), which focuses on feminist analysis of and resistance to fascisms and fundamentalisms. Before joining AWID, Isabel worked with Women Living Under Muslim Laws.

Daniela Marin Platero is Coordinator of the Advancing Universal Rights and Justice Program at the Association for Women's Rights in Development (AWID). She is a migrant, queer, Nonualca woman from El Salvador. She is passionate about work centred at the intersections of youth, defence of the body-territory, migration, and autonomy.

Felogene Anumo is Coordinator of the Building Feminist Economies initiative at the Association of Women's Rights in Development (AWID). She was formerly Manager of the Young Feminist Activism Program at AWID. Prior to joining AWID, she worked with Women in Law and Development in Africa – Kenya Chapter (WiLDAF-K) and the African Women's Development and Communication Network (FEMNET).

References

African Population and Health Research Centre Ministry of Health (APHRC), Kenya Ipas and Guttmacher Institute (2013) 'Incidence and Complications of Unsafe Abortion in Kenya: Key Findings of a National Study', http://aphrc.org/wp-content/uploads/2013/11/Incidence-and-Complications-of-Unsafe-Abortion-in-Kenya-Key-Findings-of-a-National-Study.pdf (last checked 11 September 2018)
Agoya, Victor (2014) 'Court allows transgender activists to register lobby group', *The Daily Nation*, 23 July, https://www.nation.co.ke/news/Court-allows-transsexuals-to-register-lobby-group/1056-2394700-cox9b8z/index.html (last checked 11 September 2018)
Al Jazeera (2015) 'Garissa attack: could it have been prevented?', 6 April, https://www.aljazeera.com/programmes/insidestory/2015/04/garissa-attack-prevented-150406190521777.html (last checked 11 September 2018)

Amnesty International (2017) *Amnesty International Report 2016/17: The State of the World's Human Rights*, https://www.amnesty.org/download/Documents/POL1048002017ENGLISH.PDF (last checked 11 September 2018)

Anami, Luke (2017) 'Government slapped with Sh30 million over transgender lady Audrey', *Standard Media*, 15 November, https://www.standardmedia.co.ke/article/2001260346/government-slapped-with-sh30-million-over-transgender-lady-audrey (last checked 11 September 2018)

Association for Women's Rights in Development (AWID) (2018) *Strategic Plan 2018–2022: Co-creating Feminist Realities*

Bhavnani, Kum-Kum, John Foran and Priya A. Kurian (2003) *Feminist Futures: Re-imagining Women, Culture and Development*, London: Zed Books

Blessol, Gathoni (2017) 'State of Power: White Supremacy as Cultural Cannibalism', Transational Institute (TNI), http://longreads.tni.org/state-of-power/white-supremacy/ (last checked 11 September 2018)

Comissão de combate a Intolerancia Religiosa (CCIR), Centro de Articulação de Populações Marginalizadas (CEAP), Laboratório de História das Experiências Religiosas - Instituto de História da Universidade Federal do Rio e Janeiro (LHER-IH), Movimiento Inter-Religioso (MIR) (2015) 'Pré-Relatório Sobre Intolerância Religiosa No Brasil: Informações, estudos de casos, números na tentativa de entender e intervir nos processos de preconceitos', http://www.ceubrio.com.br/downloads/relatorio-Intolerancia-religiosa-18-08-2015.pdf (last checked 11 September 2018)

Cunha, Magali do Nasciemiento (2017) 'Precisamos falar sobre fundamentalismo', *Carta Capital*, 24 August, https://www.cartacapital.com.br/blogs/dialogos-da-fe/precisamos-falar-sobre-fundamentalismo (last checked 11 September 2018)

Delalibera, Graziela (2015) 'Turbante é símbolo de resistência da mulher negra', *Diário da Região*, 23 August, https://www.diariodaregiao.com.br/_conteudo/cultura/turbante-%C3%A9-s%C3%ADmbolo-de-resist%C3%AAncia-da-mulher-negra-1.359598.html (last checked 11 September 2018)

Douglas, Bruce (2015) 'Brazil's "bullets, beef and bible" caucus wants to imprison 16-year-olds', *The Guardian*, 17 April, https://www.theguardian.com/world/2015/apr/17/brazil-rightwing-caucus-lower-age-criminal-responsibility (last checked 11 September 2018)

Egan, Katie (2018) 'Federal crackdown on immigration activists threatens to chill free speech', American Civil Liberties Union, 30 January, https://www.aclu.org/blog/free-speech/rights-protesters/federal-crackdown-immigration-activists-threatens-chill-free (last checked 11 September 2018)

Encarnación, Omar (2017) 'Amid Crisis in Brazil, the Evangelical Bloc Emerges as a Political Power', *The Nation*, 16 August, https://www.thenation.com/article/amid-crisis-in-brazil-the-evangelical-bloc-emerges-as-a-political-power/ (last checked 11 September 2018)

Finerty, Courtney (2012) 'Being gay in Kenya: the implication of Kenya's New constitution for its anti-sodomy laws', *Cornell International Law Journal* 45(2): 436–438, https://www.lawschool.cornell.edu/research/ILJ/upload/Finerty-final-version.pdf (last checked 11 September 2018)

Fortes, Camila (2016) 'Resistência, política e elegância: O empoderamento através do turbante', *EntreCultura*, 11 August, http://entrecultura.com.

br/2016/08/11/resistencia-politica-e-elegancia-o-empoderamento-at-raves-do-turbante/ (last checked 11 September 2018)

Fraga, Vitor (2013) 'Projeto relaciona Direito Penal e criminalização do samba', *OABRJ Digital*, May, http://www.oabrj.org.br/materia-tribuna-do-advogado/17720-Aquela-tal-malandragem-nao-existe-mais (last checked 11 September 2018)

Freelon, Kiratiana (2017) 'For the Love of God? Evangelical Drug Traffickers are Terrorizing Practitioners of Afro-Brazilian Religions', *The Root*, 16 December, https://www.theroot.com/for-the-love-of-god-evangelical-drug-traffickers-are-t-1821321682 (last checked 11 September 2018)

FRIDA | The Young Feminist Fund and AWID (2016) *Brave, Creative, Resilient: The Global State of Young Feminist Organizing*, https://www.awid.org/sites/default/files/atoms/files/frida-awid_field-report_final_web_issuu.pdf (last checked 11 September 2018)

Gay and Lesbian Coalition of Kenya (GALCK) (2016) 'What Are LGBQ Rights?', https://www.galck. org/know-your-rights/ (last checked 11 September 2018)

Gateru, Njeri (2017) 'Journeying Through Sexuality, Activism and the Internet', *GenderIT.org*, https://www.genderit.org/node/5032/ (last checked 11 September 2018)

Ghai, Jill Cottrell and Yash Pal Ghai (2018) 'Understanding the gay rights case and Penal Code penalties', *The Star*, 24 February, https://www.the-star.co.ke/news/2018/02/24/understanding-the-gay-rights-case-and-penal-code-penalties_c1719184 (last checked 11 September 2018)

Gikandi, Halima and Ryan Lenora Brown (2018) 'Gay Kenyans hope for legal win, eyeing broader shift in Africa', *Christian Science Monitor*, 13 June, https://www.csmonitor.com/World/Africa/2018/0613/Gay-Kenyans-hope-for-legal-win-eyeing-broader-shift-in-Africa (last checked 11 September 2018)

Greene, Heather (2014) 'A Brazil federal ruling states Candomblé and Umbanda are not religions', *The Wild Hunt*, 21 May, http://wildhunt.org/2014/05/a-brazil-federal-ruling-states-candomble-and-umbanda-are-not-religions.html (last checked 11 September 2018)

Hernández, Tanya Katerí (2012) *Racial Subordination in Latin America: The Role of the State, Customary Law, and the New Civil Rights Response*, New York: Cambridge University Press

Imam, Ayesha (2006) 'Fundamentalism and women's rights in Africa', presented at the African Feminist Forum, 15–19 November, Accra, Ghana

Kenya Legal & Ethical Issues Network on HIV & AIDS (KELIN) (2018) 'Petition no. 150 of 2016 consolidated with Petition no. 234 of 2016', http://www.kelinkenya.org/wp-content/uploads/2018/03/Mathenge-FINAL-.pdf (last checked 11 September 2018)

Kenya Gazette Supplement (2014) 'The Security Laws (Amendment) Act, No.19 of 2014', http://kenyalaw.org/kl/fileadmin/pdfdownloads/AmendmentActs/2014/SecurityLaws_Amendment_Act_2014.pdf (last checked 11 September 2018)

Kenya Law (n.d.) 'Constitution of Kenya, 2010', http://www.kenyalaw.org/lex/actview.xql?actid=Const2010 (last checked 4 October 2018)

Kenya National Commission on Human Rights (KNCHR) (2016) 'Compendium on Submissions to ICESRC: Committee on Economic Social and Cultural

Rights, Vol 1', http://www.knchr.org/Portals/0/InternationalObligations Reports/ICESRCE%20A4%20.pdf?ver=2016-08-18-115852-683 (last checked 11 September 2018)

Langat, Anthony (2016) 'Ban on sexy music video raises gay rights campaign profile in Kenya', *Reuters*, 11 March, https://af.reuters.com/article/topNews/ idAFKCN0WD0KX (last checked 11 September 2018)

Machado, Tamirys (2015) 'Marcha do Empoderamento Crespo toma as ruas do centro da cidade', *Bocao News*, 8 November, https://www.bocaonews.com. br/noticias/principal/polatica/128478,marcha-do-empoderamento-crespo-toma-as-ruas-do-centro-da-cidade.html (last checked 11 September 2018)

Malek, Ghadeer (2010) 'Warembo Ni yes launches!', *Young Feminist Wire*, 7 June, http://yfa.awid.org/2010/06/warembo-ni-yes-launches/ (last checked 11 September 2018)

Malia, Ashley (2017) 'Negros em marcha pelo direito do cabelo encrespar e contra o racismo religioso', *Portal Correio Nagô*, 19 November, http:// correionago.com.br/portal/negros-em-marcha-pelo-direito-do-cabelo-encrespar-e-contra-o-racismo-religioso/ (last checked 11 September 2018)

Mathare Social Justice Center (MSJC) (2017) *Who Is Next? A Participatory Action Research Report Against the Normalization of Extrajudicial Executions in Mathare*, https://www.matharesocialjustice.org/who-is-next/ (last checked 13 May 2021)

Mbenywe, Mactilda (2018) 'KFCB bans "Rafiki" film for depicting homosexual content', *Standard Digital*, 27 April, https://www.standardmedia.co.ke/ article/2001278422/kfcb-bans-rafiki-film-for-depicting-homosexual-content (last checked 11 September 2018)

Menon, Harish C. (2016) 'India is displaying classic signs that foreshadow fascism', *Quartz India*, 24 November, https://qz.com/india/844672/along-with-narendra-modis-rise-india-has-displayed-classic-signs-that-foreshad-ow-fascism/ (last checked 11 September 2018)

Ministry of Medical Services (2012) 'Standards and guidelines for reduction of morbidity and mortality from unsafe abortion in Kenya', http://www. safeabortionwomensright.org/wp-content/uploads/2018/02/Standards-Guidelines-for-the-Reduction-of-Morbidity-and-Mortality-from-Unsafe-Abortion.pdf (last checked 11 September 2018)

Mishra, Pankaj (2017) *Age of Anger: A History of the Present*, London: Allen Lane

Moore, Jina (2018) 'Kenya bans film about 2 girls in love because it's "too hopeful"', *New York Times*, 27 April, https://www.nytimes.com/2018/04/27/ world/africa/kenya-cannes-film-lesbians-banned.html? smid=tw-share (last checked 11 September 2018)

Moraes, André (n.d.) 'Carta Histórico da Juventude de Terreiro RMC', https:// juventudedeterreirormc.wordpress.com/sobre/carta-historico/ (last checked 11 September 2018)

Muggah, Robert (2017) 'In Brazil, religious gang leaders say they're waging a holy war', *Chicago Tribune*, 2 November, http://www.chicagotribune.com/ sns-in-brazil-religious-gang-leaders-say-theyre-waging-a-holy-war-86097-20171102-story.html (last checked 11 September 2018)

Murumba, Stellar (2016) 'Films board gives Google a week to take down gay song video', *Business Daily*, 24 February, https://www.businessdailyafrica.

com/corporate/Films-board-gives-Google-a-week-to-take-down-gay-song-video/539550-3089994-as8todz/index.html (last checked 11 September 2018)

National Gay and Lesbian Human Rights Commission (NGLHRC) (2017) 'Case digest', https://static1.squarespace.com/static/581a-19852994ca08211faca4/t/58d36f88e58c62dead2f5924/1490251659581/NGLHRCCaseDigestFeb2017.docx.pdf (last checked 11 September 2018)

Nest Collective (2014) 'Stories of Our Lives: On George's Arrest', *The Nest Collective*, 16 October, http://www.thisisthenest.com/news/2015/1/13/stories-of-our-lives-on-georges-arrest (last checked 11 September 2018)

Njagi, Cera (2015) 'I am because we are', *Kenyan Feminist*, 26 November, https://ceranjagi.wordpress.com/ (last checked 11 September 2018)

Njeri Thuo, Jane (n.d.) 'How to Improve Security in Universities in Kenya', *Study in Kenya*, https://studyinkenya.co.ke/blog/how-to-improve-security-in-universities-in-kenya (last checked 11 September 2018)

Nkowane, Chilemwa Harriet (2004) 'Samba Brasileiro – A History', *World Music Central.org*, 1 July, https://worldmusiccentral.org/2004/07/01/samba-brasileiro-%E2%80%93-a-history/ (last checked 11 September 2018)

Norton, Ben and Amrit Wilson (2018) 'India's Ruling Hindu-Nationalist Party Combines Fascism and Neoliberalism', *The Real News Network*, 24 April, https://therealnews.com/stories/indias-ruling-hindu-nationalist-party-combines-fascism-and-neoliberalism (last checked 11 September 2018)

Okumu, Patel (2017) 'Matatu crew caught on camera stripping woman, sentenced to death', *Standard Digital*, 19 July, https://www.standardmedia.co.ke/article/2001248234/matatu-crew-caught-on-camera-stripping-woman-sentenced-to-death (last checked 11 September 2018)

Osborne, Samuel (2018) 'Victor Orban's right-wing Hungarian government announces plan to stop people helping refugees and migrants', *The Independent*, 10 April, https://www.independent.co.uk/news/world/europe/victor-orban-hungary-migrant-refugees-george-soros-ngo-far-right-a8297441.html (last checked 11 September 2018)

Pavão, Fábio Oliveira (2004) 'Entre o Batuque e a Navalha', *Universidade do Estado do Rio de Janeiro Instituto de Filosofia e Ciências Humanas*, June, http://academiadosamba.com.br/monografias/fabiopavao-1.pdf (last checked 11 September 2018)

Paxton, Robert O. (2004) *The Anatomy of Fascism*, New York: Alfred A. Knopf

Reuters (2015) 'No room' for gays in Kenya, says deputy president', *Reuters*, 4 May, https://af.reuters.com/article/topNews/idAFKBN0NP11T20150504?pageNumber=1&virtualBrandChannel=0 (last checked 11 September 2018)

Schipani, Andres and Joe Leahy (2017) '"Drug traffickers of Jesus" drive Brazil slum violence', *Financial Times*, 27 October, https://www.ft.com/content/b5096a18-b548-11e7-aa26-bb002965bce8 (last checked 11 September 2018)

Shameem, Naureen (2017) *Rights at Risk: Observatory on the Universality of Rights Trends Report* 2017 Toronto: Association for Women's Rights in Development (AWID) and The Observatory on the Universality of Rights (OURS) https://www.oursplatform.org/wp-content/uploads/Rights-At-Risk-OURs-Trends-Report-2017.pdf (last checked 11 September 2018)

Strobl, Tyler (2017) 'Thousands March in support of religious tolerance amid rising hate-based vio- lence', *RioOnWatch*, 20 November, http://www.rioon-watch.org/?p=38786 (last checked 11 September 2018)

Taspinar, Omer (2018) 'Turkey takes a big step toward nationalist fascism', *The Washington Post*, 25 June, https://www.washingtonpost.com/news/theworldpost/wp/2018/06/25/erdogan/?noredirect=on&utm_term=.05fafb687969 (last checked 11 September 2018)

Thatiah, Joan (2017) 'What happened after My Dress My Choice?', *Daily Nation*, 3 March, https://www.nation.co.ke/lifestyle/saturday/What-happened-after-My-Dress-My-Choice/1216-3835382-yasgfnz/index.html (last checked 11 September 2018)

Tumulty, Karen (2017) 'President Trump isn't a fan of dissent – inside or outside the government', *The Washington Post*, 1 February, https://www.washingtonpost.com/politics/president-trump-seeks-to-quash-dissent-inside-the-government/2017/02/01/788bdefa-e7ed-11e6-b82f-687d6e6a3e7c_story.html?utm_term=.41de6f28d398 (last checked 11 September 2018)

Weiss, John (1967) *The Fascist Tradition: Radical Right-Wing Extremism in Modern Europe*, New York: Harper & Row

Wood, Peter David Arnould (2018) 'Brazilian evangelicals, swinging hard to the right, could put a Trump-like populist in the presidency', *The Conversation*, 6 August, https://theconversation.com/brazilian-evangelicals-swinging-hard-to-the-right-could-put-a-trump-like-populist-in-the-presidency-96845 (last checked 11 September 2018)

CHAPTER 9

A young feminist new order: an exploration of why young feminists organise the way they do

Devi Leiper O'Malley and Ruby Johnson

Abstract

This chapter draws on FRIDA/The Young Feminist Fund's experience of young feminist activism. It explores a range of examples from around the world of how young feminists are reinventing and building different institutions based on new cultures of leadership, greater emphasis on the collective, and more holistic compensation for activist work. These strategies are needed in a world where progressive activism for social justice is under fire: not only from right-wing movements, but also from development that is seen widely as apolitical, yet fails to challenge patriarchal elites who benefit from inequality and poverty.

Keywords: Young feminist activism; organising; international development; young women's leadership; non-government organisations (NGOs)

Introduction

In the last few years we have seen young feminists take the world by storm. They sit at the forefront of movements, drawing on direct action and social norm change, both creating and realising transformative leadership styles. Young people around the world are increasingly distrustful of institutions such as governments and democracy itself. While this wariness can be instrumentalised by extremists and contribute to more dangerous environments, there is also a positive but less-reported wave of questioning happening among young feminist organisers. In their rejection of the development industrial complex, young women, girls, and trans* youth around the world are deconstructing practices and rebuilding new ways of organising themselves

Founded in 2010, FRIDA – also known as the Young Feminist Fund – is the only youth-led fund focused exclusively on supporting young feminist activism to advance social justice movements and agendas across the globe.[1] It provides small flexible grants and runs an annual global participatory grant-making process in seven different languages, whereby all eligible applicants vote on the best proposals and this informs the final funding decisions. The money which we disburse in grants comes from a wide range of donors including private foundations, international non-government organisations (INGOs), corporate foundations, women's funds, and individuals. We are increasingly asked for advice and provide inputs to INGOs, bilateral funders, and other private foundations who are also creating their own new programmes and strategies on young feminist organising.

In addition to grants, FRIDA offers opportunities for capacity development that are accessible and responsive to the needs of young feminist organisers, and based on linking and learning relationships that strengthen networks of young feminist activists within multi-generational movements. Finally, it mobilises resources from both traditional and non-traditional sources, with new and modern methods, to enhance the quality and quantity of funding for women's human rights; while building knowledge for advocacy to ensure financial and non-financial policies are inclusive and responsive to the priorities articulated by young women, girls, and trans* youth.

As Co-Executive Directors of FRIDA for the past five years, we aim to use this space in *Gender & Development*'s issue on Young Feminisms to reflect on our own experiences leading a virtual global young feminist fund, focusing in particular on what we have observed of young feminist organising around the world. We will, in particular, examine how young people are forging transformative feminist leadership models that challenge the status quo, decentralise power, and place decisions in the hands of young feminists themselves. Young feminists appear to be rejecting more formal structures and are organising in temporal, horizontal, and informal ways, in response to closing space for civil society action and backlash against progressive and rights-based activism in particular, which is placing activists at great personal risk, testing resilience, and increasingly pushing groups underground.

We focus, in particular, on the following themes:

- The *resurgence of patriarchies* and the *failure of development*. We emphasise how powerful critiques of inequality and injustice have been depoliticised by a process of 'NGO-isation' which deflects attention from entrenched race, gender, and class-based inequalities between the global South and North and fails to see the same unequal power relations operating in development itself.
- The need for new *leadership models and organisational structures that further equality and social justice,* and the *strategies of young feminist groups* – including how they deal with sharing power and leadership transition.
- How young feminist groups are *forging new understanding of resources,* including experimentation with solidarity economies and pooling resources.
- *The revolution will not be funded. Or will it?* The contradictions and tensions that such political approaches can raise, on the one hand with approaches to resource mobilisation focused on autonomous organising,

strong anti-capitalist politics, volunteer models and self-generated income, and on the other hand the reality of the unequal distribution of the resources and that activists need a living wage to survive and sustain their work.

This chapter draws on examples of young feminist collectives and organisations from Nigeria, Cambodia, Kyrgyzstan, Peru, Algeria, and Hungary. We conducted qualitative interviews from April to June 2018, with informants from these organisations who we list in the Acknowledgements. Unless otherwise stated, all the quotations from activists in this chapter are taken from these interviews. We also draw here on secondary data emerging from desk research in June 2018, spanning key journals, reports, and research, and data from FRIDA/The Young Feminist Fund's grantee partners and applicants.

Mapping the context for feminisms and feminist leadership

To frame our discussion of feminist strategies and leadership, in this section we offer a – necessarily brief – outline of some of the key issues challenging young feminists today, to frame our discussion of the strategies young feminists are evolving in response.

A scan of the world at this moment reveals increasingly conservative and repressive governments, insular and inhumane approaches to migrants, and sustained influence of religious fundamentalism. The election of Trump, changes of Brexit, the rollback on rights to LGBTQI communities, and the attack on sexual and reproductive rights in Central America are all emblematic of the spirit in the air. In the past year, civil society groups have come under increasing pressure worldwide. According to CIVICUS' 'State of Civil Society Report', over 100 countries have closed, repressed, or obstructed civic space in 2017 (2018, 4).

In response to this context, political action is desperately needed. Yet the challenges above have particularly sharp impact on the lives and bodies of young women, as patriarchy morphs and resurfaces (Enloe 2017). Young feminist groups commonly experience state and cultural oppression across the world. In response to the risks of working in these environments, some groups, including young feminist groups, need to operate in a clandestine and 'off-the-grid' way. They use covert communication mechanisms due to the high risks of surveillance and monitoring, and employ different technological apps and platforms and coded ways to communicate. In some cases, groups will have varied ways to describe their work publicly – omitting key details on the nature of the work in the public eye, or abstain from public platforms and public work at all. This is particularly the case when working on LGBTQI+ issues and on sexual and reproductive rights, including abortion rights, in difficult contexts where the work is criminalised.

Depoliticisation of the gender agenda is a key issue facing young feminists. With the expansion of the global development industry and the acceptance of 'gender mainstreaming' in development,[2] young feminist organisers have grown up in an environment where in fact, you do not have to be feminist in order to work for a women's NGO or programme. Donna Murdock's (2003) study of NGOs in Colombia presents the argument that the neoliberal state and development discourse has institutionalised 'gender' without the politics of feminist struggle. Similarly, T. K. Sundari Ravindran and Aarti Kelkar-Khambete (2008, 121) reviewed published literature on experiences in mainstreaming gender within the health sector since the 1990s and found that 'apparent lack of progress in mainstreaming gender in health may be [partly] attributed to: depoliticization and delinking of gender mainstreaming from social transformation and social justice agendas'. Finally, in her study of GROOTS[3] Kenya, Awino Okech says that

> the de-politicization of gender that has arisen with the packaging of gender as a development tool results in most gender-oriented organizations being acutely unaware of the political and ideological influences of the broader feminist ideology and movement to their work. (Okech 2009, 225)

Another closely related example of depoliticisation of the feminist agenda is the way that 'intersectionality' – an analysis and agenda for political action based on an understanding of the intersections between race, gender, and class shaping the realities for African-American women in poverty (Crenshaw 1989) – has been taken up by international development and other actors. In agendas such as the United Nations' Leave No-one Behind, the politically radical focus of intersectionality and its critique of patriarchy is derailed and reduced to a focus on technical aspects of 'development'.

An example of young feminist responses to depoliticisation is the #PracticeSolidarity campaign by the Young Feminist Wire at the Association for Women's Rights in Development (AWID) in 2016:

> #PracticeSolidarity is a campaign exploring what solidarity means for young feminists across gender, racial, economic, social and ecological justice movements ... The #PracticeSolidarity campaign aims to promote young feminist discourses on solidarity, as well as practices, that do not separate themselves from struggles against colonialism, racism, sexism, homonationalism, Pink-washing, islamophobia, cultural imperialism and neoliberalism, and to advocate for concrete cross-movement solidarity and joint action. (AWID 2016; Young Feminist Wire 2016)

The #PracticeSolidarity campaign informed a larger question discussed at the AWID forum of the same year: asking what the feminist future could look like. The campaign demonstrated that the young feminists in the present are intentionally working to connect each other's struggles – and that practising solidarity is work. It illustrated many of the values that many young feminist activists are trying to illuminate in their leadership: checking one's privilege, adjusting habits, and questioning practices.

INGOs have played – and continue to play – an important role in community development, and many were founded with progressive intentions underpinned by analyses of inequality and a mission to challenge power relations to right the wrongs of the colonial era. In their DNA was a critique of neo-liberal development and they presented themselves as focusing on rights, and on a race- and class-based critique of ideas of development as modernisation in the wake of the Second World War and the end of colonialism. However, even where these politics may have existed, in the eyes of many they have been lost in recent years. It is possible that they never really existed. The underlying power dynamics of moving money from North to South, and of large international organisations driving development, suggests the need to question and reflect. NGOs in the global South being heavily dependent on foreign funds (mainly from the global North) has widely been accepted as the norm.

Critiques from both academics and practitioners point out that most large well-funded NGOs are financed and backed historically by Western aid and development agencies, which are in turn funded by Western governments, the World Bank, the UN, some multinational corporations, and private philanthropists (Brehm 2004; Cohen *et al.* 2009; Roy 2014; Wright 2012). The notion of this relationship as a 'non-profit industrial complex' (INCITE 2007) argues that this system reinforces and sustains existing elite dominance. This perspective highlights that non-profit organisation staff are often dependent upon wealthy white elites for their salaries, and are therefore accountable to those elites instead of marginalised people (Oyakawa 2017).

The ground beneath NGOs is rapidly shifting, and their existence is being questioned more strongly than ever. For example, INGOs are moving their headquarters to the global South, with intentions of staying relevant and being grounded in the communities they serve. More recently, the sexual harassment cases against Oxfam Great Britain and other organisations in the aid sector suggest a range of complexities in understanding the current challenges and contextual realities of the aid sector. Questions of power and politics are critical and increasingly hard to ignore. As Joanna Moorhead and Joe Sandler Clark put it:

> A hurricane is blowing through the world of international development and when the dust settles, the landscape is going to look entirely different. At the centre of the storm is a mix of acknowledgement and fear around a simple principle, which is that to be effective and meaningful in the 21st century, NGOs have no business continuing to hole up in headquarters in the north. (Moorhead and Sandler Clark 2015)

NGOs still absorb an enormously disproportionate amount of funding compared to grassroots organisations or women's funds. AWID's 2013 report, 'Watering the Leaves, Starving the Roots' (Arutyunova and Clark 2013), highlighted the fact that in 2010, the median annual income of over 740 women's organisations around the world was US$20,000, compared to large INGOs such as Save the Children with US$1.442 billion and World Vision with US$2.611 billion (*ibid.*, 16). Not all NGOs are bad, but growing up in an environment where NGOs have become giant and powerful institutions, young feminists have become increasingly jaded.

This analysis reveals profound problems about the apparent 'solutions' offered by development agendas and activism, which are shaped by existing elites shaped by patriarchal values. We see patriarchy persisting and morphing in institutionalised and depoliticised environments. In response, many young feminist groups are specifically and intentionally working to repoliticise 'development' and experiment with new systems and practices. In the next section, we look at the different ways this is happening through leadership, organising structures, and resource mobilisation.

Leadership models and organisational structures of young feminist groups

In this section, we want to highlight the new positive and transformative models of leadership that young feminists are already offering. Many of our insights offer new ways forward for other organisations – including INGOs – which want to renew their commitment to realising social justice. Powerful, visionary leadership rooted in a commitment to social justice is required to ensure development – and INGOs – are part of the solution to global inequalities and poverty. In the 2015 survey, *Outlook on the Global Agenda* (World Economic Forum 2015, 14), a staggering 86 per cent of respondents agreed that the world is in the middle of a leadership crisis – indeed, this was the third most critical issue amongst respondents. In the Survey Report, Shiza Shahid puts forward rising income inequalities, the failure to address climate change, and protracted armed conflict as factors leading to many young people around the world becoming more and more disillusioned with representative democratic systems or current leadership (*ibid.*). Shahid also links to young people being increasingly interested in or lured by more populist and/ or right-wing agendas (*ibid.*).

Feminist activists, movements, and academics have a long history of exploring and critiquing conventional – patriarchal – notions of leadership (Batliwala 2011; Sinclair 2014). The way that feminists redefine leadership is one of the ways they offer alternative models to development, to human rights, to civil society, deconstructing the organisational models and leadership styles that they themselves have found oppressive and limiting. If we really want to see change, we need to ensure we do not re-create the same oppressive structures and internalise patriarchy in our own organisations, groups, and collectives. Sometimes this starts with a process of unlearning and questioning the very notion of leadership.

Many young feminist groups are rejecting traditional leadership models and organisational structures, contesting notions of hierarchy. The FRIDA/ AWID research report *Brave, Creative, Resilient: The Global State of Young Feminist Organizing* (FRIDA and AWID 2016) showed the majority of young feminist groups using consensus and participatory decision-making models. This manifests in many ways in different contexts, in the legal aspects of whether groups are registered or not, in how they make decisions, if they have volunteer or paid staff. Today's generation of young feminists have grown up using digital technologies for collective action that challenges traditional ideas of leadership. In the words of one commentator, we have:

> grown up with the Internet and embrace its efficiency, transparency, bottom-up action, and co-creation ethos. Young people are also challenging conventional notions of hierarchical leadership, preferring collaboration and horizontal arrangements in which 'everyone's a leader'. (Gibson 2018, 8)

Young feminist choices and experiences on leadership and registration

Bishkek Feminist Initiatives[4] aims to build and strengthen intersectional social justice movement(s) from the perspective of feminist ethics and communities' lived experiences in Kyrgyzstan and Central Asia. It uses public campaigns and social media, provides training, and runs a feminist library. It aims to challenge sexism, promote women's rights, and challenge the normalisation of violence against women. A member of the initiative – Aizat – explained the group's view on their leadership model in her written interview with us for this chapter:

> We never call it a 'leadership model', leadership itself sounds very capitalist and patriarchal and demands us to always be successful. Though I understand the need to raise our voice and to solve our issues we have to be leaders, right? We are a non-hierarchical organization and we are all somehow leaders in very 'non-traditional' and unexplainable ways. Society and community is not used to such leadership. We all should be equal leaders what we are practising is a very great rare way. We listen to each other, we listen to every single voice of us.

The Radical Queer Affinity Collective (RQAC) was founded in 2011 in Budapest, Hungary, as a transnational queer and trans feminist collective committed to building a network of young queer and trans activists in Hungary and the Central and Eastern European region. One of their founders, Marianna Szczygielska, explained:

> From the start, we wanted to avoid having leaders. This was key in our model because a lot of us were already part of other movements. We decided on consensus based decision-making, and all decision-making had to made by all members … It was time consuming so later on we developed some faster ways when decisions needed to be made more urgently. But financial decisions stayed with [were still made by] consensus.

TierrActiva[5] is a Peruvian movement, network, and collective made up of young people seeking to strengthen the climate justice movement in Peru by providing a focal point for activism, emphasising diversity, collective action, and deep and systemic change. Almost half of the network is made up of young women. One of its members, Majandra Rodriguez Acha, shared how she and other members are pushing against centralised models where power and information have historically flowed from the capital city of Lima:

> Part of the legacy of centralisation, traditional charity models, paternalism, and top-down models is that people will wait to hear what those in Lima have to say and not take the lead. We have been really clear from the beginning, foster autonomy and independence, and having people take charge and take the lead and feel confident that they can do that without having to look for approval or authorisation from Lima. It is not an explicit thing but a subtle cultural thing that is just there.

Reflecting on our own leadership at FRIDA

Reflecting on our own leadership at FRIDA over the last five years, we have found growing support for redefining the rules of what leadership is. We use a co-leadership model, and have done from this start. This means that leadership can be shared by multiple people – rather than just one person. For FRIDA, this model works in different ways. We have two Executive Directors (rather than one Chief Executive Officer), and engage our community in decisions related to strategic direction, certain policies, and public representation. While we had to defend this model in our earlier stages, we now find the idea gaining momentum and it is gaining acceptance not only in the non-profit sector, but also in the for-profit sectors. We are increasingly receiving opportunities to co-represent FRIDA – that is, event organisers are happy to accommodate multiple representatives of FRIDA to speak, as staff, Board, Advisors, and/or grantee partners.

By adopting and sustaining the use of participatory approaches throughout our decision-making and regularly consulting our community (that is, our grantee partners, Advisory Committee, staff, and Board), we have been able to attain and maintain legitimacy, and gain greater influence and authority – especially in sectors looking to work more with young women, girls, and trans* youth. Some examples have been the democratic election of our Board of Directors by grantee partners and advisors; and polls we ran in 2014 on how we should manage age dynamics in our own structure.

In line with our commitment not to follow conventional leadership models, we have also chosen not to set up a physical office. FRIDA currently has no head office – in fact, no office at all. We have staff based in over 14 countries from India to Morocco, to Mexico to Serbia. People link with local community-based organisations or shared office spaces to connect and ground in context and have a space to work, but everything we do is virtual. This model was met with some scepticism from the donors, but increasingly we are finding funders for our work that are supportive of our model and structures, and willing to be bold and take some risks. Principles that have guided our leadership include: finding a way to trust yourself; active experimentation, piloting things with a close eye to evaluation and assessment; and ensuring iterative communications with our constituencies, forming an 'open loop'.

Resisting cultural pressure and conformity

Many young feminist groups are wary of being trapped in the system, replicating unequal patterns but still facing pressure to conform. For example, when Akudo Oguaghamba founded the Women's Health and Equal Rights Initiative (WHER),[6] one of the first lesbian, bisexual, trans* women's organisations in Nigeria, she faced a lot of insistence from others to quit her current full-time job (in another sector) and make WHER her full-time job. In an interview with us, she stated:

> There is pressure to conform, to be like other organisations. A lot of people felt like it was cheating – saying if you do this, you have to do it full-time.

Similarly, founders of the RQAC in Hungary also pushed back against expectations, specifically

> wanting to avoid pitfalls of 'needing office, needing funding' that turns your purpose to focus on existence rather than actually community.

Challenging the normal ways of working, and ensuring flexibility is also something we have experimented with in the area of our virtual office set-up, described above. This requires a commitment to a range of things that make this work for us, from excellent documentation of meetings to flexibility with time zones and the hours we work, to making an additional effort to practise inclusive collective feminist leadership principles across diverse geographies. With the realities of geographic isolation that come from not sharing a physical office in one location, come the requirement that we should support each other via a commitment to 'collective care' – including consciously valuing our different contributions, no matter how far apart we are. This institutional commitment to collective care is joined by a similarly conscious commitment to self-care, and to active creation of an organisational culture based on a Happiness Manifestx[7] – a declaration of our feminist principles and practices to preserve the well-being of our community, as individuals and as a whole – especially in a global virtual context. For example, it promotes healthy working hours, constructive conversation, and respect to each other as fellow feminists, despite differences.

Benefits of young feminist leadership models

In our analysis and experience, the alternative leadership models described in this section have several benefits. They benefit the quality of the work and its relevance to the women it seeks to support, through its emphasis on consultation and participation. Young feminist collectives rooted in the very community they are working with, and self-led, will be more in sync with their community and/or have in-built accountability mechanisms, driven from their community and actively sharing power within their structure. This may sometimes mean things take longer, but the activities are more likely to be considered appropriate and useful by the people they are intended to support. This argument will be familiar to development policymakers and practitioners from literature focusing on participatory development (Cornwall 2006).

Second, co-leadership or shared decision-making is better for leaders. It ensures there are built-in support mechanisms and mentoring. Young leaders are less isolated when they can share responsibility and risk and feel less alone. In addition, younger members will often be incubated within groups, exposed to leadership through democratic or consensus models, and shared processes.

Mobilising resources today

In this section, we explore how young feminist groups are forging new feminist resource mobilisation strategies as a direct response to the contexts they have grown up in. AWID explains feminist resource mobilisation as:

> A strategy that addresses financial sustainability for our organizations and our movements, where processes of resource mobilization are political acts and built upon feminist values. (AWID n.d., 3)

In this section, we explore this concept, and look at five ways in which we see it being practised by young feminists. While we are not saying that these practices are restricted only to young feminist groups, we think the next generation is taking up these new ways of working with great momentum and vigour.

Expanding the definition of resources and focusing on abundance

Resources can be material or non-material, tangible or intangible (Edwards and McCarthy 2004). In our capitalist societies, there is a tendency to over-emphasise material resources (money, staff, means of communication) and under-value non-material resources (legitimacy, social relationships, networks, personal connections, and solidarity) (Fuchs 2006). An example of this over-emphasis on material resources is a common donor requirement on development and humanitarian interventions in the non-profit and aid industries that they use only 20 per cent of their budgets to fund overhead costs (e.g. salaries or training for staff). Unequal power dynamics between funder and grantee make it difficult for groups to push back on this (Gregory and Howard 2009).

With a wider perspective on the importance of resources for investing in people and movement building, as well as the desire to break traditional dependence on foreign funders, we see many young feminist groups rejecting funding or exploring other resources they already have or see in their communities. In our interview with her for this chapter, Chansittha Mark, Coordinator of the United Sisterhood Alliance in Cambodia, explained:

> We advocate with funders that it's not a 20:80 per cent overhead versus programmes. We can proudly say we advocate 40:60 per cent, sometimes 55 per cent. We are not just transactionally paying people, we need people on the ground and a lot of resources for sustaining these people.

Moving from an individual to collective focus and breaking competition

Alternative ways of funding transformative work are required. Participatory grant-making models identify community-building, solidarity, encouragement of collaboration, and opportunities for more learning and capacity building as key benefits for both donors and activists (Gibson 2018). As such, these models are a potential solution to enable more feminist resource mobilisation, reflecting value placed on movement building, investing in capacity of people, and in processes that reflect feminist values, ultimately shifting traditional power dynamics in philanthropy.

The Guerrilla Foundation, a new foundation exploring the approach, talks about a collective approach from their perspective as a funder:

> Taking a systems perspective and considering wealth accumulation as the result of an extractive economy that does not account for all of its social and environmental side-effects, philanthropic money can be seen as a common good that should be managed for the benefit of all. (Guerrilla Foundation, n.d.)

A participatory grantmaker in the Lafayette Practice's *Who Decides* report also explains the link between this perspective on funding, and co-leadership as a principle to be used by funding bodies when deciding what to support:

> Grant decision-making should never depend on an individual, and peer-led funding will always have larger group involvement as a frame for those decisions. Most Peer-Review Funds are related to movements and movement-building. So there's always a larger vision of what's best for the movement. Not asking 'Which group am I personally most comfortable with, or excited by?', but 'For the movement, what would be the smartest choice?' (The Lafayette Practice 2014, 22)

FRIDA's experience of working in collaborative and participatory ways with young feminists in our own decision-making echoes this view. In our methodology, feminist groups review each other's proposals, making groups more aware of other initiatives and strategies that may complement their work. This contributes to their overall awareness of larger networks and potential movements they can join – which are important resources for their work beyond funding. Additionally, we find some groups declining funds or choosing not to re-apply for renewal funding, but saying they prefer to receive other resources – such as remaining in the networks and having access to learning opportunities.

While we cannot say these approaches to funding decisions are unique to young feminists, we are working in a virtual online context and this creates opportunities to work in collaborative and consensual ways. Perhaps these ways of working are more 'natural' to our generation! In a Ford Foundation-commissioned report on participatory grantmaking, Gibson (2018, 8) reflects on young people's preference for consensus-based decision-making in philanthropy, 'as evidenced by their preference for giving circles, crowdfunding, and other giving vehicles'.

Pooling and sharing resources

In using a more collective approach, there is greater capacity to turn away from competitive attitudes. While still comparatively rare, there are instances of young feminist groups in FRIDA's network that decline funds after participating in the participatory grantmaking process because they decide other groups are in greater need than them. Additionally, by not being influenced by a feeling of competition, young feminists are better able to practise their own intersectional politics. Mark of United Sisterhood explains:

> For example, lots of donors only want to work with garment workers, but not with sex workers. So what we do is apply for core funds and make this decision ourselves ... We've actually had success in raising awareness of donors of why it's important.

We see many young feminist organisers sharing resources with multiple identities, for different causes, and with groups that use diverse strategies. One key example is the United Sisterhood Alliance (US) in Cambodia,[8] an alliance of four social groups dedicated to addressing the needs of the people in Cambodia as well as realising social development, change, and justice. These four groups are: The Women's Network for Unity founded by male, transgender, lesbian, and heterosexual female sex workers; Workers' Information Center, an association of garment factory workers; Messenger Band, a musical band of garment factory workers; and Social Action for Change (SAC), a group of women activists whose aims are to build, strengthen, and support grassroots movements, workers, and women activists. These four groups decided to form an alliance; acquire a common space; and pool administrative, financial, and human resources so as not to recreate multiple systems of bureaucracy and overheads.

The revolution will not be funded. Or will it?

The reality of funding movements and funding young feminist activist-led groups and collectives raises many contradictions and tensions; on the one hand, with approaches to resource mobilisation focused on autonomous organising, strong anti-capitalist politics, volunteer models, and self-generated income and, on the other hand, the reality of the unequal distribution of the resources, the intensive labour, energy, and time, and the need for a living wage for activists to survive and sustain their work.

Groups are motivated to reject funding from donors in order to escape restrictions, added pressure from reporting, and competition that arises from others in the community. As Acha from TierrActiva shared in our interview with her:

> Culturally, groups that don't receive funding are in the eyes of some people seen as more legit than groups that receive funding because groups that receive funding have it easy in a sense.

This is a reality for many groups in many contexts.

Additionally, many groups will not accept funding from many sources to ensure that they do not become dependent on donor funding and to ensure the coherence and authenticity of their politics. Since United Sisterhood works with garment factory workers, they specifically state that they would never accept funds from corporations. Szczygielska from RQAC told us the organisation:

> would never accept money from companies. We don't want to commodify our organisation.

On the question of whether radical work can find funding, Acha from TierrActiva stated:

> Yes the revolution will not be funded and yes we need more resources to fund the revolution ... donor funding should have a role and a necessary role, and a political role, but this role has to be limited ... When they feel that it is not helping anymore ... groups should be putting restrictions in place, you are going too far, we want more space.

Funding movements and activists should be seen as a privilege. In a world that is so unequal and those with money and resources have for so long held the power, it is normal for us to function in a system where funders hold grantees or activists to account to follow their restrictions. But if we really want to shift power and start to unravel oppressive and unequal systems, we need to ensure that when money flows, funders are not only focusing on accountability to donors, but to the activists to whom they channel funds. The expertise and time and change work done by activists needs to be valued as important resources in their own right. The exploitation of free labour and the 'strategy mining'[9] that we see going on needs questioning.

Tensions between resisting 'NGO-isation' and needing to value the labour of activists

The activist and writer Arundhati Roy has this to say about the NGO-isation of resistance:

> Real political resistance offers no ... short cuts. The NGO-ization of politics threatens to turn resistance into a well-mannered, reasonable, salaried, 9-to-5 job. With a few perks thrown in. Real resistance has real consequences. And no salary. (Roy 2014)

Many activists, scholars, and observers echo this sentiment (Bah and Anumo 2017; Carty and Mohanty 2015; Choudry and Kapoor 2013).

While we fully understand the pitfalls of becoming over-professionalised, we cannot be silent on demanding compensation when it is due – and especially when it is overdue. Activists are regularly exploited for their time, creativity, knowledge, skills, and energy, and often experience guilt because they accept a salary. They may be seen as 'selling out' because of this, or devalued by funders who have unjust expectations of activist labour. Szczygielska from RQAC reflected:

> Free labour was the key resource. We never took any money for our work. But then we realised it wasn't sustainable. So if some us had a job it was ok, but some members didn't have a job and it became an issue. So we had conversations on [compensation based on] individual needs ... It was hard to realise this, and it's hard with the grant to suddenly think about salary/compensation when dealing with community needs.

Acha from TierrActiva shares about her experience in the sector:

> People should be paid for the work that they do ... There are real systemic problems, deep problems with people not getting compensated in life. But I also think that money is dangerous and money is risky and money can change dynamics and influence things, because we live in an unequal world, so it needs to be done really carefully.

Good practices and examples

There are no easy answers, but it is critical that funders find ways to support and show up for autonomous and independent groups and movements today in ways that are not harmful. Solomé Lemma of Thousand Currents[10] shares '25 Powerful Ways that Funders Can Support Social Movements' (Lemma 2018). While all are critical, one of our favourites is:

> Be clear: Funders don't start movements: They fund. They can connect. They may convene. They can facilitate (sometimes, if requested to do so). They can encourage. They back, but they don't build. Building is the work of movement leadership. (*ibid.*)

A clear understanding of the role of funders in the complex moment we are in is critical.

While there is still much to be learnt, there are concrete examples of good practice on the part of donors and institutions that are responding to the realities of activists. The United Nations Trust Fund to End Violence Against Women (2012) includes a specific section on self-care in their grant application guidelines. Self-care costs (of up to US$2,000 over three years) are available to small women's organisations (those with an annual budget of less than US$200,000):

> Self-care costs can be used for a variety of expenses for the organization to respond to issues of staff burn-out and vicarious trauma as well as to promote overall staff well-being. Organizations have the flexibility to choose how to expend resources under this budget line so long as they demonstrate that the funds were utilized to promote self-care and benefit multiple staff members across the organization. (United Nations Trust Fund to End Violence Against Women 2012)

However, the small amount of money available here is unlikely to be a real quantification of the actual costs of self-care. We feel this is a great start, but the time is now for funders to be bolder and respond to the holistic needs of activists.

Another positive example of a donor recognising activist labour comes from the NoVo Foundation. In addition to the US$34 million committed to successful applications of their Radical Hope Fund,[11] the Foundation awarded small grants to unsuccessful applicants (who had made it to the final stages) to be used how the groups chose, so long as it was related to the group's original mission (personal communication, 15 May 2018). A final example comes from the Whitman Institute's[12] philosophy of 'trust-based philanthropy' (Whitman Institute 2018), which embodies what FRIDA and many other women's funds practise. This philosophy is based on the importance of embedding 'trust, dialogue, and relationship-building' (*ibid.*) between funders and grantees as part of a larger effort to create 'social, political, and economic equity' (*ibid.*). These practices are not necessarily designed only for young feminist organisers. They represent serious responses to today's contexts, and deeper understandings of social movements. But they are substantially compatible with the values and priorities of young feminist organisers, and represent pathways for activists and funders to work more meaningfully alongside each other.

As funders of movements committed to social transformation, it is our duty to start with ourselves, to change our institutions from within, and to question the power we hold. It is our job to talk about and to fund the hard issues and to co-ordinate between ourselves to reduce the burden on activists. It is our job to take holistic security and self-care seriously, and put it into our funding mechanisms to ensure it too is resourced. Below are some concrete suggestions for specific sectors.

Funding mechanisms may need to be restructured to ensure resources are reaching groups that need this support most – including young feminist groups. This may require changes to overseas development assistance (ODA) architecture, to ensure recipients of ODA (whether governments, INGOs, or funding organisations) have a clear mandate to include young people – and in particular, young women, girls, and trans* youth – in the design and decisions of programmes relating to them. It also requires funds channelled through intermediary funding organisations to be re-granted to girl or young women-led initiatives. This may mean funding consortiums with youth-led organisations. It will require increased flexibility and risk-taking, given the very informal and dynamic nature of young feminist organisations. It also requires funders to change their approaches and conceptual frameworks.

To give an example: to determine a group's sustainability, funders often rely on reviewing group's budgets. This is problematic for young feminist groups who have just started or deliberately choose a non-linear growth model. Our perspective is that asking for more detail and evaluation of non-material resources that are essential to movement success – and are actually harder to mobilise – like legitimacy with constituencies, or authority (e.g. evidence that a group's voice is respected in wider movements) – may allow for a more holistic view.

Similarly, we need to deconstruct what funders count as impact, and challenge the notion that change is only equated with scale. Sometimes it is the smaller pockets of change that build meaningful power at an individual and collective level, create safe spaces to thrive in these volatile contexts, and fuel movements that make ripples in our history. Even if they do not fit into large-scale definitions of change, with perfect logframes, young feminists are doing the life risk-taking, ground-breaking, time-shaking work on the frontlines of change.

Funders also need to support groups morally and financially to explore and implement new resource mobilisation strategies. A few ways they can do so are to invest in groups to test new resource mobilisation tactics that are not dependent on grant-writing and to play an active role in growing philanthropic culture outside the global North/West. Changes might also be made in the worth funders see in different interventions. What do funders attach value to? Do they need to change their attitudes? In the current global context it is essential to find funders keen to support work that does not see the solution to women's interests as lying in legal or policy changes alone. Work is needed to challenge what is seen as cultural or traditional, and social norm-change.

We see many young feminist groups employing local resource mobilisation strategies for their work – some more successfully than others. But this is very important nonetheless, especially when their work directly addresses power structures in communities. Direct funding, trust, and other creative ways to support activists to cultivate autonomous and independent activist structures and movements will be critical in the years to come. Investment in intergenerational healing and collective learning processes will also pave the way for more effective movement collaborations.

Conclusions

A restock of the first half of 2018 shows us that young people are making bold and courageous contributions to change worldwide, from representing larger numbers in the #NiUnaMenos movements in Latin America to being major players in the toppling of the dictator in Armenia. This generation are playing a greater role as social media revolutionaries, as activists, as UN advocates and lobbyists, as campaigners organising for gender equality, and warriors for climate justice.

Their leadership is informed by growing up in an era of shrinking civic space and in a time when the questioning of depoliticised agendas and NGOs' models is becoming more mainstream. They are contesting narrow definitions of identity, and reclaiming and reconstructing democratic and secular spaces. It is critical to understand that it is their autonomy and the very rejection of institutions, be it government, INGOs, or funders, that so often makes the change that young feminists are creating so genuine and impactful. Their choices to challenge traditional structures of organising, and to develop new forms of leadership including practising collective decision-making build our consciousness of the importance of linking the way we work to the social justice outcomes we all want to see in the world.

As a feminist funding organisation, we see how young feminist groups are challenging funders as they challenge unequal power relations and ways of thinking about funding relationships and accountability. Young feminist groups are developing new ways of mobilising resources – focusing more on abundance than scarcity, breaking competition, and questioning where resources come from.

With these new opportunities come certain risks and contradictions. The question remains of whether funding and institutionalisation inherently damages political movements but so does the question of how we keep activists sustained with adequate pay and security for their own physical and mental well-being. These questions are yet to be fully resolved, but need to be given more attention in order to support the leaders of the future. In the current state of the world, it is necessary for both activists and funders to engage in meaningful dialogue and begin to work through the power imbalances between them.

Notes

1. See www.youngfeministfund.org.
2. 'Gender mainstreaming' was originally developed as an approach by feminists but its original radical political vision has been lost in translation to become a technical concern (Mannell 2012).
3. See http://grootskenya.org.
4. See https://bishkekfeminists.wordpress.com/.
5. See https://tierractiva.pe/.
6. See https://whernigeria.org/.
7. Manifestx is a gender-neutral spelling of 'manifesto' or 'manifesta'. FRIDA's Happiness Manifestx will be publicly available by the end of 2018.
8. See www.unitedsisterhood.org/.
9. By 'strategy mining' we mean 'outsiders' extracting information about different strategies used by another organisation, group, or individual – who may not have formally written down their strategy, but rather have

naturally come to practise the strategy regularly over time through their inherent knowledge of their community. This is problematic when outsiders do so without transparency and equal understanding from the group that holds the strategy and credit is not given. In most extreme cases, we see this happening by larger, more resourced and privileged institutions in the global North, who do not involve global South activists and institutions in developing the formal articulation of these strategies.

10. See https://thousandcurrents.org/.
11. See https://novofoundation.org/radicalhope/.
12. See https://thewhitmaninstitute.org/.

Acknowledgements

With thanks to our interviewees: Majandra Rodriguez Acha, TierrActiva, Peru; Akudo Oguaghamba, WHER, Nigeria; Channsitha Mark, United Sisterhood Alliance, Cambodia; Aizat Shakieva, Bishkek Feminist Initiative, Kyrgyzstan; and Marianna Szczygielska, RQAC, Hungary.

Notes on contributors

Devi Leiper O'Malley was previously a Co-Executive Director of FRIDA | The Young Feminist Fund.

Ruby Johnson was previously a Co-Executive Director of FRIDA | The Young Feminist Fund.

References

Arutyunova, Angelika and Cindy Clark (2013) *Watering the Leaves, Starving the Roots: The State of Financing for Women's Rights Organising and Gender Equality*, Toronto: AWID, https://www.awid.org/sites/default/files/atoms/files/WTL_Starving_Roots.pdf (last checked 17 September 2018)

Association for Women's Rights in Development (AWID) (2016) '#PracticeSolidarity: How We Build Feminist Futures', https://www.awid.org/resources/practicesolidarity-how-we-build-feminist-futures (last checked 17 September 2018)

AWID (n.d.) *Building a Feminist Resource Mobilisation Strategy*, https://www.awid.org/sites/default/files/atoms/files/building_a_feminist_resource_mobilization_strategy_2.pdf (last checked 17 September 2018)

Bah, Valerie and Felogene Anumo (2017) '"The revolution will not be NGO-ised": four lessons from African feminist organising', 50:50 openDemocracy, 31 July, https://www.opendemocracy.net/5050/felogene-anumo-and-valerie-bah/four-lessons-african-feminist-organising (last checked 4 October 2018)

Batliwala, Srilatha (2011) *Feminist Leadership for Social Transformation: Clearing the Conceptual Cloud*, New Delhi: CREA, https://www.uc.edu/content/dam/uc/ucwc/docs/CREA.pdf (last checked 4 October 2018)

Brehm, Vicky Mancuso (2004) 'Autonomy or Dependence? North–South NGO Partnerships'. INTRAC Briefing Paper No. 6, http://cercle.lu/download/

partenariats/INTRAC1autonomy1or1dependence.pdf (last checked 17 September 2018)

Carty, Linda and Chandra Talpade Mohanty (2015) 'Transnational Feminist Engagements: Neoliberalism and the Politics of Solidarity', in Rawwida Baksh and Wendy Harcourt (eds.) *The Oxford Handbook of Transnational Feminist Movements*, New York: Oxford University Press, 82–115

Choudry, Aziz and Dip Kapoor (eds.) (2013) *NGOization*, London: Zed Books

CIVICUS (2018) 'State of Civil Society Report', https://www.civicus.org/index.php/state-of-civil-society-report-2018 (last checked 9 September 2018)

Cohen, Michael, Maria Figueroa Küpçü and Parag Khanna (2009) 'The New Colonialists', *Foreign Policy*, http://foreignpolicy.com/2009/10/07/the-new-colonialists/ (last checked 30 July 2018)

Cornwall, Andrea (2006) 'Historical perspectives on participation in development', *Commonwealth & Comparative Politics* 44(1): 62–83

Crenshaw, Kimberle (1989) 'Demarginalizing the Intersection of Race and Sex: A Black Feminist Critique of Antidiscrimination Doctrine, Feminist Theory and Antiracist Politics', *University of Chicago Legal Forum*, vol. 1989, Article 8, https://chicagounbound.uchicago.edu/cgi/viewcontent.cgi?article=1052&context=uclf (last checked 17 September 2018)

Edwards, Bob and John D. McCarthy (2004) 'Resources and Social Movement Mobilization', in David Snow, Sarah A. Soule and Hanspeter Kriesi (eds.), *The Blackwell Companion to Social Movements*, Malden, MA: Blackwell Publishing, 116–52

Enloe, Cynthia (2017) *The Big Push: Exposing and Challenging the Persistence of Patriarchy*, Oakland, CA: University of California Press

FRIDA | The Young Feminist Fund and AWID (2016) *Brave, Creative, Resilient: The State of Young Feminist Organizing*, https://youngfeministfund.org/joint-research-by-frida-awid (last checked 17 September 2018)

Fuchs, Christian (2006) 'The self-organization of social movements', *Systemic Practice and Action Research* 19(1): 101–137

Gibson, Cynthia (2018) 'Participatory Grantmaking, Has Its Time Come?', Ford Foundation, https://www.fordfoundation.org/media/3599/participatory_grantmaking-lmv7.pdf, (last checked 13 September 2018)

Gregory, Ann Goggins and Don Howard (2009) 'The Non Profit Starvation Cycle', *Stanford Innovation Review*, https://ssir.org/articles/entry/the_nonprofit_starvation_cycle (last checked 30 July 2018)

Guerrilla Foundation (no date) 'A journey towards participatory grantmaking – Part 1', http:// guerrillafoundation.org/journey-participatory-grantmaking/ (last checked 13 May 2021)

INCITE! Women Of Color Against Violence (2007) *The Revolution Will Not Be Funded: Beyond the Non-Profit Industrial Complex*, Cambridge, MA: South End Press

The Lafayette Practice (2014) *Who Decides? How Participatory Grantmaking Benefits Donors, Communities, and Movements*, Paris: The Lafayette Practice

Lemma, Solome (2018) '25 Powerful Ways that Funders Can Support Social Movements', *Inside Philanthropy*, https://www.insidephilanthropy.com/home/2018/5/10/25-powerful-ways-funders-can-support-social-movements (last checked 12 September 2018)

Mannell, Jenevieve (2012) '"It's just been such a horrible experience." Perceptions of gender main-streaming by practitioners in South African organisations', *Gender & Development* 20(3): 423–434, https://policy-practice. oxfam.org.uk/publications/search?q=mannell;sort=publication_date (last checked 4 October 2018)

Moorhead, Joanna and Joe Sandler Clarke (2015) 'Big NGOs prepare to move south, but will it make a difference?', *The Guardian*, https://www.theguardian. com/global-development-professionals-network/2015/nov/16/big-ngos-africa-amnesty-oxfam-actionaid (last checked 10 September 2018)

Murdock, Donna (2003) 'Neoliberalism, gender, and development: institutionalizing "post–feminism" in Medellin, Colombia', *Women's Studies Quarterly* 31: 129–53

Okech, Awino (2009) 'Building a grassroots based movement: GROOTS Kenya', *Development* 52(2): 224–9

Oyakawa, Michele (2017) 'Building A Movement in The Non-Profit Industrial Complex'. Unpublished Dissertation, University of Ohio, http://rave. ohiolink.edu/etdc/view?acc_num=osu1500393653574528 (last checked 30 June 2018)

Ravindran, T. K. Sundari and Aarti Kelkar-Khambete (2008) 'Gender mainstreaming in health: looking back, looking forward', *Global Public Health* 2008(3 Suppl 1): 121–42

Roy, Arundhati (2014) 'The NGO-ization of Resistance', Massalijn, http:// massalijn.nl/new/the-ngoization-of-resistance/ (last checked 5 September 2018)

Sinclair, Amanda (2014) 'A Feminist Case for Leadership', in Joy Damousi, Kim Rubenstein and Mary Tomsic (eds.) *Diversity in Leadership: Australian women, past and present*, Canberra: ANU Press, 17–35

United Nations Trust Fund to End Violence Against Women (2012) 'Grant Guidelines', https://grants.unwomen.org/untf/cfp/guidelines (last checked 17 September 2018)

The Whitman Institute (2018) 'Trust-Based Philanthropy', http://thewhitman institute.org/grantmaking/trust-based-philanthropy/ (last checked 12 September 2018)

World Economic Forum (2015) *Outlook on the Global Agenda 2015*, Cologny: WEF

Wright, Glen (2012) 'NGOs and western hegemony: causes for concern and ideas for change', *Development in Practice* 22(1): 123–34

Young Feminist Wire (2016) 'Call for blogs: #PracticeSolidarity', http://yfa. awid.org/2016/05/call-for-blogs-practicesolidarity/ (last checked 13 May 2021)

CHAPTER 10

Paid work: the magic solution for young women to achieve empowerment? Evidence from the Empower Youth for Work project in Bangladesh

Pushpita Saha, Saskia Van Veen, Imogen Davies, Khalid Hossain, Ronald van Moorten and Lien van Mellaert

Abstract

Recently the 'demographic dividend' has attracted attention from policymakers because of the promise it delivers for development. But it has attracted criticism for taking an instrumental approach to young people rather than focusing on equality and rights. A similar critique has come from feminists evaluating livelihoods programming focusing on women's 'economic empowerment'. In this chapter, we draw on evidence from the Empower Youth for Work (EYW) project in Bangladesh to show why youth employment programmes need to challenge complex gender- and age-related barriers to young women's full participation. Research findings confirm young women's sizeable contribution to the economy through unpaid care work and informal employment. They also highlight the powerful role of gendered social norms that prevent young women from taking full advantage of training and income-generating opportunities. Youth employment programming needs to move beyond a narrow focus on 'economic empowerment' and instrumentalist approaches to ensure the current focus on youth is as empowering as it can be to young women.

Keywords: Young women; paid work; holistic empowerment; transformational change; social norms

Introduction

Alleviating poverty and enabling women to make some income can better lives, but the enabling environment that confirms the right to work, to property, to safety, to voice, to sexuality, and to freedom is not created by sewing machines or micro-credit alone (Sholkamy 2010, 257).

Gender equality and the empowerment of women have been development priorities for many years now, even while much remains to realise policy commitments (Porter 2013). In contrast, young people are only now being recognised as a constituency in which development funders, the international development agencies, and governments are taking an interest, beyond traditional concerns including child and adolescent education and health (Matin and Hulme 2003). Amid awareness of changing demographics in many developing countries where populations are becoming younger, many international development communities and governments are directing their funding and policy energies towards youth employment initiatives. Gender equality and women's rights are also policy imperatives for governments and development funders, and some youth employment initiatives are focused solely or mainly on young women's access to vocational skills training and economic engagement.

This chapter reflects on our progress in Oxfam Bangladesh to understand the relationship between paid work/employment and empowerment, focusing on projects we have been undertaking with young women. We focus in particular on the Empower Youth for Work (EYW) project in Bangladesh, which started in June 2016. In EYW, our approach to economic empowerment is anchored in relation to those broader empowerment issues and to the wider structural change Oxfam seeks for women in its gender justice approach.[1]

The EYW project is a multi-country project that focuses on the economic and overall empowerment of young women and men in rural climate-affected areas in Bangladesh, Pakistan, Indonesia, and Ethiopia. It has a strong emphasis on young women, and systematic consideration of the effects on climate change and food security. It started in 2016, and is due to conclude in 2021. The EYW project has a holistic approach to empowerment, where the agency and skills of young people, economic opportunities, and an enabling environment all contribute to the empowerment of young women and men.

In line with Rys Farthing's (2012) conceptualisation of youth participation, the EYW project sees young women and men as having a right to participation; they are not merely considered as project beneficiaries, but expected to take part in, express their views on, and share decision-making power in the implementation of project activities as leaders and partners. The EYW programme's theory of change reflects this thinking and applies a holistic approach to drive young women's economic and overall empowerment through effectively: (1) our work on agency, capacity, and skills; (2) linking young people to existing and new economic opportunities, including access to finance; and (3) addressing restrictive social norms and policies.[2]

In the next section, we offer a short account of current policy approaches to youth in Bangladesh, from a gender perspective, before looking in detail at the EYW project.

Youth and the 'demographic dividend' in Bangladesh: a gender perspective

In Bangladesh, as in many other countries, the youth population is at an all-time high (The Commonwealth 2016), with 15–24-year-olds making up 18.16 per cent of the total population, with more young women than young men (Bangladesh Bureau of Statistics 2013, 5). The large proportion of youth within the working age range is seen as a one-time demographic 'window of opportunity', decreasing dependency ratios (that is, the proportion of the population of working age compared to the proportion of children and elderly) and increasing the labour force. This is seen as a 'demographic dividend', promising unprecedented economic growth (Bloom *et al.* 2003).

However, the relationship between growth in the youth population, youth employment, and economic development is not straightforward. Only 42 per cent of the youth labour force is involved in economic activities (Bangladesh Bureau of Statistics 2017, 24). Young women, in particular, are unable to make use of economic opportunities; the youth labour force participation rates for men and women are recorded at 62.9 and 21.5 per cent, respectively (*ibid.*). However, these statistics hide the participation of young people – and particularly women – in informal jobs and unpaid care (UNICEF Bangladesh 2011). Young women's existing contribution to the economy goes largely marked and measured, and policies are needed that address their need for decent work (ILO 2013, 37). Keeping to its commitments on both gender equality and promoting youth employment, the government has carried out various initiatives to help promote young women's employment and economic empowerment. Development experts have recommended heavy investment in education, skills development, and employment generation for youth, and specifically for young women (World Bank 2017).

Seizing on this recommendation, and encouraged by increasing donor interest in funding youth employment programmes, the government of Bangladesh has set a national target to increase enrolment in vocational education to 20 per cent of the entire student cohort in its 7th Five Year Plan, including increasing the proportion of young women in training programmes (World Bank Office Dhaka 2017, 16). The theory behind the strategy is simple: equipping young women with vocational skills and expanding their labour force participation will enable them to contribute more than they do at present to national development. This is widely spoken of as 'economic empowerment', and some conflate this term with the wider goal of 'empowerment' and 'gender equality'.

But paid work and employment cannot deliver change for individual women facing multiple forms of discrimination, which are social and political in nature as well as economic. They are also not sufficient to deliver change for women as a collective marginalised group, as we show in the next section which recalls key contributions to the feminist literature on women, empowerment, and gender equality.

Feminist insights into empowerment and the importance of paid work

Amartya Sen defines empowerment using the language of capabilities: people's potential to live the lives they desire and to achieve valued ways of 'being and doing' (Sen 1985). There is a recurring debate in international development policy and practice around the relationship between paid work and women's empowerment. Much of this has focused on one country: Bangladesh (Kabeer 1998; Kabeer *et al.* 2011). Many development actors focus on the empowering potential of livelihoods and decent work, to argue that women's integration on fairer terms into markets is key to their empowerment.

Paid work that puts money in women's control can be a critical step towards empowerment, and it is important to recognise this. Naila Kabeer (1999) has outlined the importance of resources – including material resources – as an essential underpinning of women's empowerment. However, as Kabeer reminds us, resources include 'not only material resources in the more conventional economic sense, but also the various human and social resources which serve to enhance the ability to exercise choice' (*ibid.*, 3). In addition, empowerment also requires structural change – including challenging social norms – to transform gender-biased institutions that discriminate against women (Kabeer 1994).

In recent years, development actors have adopted the phrase 'economic empowerment' to denote the importance of resources to women's empowerment. Women's economic empowerment refers to the ability of women to enjoy their right to control and benefit from the resources, assets, income, and their own time, and to manage risk and improve their economic status and well-being (DAC Network on Gender Equality 2011). This terminology is not always welcomed by feminists, who recognise the danger of individual women producers being seen as a sufficient aim for those development actors who are more reluctant to call for genuine transformation of gender, race, and class power relations (Chant and Sweetman 2012). Feminists have also critiqued the idea of inclusion in markets when the inequalities that underpin economic relations are not addressed, arguing that this may result in worsening women's living conditions and adding to their stress (Lairap-Fonderson 2002).

Feminist writers emphasise the need for women themselves to lead development, and point out that development practice needs to consciously step back from prescribing solutions or developing programming without women's participation (Moser 1989). Current approaches to youth programming could learn from these insights. Young people have the right to participate as leaders in development initiatives, instead of being considered as passive recipients of project interventions (International Planned Parenthood Federation 2016).

Young women's empowerment in Bangladesh: what does the literature tell us?

It is a consensus among many development experts and feminist activists that Bangladeshi women have made considerable gains on the gender equality front since the country's independence in 1971 (Nazneen *et al.* 2011). Various economic and social development indicators demonstrate that Bangladesh has made substantial progress in increasing women's access to education and health care and in improving women's participation in the labour force. There is comprehensive literature on the economic opportunities of microfinance and the garment industry (see Goetz and Sen Gupta 1996; Kabeer 2001a, 2001b; Mahmud 2003), even while there is debate about the extent to which the employment opportunities open to women can deliver empowerment worthy of the name. At the same time, however, there are also attacks on women's rights and reversals in gender equity, including a generalised shift to fundamentalism in religion and religious politics (Adams 2015).

In keeping with the invisibility of young women from employment statistics, there is little literature focusing specifically on the empowerment of young Bangladeshi women as a specific group. The literature on young women from a feminist perspective tilts heavily on the impact of early marriage on young women, and their sexual and reproductive health rights (SRHR), recognising that most female adolescents aged over 18–20 in rural Bangladesh are married with children (e.g. Deeba Chowdhury 2004; Field *et al.* 2008). However, what has been less explored is the role early marriage and poor access to SRHR services play in preventing young women doing paid work.

Literature on women's responsibilities as providers of unpaid care in the global South is only beginning to emerge, and has not focused on a thorough life-cycle analysis and the specific limitations that these roles place on young women. Empirical data reveal that women of all ages receive less income for their labour than men, and are more likely to be found in irregular, informal, and vulnerable forms of employment. The growth rates and profitability levels of businesses led by women are also lower than those led by men, and fewer women are found in positions of economic leadership. Women also move in and out of the paid work force more frequently than men.[3] We also know that women, young or adult, living in rural or urban areas, have difficulty obtaining the same specialised knowledge and skills as men (Government of Canada 2013, 2). Women are less likely to attend training opportunities that are provided far from home and, as such, often end up accessing low-quality programmes close to home. Women also have limited capacity to access equivalent business and financial services, and profitable market linkages, even after receiving training or financial support to start a business. Women also face institutional constraints, such as biased legal environments, that limit their ability to control or own productive resources or to engage in economic work.

The EYW project in Bangladesh

The EYW project in Bangladesh began in June 2016, and involves 67,000 young women and men (70 per cent women and 30 per cent men). The project consciously takes an approach which draws on feminist insights into gender inequality and the empowerment of women, as well as insights into youth rights and participation.

Learning from earlier programme experience

Our approach in EYW in Bangladesh draws on experience gained in the first phase of another programme, the Resilience through Economic Empowerment Climate Adaptation Leadership and Learning (REE-CALL) programme (Oxfam 2017a). REE-CALL aims to ensure that women and men most at risk of disaster and climate change in Bangladesh are able to thrive in spite of shocks and change. The project aimed to facilitate sustainable income and employment options for vulnerable women and men by creating access to training services, natural resources, and market linkages, and forming community-based organisations (CBOs), to strengthen collective and individual actions towards fulfilment of rights and entitlements of vulnerable households and promote transformational leadership of women.

The first phase of REE-CALL ran from 2013 to 2017, and worked with 76,000 adult participants above the age of 18, both women and men. The project did not target younger participants separately within the adult group. It worked through 800 CBOs in 12 districts, representing three distinct disaster-prone ecological zones of Bangladesh: Haors, Chars, and Coast (Oxfam 2017a).

The endline evaluation of the project conducted in late 2017 (Oxfam 2017b) revealed that 81 per cent of men and 75 per cent of women in the project areas now had fulltime paid work. In contrast, before the project began, 53 per cent of men and 45 per cent of women in the project areas had been in full-time paid work.

However, we found women had not necessarily experienced an increase in control over resources, or increased ability to act independently. Only 15 per cent of women reported being able to sell their products by themselves, or negotiate selling prices, delivery times, and other market-related actions in connection with their business. Only just over one-third (38 per cent) of the women reported having greater control over household and community-level decision-making processes and resources, and receiving more co-operation from their husbands and other male household and community members.

Strikingly, women members of CBOs that approached women's economic empowerment more holistically, using a feminist approach, reported more positive changes that went beyond just earning an income. One hundred CBOs in four districts – Jamalpur, Kishoreganj, Nilphari, and Satkhira – were managed by women, and, in these cases, more than 1,700 women members had some control over markets in terms of price negotiations. These CBOs facilitated connections to financial institutions, such as microfinance institutes and banks, and provided specialised capacity-building support in terms of knowledge and skills required for sustainable saving and access to credit, cash, and capital by its female members.

Also striking was that 28 producer groups with a particularly high level of business success had 75 per cent female management committees. Fifty-two per cent of the members of these CBOs also became active members of other community groups, including groups that supported local government activities and mediated village *Shalish* (arbitration). The female members of these groups reported more freedom of mobility and control over household resources. The CBOs which conducted effective couples' training, family-level consultations on gender equality, care work analyses, and awareness activities on gender-based violence with community members, and engaged men as champions for women's empowerment, saw improved qualitative outcomes in their communities on indicators related to women's holistic empowerment.

Despite not having considered young women as a distinct group within the project participants, our research revealed that the demands, needs, barriers, and opportunities for women of different ages varied significantly. Unmarried young women, mostly aged between 15 and 24 in rural Bangladesh, had less care work than married women with children, so potentially had more time for paid work. However, social norms held them back. Some were reluctant to get engaged in paid work outside the home as they felt it would negatively impact their prospects of making a good marriage. Their families were concerned that a young unmarried woman working outside with male employers would lead to community censure concerning a young woman's 'moral character', and stigmatise the family. We learnt that programmes needed to encourage greater acceptance of young women going outside the home. In addition, young women needed skills training and economic opportunities in environments with more security, to lower their risks of sexual harassment and gender-based violence.

Another set of insights from REE-CALL concerned differences in financial resources available to older and younger women. Although the husbands of adult married women exercised control over their wives' income and decision-making in most instances, they were sometimes willing to provide business capital. Unmarried young women, in contrast, were less likely to secure the capital needed to start any new business venture, either from formal or informal channels, due to lack of support from family members and a culturally entrenched distrust within financial institutions regarding giving finance to young people, especially young women, without high collaterals. Family members of unmarried young women were reluctant to provide collateral for two reasons: first, they believed young women were not equipped to run a business and, second, they feared that any income arising from that business would eventually go to her in-laws' family. Age-related norms, which deemed young people as incapable of managing finances, starting businesses, or making decisions, were therefore intersecting with gender-related norms, resulting in the double marginalisation for young women.

These observations further solidified our realisation that our interventions, especially those around creating an enabling environment to facilitate young women's holistic empowerment, must be tailored to reflect these diverse needs and challenges of women of varying ages and marital status. Specifically, we recognised that a youth-led approach is critical, building the knowledge and capacities of young women, supporting their participation and agency, and shifting social norms which exclude them from the decision-making processes affecting their lives.

Learning from EYW's Baseline Survey

As part of the EYW project inception phase, we conducted a large-scale Baseline Survey in the project areas (Rangpur, Rajshahi, Barisal, and Khulna), among youth and in the wider community (Oxfam 2017b). Our sample included 915 Bangladeshi youth aged 15–29, mostly from rural areas, of whom 70 per cent are female and 30 per cent male.[4]

The Baseline Survey (Oxfam 2017b) revealed many important insights into the sample population. We asked the sample about their current occupations, including details of work or education. Due to the age of the sample, education was a main activity for many: 67 per cent of young men and 45 per cent of young women said they were students. The current level of education of the participants in our sample was relatively low: 42 per cent of men and 25 per cent of women had an upper secondary diploma or higher degree, compared to the national averages of 53 and 46 per cent for boys and girls, respectively (Bangladesh Bureau of Educational Information and Statistics 2017, 53). This can be explained by the fact that the EYW project is focused on rural areas that generally have lower levels of education. Clearly, however, since many of our sample are still receiving education, this picture will change and evolve as each participant continues through the system.

The Baseline Survey also revealed a very clear and absolute gender difference in terms of paid employment. Some 21 per cent of young men currently had a paid occupation, as compared to only 5 per cent of young women. Again, this is not very surprising given the overall country context and the project's focus on climate-affected and often more remote areas, with strong traditional gender norms. The high number of students in our sample also explains the low paid employment percentages, since they were questioned about their main occupation and, as outlined above, the majority of our sample was still involved in education. Forty-three per cent of young women said that they were housewives (and hence working unpaid as carers), while just 2 per cent of young men said they worked similarly in the home. These statistics reveal striking differences, even when accounting for some respondents combining several occupations, e.g. spending most of their time at home while being in part-time work or education. Eleven per cent of men and 7 per cent of women said they were unemployed. Three per cent of young men and 1 per cent of women said they owned a business. Other categories chosen by respondents related to, for example, agricultural business and daily wage labour to get a clear view of the type of paid employment in our sample (14 per cent of men and 2 per cent women).

The Baseline Survey revealed interesting findings on a range of key areas, two of which we focus on below. These are gender differences in agency between young women and men, and differences in young women's and young men's occupational preferences.

Gender differences in agency between young men and women

At the start of this chapter, we highlighted that without access to money and material resources, people cannot exercise meaningful agency. We explored the importance of agency in our Baseline Survey, and aimed to expose gender differences in the degree of agency young women have, compared to that of young men. Based on Scales (2011), our complete working definition of agency in the Baseline Survey was as follows: 'The ability of and opportunity for young people to confidently express their views, needs and aspirations among peers, their community and towards power holders, leading to their meaningful involvement and/or leadership in decisions related to social and economic empowerment.'

We asked young women and men involved in the Baseline Survey whether their current income covers their household needs, giving their answers on a four-point scale ranging from 'To a great extent' = 4 to 'Not at all' = 1). We found a significant difference between our male and female respondents, with an average of 1.06 for young women and 1.44 for young men. This shows that for both young women and men, their income is not enough to cover the economic needs of themselves and often their parents and siblings or their own young families. For women, however, the disparity was greater, showing that the income gap between young women and men already exists at a young age.

The survey results revealed gendered differences in terms of agency. We measured agency by focusing on two of the four underlying dimensions proposed by Peter Scales (2011), one being 'empowerment' and the other 'comfort expressing voice' (*ibid.*). 'Empowerment' was defined as the extent to which a young person feels that they are being taken seriously by adults and the wider community. As this does not unambiguously mean they feel comfortable to voice their concerns, for example due to of a lack of knowledge or confidence to speak up, we included the additional measure of 'comfort expressing voice', meaning young people's perceived abilities to voice their concerns towards other youth, adults, and decision-makers within the community. 'Empowerment' was rated on a four-point scale from 'Strongly agree' = 4 to 'Strongly disagree' = 1, and 'comfort expressing voice' from 'Very comfortable' = 4 to 'Very uncomfortable' = 1. Young men scored 2.71 and 2.96, respectively, while their female counterparts scored lower on both, at 2.53 and 2.63, respectively. Young women in our sample were thus clearly less comfortable than men on all aspects of empowerment and voice related to agency in Peter Scales' (2011) definition quoted above, especially in speaking out to duty bearers in their communities. In all aspects of agency, young women seemed to have less capacity to act than their male counterparts.

Further statistical analysis also revealed a direct, positive relationship between the agency measurements above and other concepts, such as soft skills, enterpreneurial ambitions, and the command of technical skills. This means that someone who has a lower level of agency is also likely to have lower skill levels, and is less likely to feel confident setting up a business. While further research is needed to verify these findings, and they do not necessarily indicate a causal relationship, the implications for young women are far-reaching. More detailed findings and accounts of our methodology are available upon request.[5] However, we did not find a relationship between agency levels and having a paid occupation or having a source of income, as respondents with paid employment did not necessarily have high agency scores. A possible explanation is the low numbers of young women in our sample with a paid occupation or other income-generating or entrepreneurial activities (5 and 7 per cent, respectively) which makes it harder to detect any statistically signficant relations. However, this does also indicate that the relationship between empowerment and paid employment is more complex than many mainstream development actors assume.

Our Baseline Survey data therefore confirmed what development practitioners working with young women in Bangladesh are well aware of empirically: as well as differences in paid employment, income (and control of income), young women are less likely to benefit from a range of other, less tangible factors, including differences in agency and core soft and technical skills related to employability compared to young men. The Baseline Survey data informed our holistic programme approach related to young women's economic empowerment, which was integrated into the design of our interventions. We cannot expect an intervention which focuses on paid employment alone to deliver economic empowerment, let alone the wider and more ambitious goal of holistic empowerment as it is understood by feminist researchers and thinkers. If we merely focus on obtaining paid employment as a short-term objective in itself, this leaves many factors that contribute to gender inequality, youth marginalisation, and disempowerment of young women unsolved.

Differences in young women's and young men's occupational preferences

In the Baseline Survey, we also asked questions about the types of skills young women and men would prefer to be trained in. In this way, we hoped the EYW programme could tailor its technical training towards youth preferences. The results showed strong and significant gendered differences in terms of preference for enrolment in specific types of technical skills training. Whereas nearly half (44 per cent) of the young women surveyed were keen to learn technical skills related to the traditionally female-dominated sectors of tailoring and dressmaking, only 1 per cent of the young men surveyed were willing to learn a similar skill. In contrast, for traditionally male-dominated jobs such as electrical installation and maintenance, one-third of young men (32 per cent) were willing to learn these skills, versus 1 per cent of young women. For modern ICT-sector jobs – the example we used was mobile phone servicing – the pattern of male preference was similar (nearly one-third [29 per cent] of young men versus 2 per cent of young women).

These gendered preferences stem from pervasive social norms, as well as lower levels of agency among women. Young women may perceive that it will be easier for them to undertake tailoring and dressmaking-related economic activities because they already have some basic skills in these areas – learned from adult female members of their households. Another potential reason for such preferences is the prevailing narrative around what it means to be empowered – that is shared by NGO-based gender programming in rural areas. The website for one India-based NGO suggests: 'You can empower poor women in slum areas and rural villages with valuable sewing skills and a sewing machine so they can earn a respectable living and help their families' (India partners website, quoted in Cronin-Furman *et al.* 2017, 11–12). Young women see their peers and other female adults training in tailoring, receiving a sewing machine, and earning a modest income, and may interpret this as the road to economic sovereignty. But however potentially useful a small amount of money is when controlled by a young woman, increasing her sense of having 'power to choose' (Kabeer 2001b), the empowerment potential of learning a trade in an already crowded market is obviously limited.

The expressed preference for technical skills training and the types of professions chosen by young women show the deeply entrenched social norms that influence women's economic choices and opportunities. For example, a gender norm formed by normative and empirical expectations around how women should 'behave' in society sees tailoring as a 'fitting' job for girls, as it can be done from home alongside care work responsibilities. Feminist research showing the likelihood that women will make such choices dates back as far as the early 1980s, and shows, too, that these jobs are disproportionately likely to be located in the most informal and low-paid areas of the market (Heyzer 1981).

Learning from a qualitative study into barriers trapping young women in low-paid work

There are other economic and social reasons for women being trapped in low-paid, insecure work which create barriers to economic empowerment. Employers are commonly unwilling to employ young women in non-traditional trades or jobs. A qualitative study conducted to complement the Baseline Survey resulted in findings that once again confirm the literature about this, that has long existed, but whose findings are still little understood in some areas of policy and practice.

We found that the majority of the employers interviewed in all four project locations perceived that automated production work is too complicated for women. The study (Oxfam 2017c) was conducted with 20 small, medium, and large formal enterprises in two project locations of Bangladesh. The objective of the study was to understand what prevents employers from employing young females in non-traditional formal jobs, internship, apprenticeship, and mentorship opportunities.

Employers in this qualitative study voiced the belief that young women are not physically equipped to carry out labour-intensive production work. A large number of the employers are also concerned that employing young women would increase security concerns in the workplace and would require them to invest more in security measures – something that can be avoided by simply employing young men. Employers also opined that, due to young women's care work responsibilities, they are unable to maintain strict working times and shifts, as they take more leave and have more 'personal issues' distracting them from their productive work.

Feminist research has, once again, led the way with its focus on employers' attitudes as a barrier to decent work. In some contexts, employing young women can increase employers' profit margins. A key study into the garment sector in Third World exporting (Elson and Pearson 1981) showed that employers preferred to employ young women because of the comparative advantage that a young, female workforce offered them, even allowing for the potential downsides mentioned above. Women were seen as naturally patient and dexterous, and suited therefore to industrial sewing. They were also seen as secondary earners, justifying low wages compared to men. Many women workers are home-based workers, who are also attractive as a workforce since they are isolated and relatively easy to manage without fear that they will organise (Rock 2001).

Today's employment programmes need to be built on an awareness of how gendered economic, cultural, and social realities limit the agency of young women, reinforcing the existing barriers that keep them restricted to traditional gender roles. This means that young women are unable to achieve real economic freedom from earning income. Trapped in low-paid areas of the economy, they cannot hope to achieve a sustainable living, let alone any greater transformational change in the areas of physical and social mobility, their experiences of gender-based violence, and communal and political participation.

Learning from focus groups: enabling environments: broader norms at play

Clearly, social norms around gender roles and about the economic value of different types of work are significantly constraining young women from gaining decent work. Various social norms were identified during focus group discussions (FGDs) with young people at the programme-design stage in the EYW project areas, using a Social Norms Diagnostic Tool (Oxfam 2017d) developed by Oxfam to identify and measure norms in the economy among young people.

Our findings confirm the story from the feminist literature. Strong gender norms around work roles have a serious impact on the division of unpaid care work and paid or productive work between young Bangladeshi women and men. Men are seen as the providers in the family. Eighty-four per cent of the respondents in the Baseline Survey were in favour of men being the achiever outside the home and the women taking care of the family and children. The focus groups confirmed these findings, and justified them on grounds of perceived ability, and also the status of the work. One male participant said, 'It is humiliating for me as a man to do all housework, even if I can' (participant of FGD, Rangpur District, May 2017).

Predictably, norms about the economic value of different types of work were important barriers to inequitable division of work between young women and men. The community regarded care work as less enjoyable, less skilled and less physically demanding than the work typically carried out by men, while men were seen to make the largest contribution to the household and community – because the work they do is likely to make a greater financial contribution. Young men are unlikely to share care tasks that are considered unskilled drudgery.

Further norms affecting young women's economic empowerment related to sanctions for transgressing accepted gender roles. Our research found that gender-based violence was seen as acceptable when women and girls failed to fulfil their expected care roles – with community censure and domestic violence considered a suitable punishment if women and girls spent a lot of time outside the house, failed to provide food for family members, or did not take care of in-laws. Harassment on the street, on public transport or in the workplace was perceived as acceptable, should women take up jobs in the public sphere, particularly in markets – which were considered as men's domain. Alongside this, jeering at men undertaking care responsibilities was thought to be socially acceptable, especially with regards to tasks considered more demeaning, such as cleaning and washing clothes.

Norms relating to young women's marriage and motherhood were also found to uphold sanctions for women undertaking non-traditional tasks, with women who undertook work in markets and interacted with unknown men being seen as 'shrewish' and 'unattractive' (FGD, Rangpur District, May 2017). Women who failed to undertake their care tasks due to paid employment outside the home were seen as undesirable wives and mothers, and women were expected to give up paid work and regular employment upon marrying, and especially when having children. Going beyond norms on gender roles and the value attributed to different types of work, to looking at how to shift harmful norms relating to gender-based violence and marriage and motherhood, is crucial in supporting young women's engagement in paid work and wider empowerment.

Creating an enabling environment that addresses a wide variety of social and cultural factors that influence women's economic empowerment is therefore imperative. There is a clear need for holistic approaches that replace these limiting social norms with positive norms that support young women's transformational leadership in Bangladesh. If left unaddressed, these multi-faceted factors will prevent young women from transferring the gains they have made from economic engagement to improved social gains in both domestic and public domains.

Towards a more holistic approach on the empowerment of young women

Building on the learning from our Baseline Survey and other sources, the first phase of the EYW project began in June 2016, adopting a holistic approach which puts feminist empowerment and youth-led models at the forefront. Oxfam is working with local partners – UCEP Bangladesh, WAVE Foundation, RDRS Bangladesh and CODEC Bangladesh – to increase young women's agency, capacity, and soft and technical skills to empower them as active citizens who are able to find or create sustainable jobs. We are forming youth groups at village, union, and national level, with young people taking on leadership positions and acting as both co-creators and co-implementers of the programme. In mixed youth groups, young people are taking measures so that young women are supported to feel confident to speak up, take up leadership roles, and enter dialogues with their parents, community, local duty-bearers, and politicians.

Through our partners, young women are receiving training in soft skills – including self-efficacy, leadership capacity, gender equality and SRHR – as well as selected technical and entrepreneurial skills based on a detailed market assessment. We are actively identifying role models and mentors for young women, and linking them to existing job opportunities, both traditional and non-traditional. Young people themselves have conducted a credit market mapping in the project areas and are working with local microfinance institutions to ensure access to finance for those aspiring to start their own climate-resilient micro-businesses.

Young people are working with partners to influence the government and the private sector to improve opportunities and working conditions for young women, especially in the informal sector. This is done through improved standards for businesses related to fair wages, social security, child care and workplace anti-harassment policies. We are also working with the private sector to provide apprenticeship opportunities to both young women and men. We are leveraging these apprenticeship and mentorship programmes to break traditional gender roles and engage young women in non-traditional and more productive and profitable trades, such as electronics servicing and graphics designing.

Recognising the importance of social norm change, and of young women identifying and taking action on the issues which affect them, the project will also be taking forward suggestions emerging from the research. Through their youth groups, young women are already initiating innovative ways of raising awareness within their communities – from interactive dramas about women cycling (as it is socially unacceptable for young women to ride bicycles in public places) to campaigns on gender-based violence and shared care work responsibilities. Young people are already participating in local government budget and policy hearings, and starting to hold duty-bearers accountable on how youth development budgets should be determined and spent. They have also co-created a series of 16 personal stories of young people who have faced, fought, and overcome tremendous challenges to achieve social and economic freedom. The young women and men who created these stories are working with Oxfam and its partners to leverage them to influence a wide range of actors, from national policymakers and local community leaders to international donors.

Other strategies for addressing traditional gender roles and unequal labour division suggested by youth participants in the programme include raising awareness of women's care workloads and the need for men to share tasks; promoting examples of alternative family models; and pushing for changes to education and curricula on the acceptability of both girls and boys being able to do unpaid care and paid or productive work. Community-level campaigning for mindset change and policy change on prevention of early marriage and violence against women in public spaces was also put forward, alongside media campaigns to stop the humiliation of men who do care work. There is also demand among young people for greater capacity development in local governments on the application of social accountability tools, and for policy-influencing on issues of women's empowerment and youth development.

This youth-led advocacy supports a more holistic approach to young women's economic empowerment, both by challenging norms and structural barriers, while also supporting young women's increased agency and political participation. The findings from our Social Norms Diagnostic Tool provide support for our approach – comparing attitudes and norms during the FGDs showed younger people demonstrating more progressive, individual attitudes than the social norms identified. Moreover, the emerging success of youth-driven, community-level campaigns and awareness-raising interventions demonstrates the social advantages that arise from giving young people the chance to understand and practise active citizenship, and of supporting young women to identify issues affecting them and take action to address them. This reiterates the importance of taking a youth-led approach to effect norm and policy changes.

Conclusion

Current approaches to youth in development often focus on what youth can do for development, but both feminist and youth rights perspectives highlight the shortcomings of instrumentalist approaches which insufficiently focus on power. Young people – and in particular young women – will do more for development if they are able to realise their right to exercise agency and choice, and participate and lead development. Policymakers and practitioners on resilience and livelihoods are (re)discovering the truths and insights in feminist literature on what empowerment is, and how to support and encourage it. Our own programme evidence from the EYW project reflects the feminist literature's insights into the relationship between paid work, economic empowerment, and wider understandings of empowerment. Drawing on our programme experience from EYW in Bangladesh, we are taking these insights forward in our current and future programming. It is essential that policymakers and practitioners understand that paid work is not a magic bullet to empower young women. However, decent work is a critical element in empowerment processes, and programmes need to support young women into such work. While the provision of regular and decent income-generating work is an important entry point, sustainable and transformative change in young women's lives depends on projects adopting a feminist, youth-led approach. Focusing on economic aspects of empowerment is too limited, because this fails to address the social norms and structural power relations that keep young women poor and distanced from genuinely profitable paid work.

Notes

1. See Oxfam Policy and Practice website, https://policy-practice.oxfam. org.uk/our-work/gender-justice/womens-economic-empowerment) (last checked 12 September 2018).
2. See the Empower Youth for Work webpage at https://www.oxfamnovib.nl/ donors-partners/about-oxfam/projects-and-programs/empower-youth-for-work) (last checked 12 September 2018).
3. See 'Women's economic empowerment: Guidance note' (n.d.) Government of Canada, http://international.gc.ca/world-monde/issues_development-enjeux_developpement/priorities-priorites/women-femmes.aspx?lang= eng (last checked 4 October 2018).
4. EYW Bangladesh also has specific interventions targeted at adults and the community as a whole, and in the Baseline Survey, we additionally surveyed 202 adult community members in the same locations, to get a better understanding of the overall environment and social norms at play.
5. For further detailed technical information on the methodology of the Baseline Survey, contact Saskia Van Veen.

Notes on contributors

Pushpita Saha was previously the Senior Monitoring Evaluation Accountability & Learning (MEAL) Officer for Oxfam in Bangladesh.

Saskia Van Veen is an Impact Measurement and Knowledge specialist at Oxfam Novib in The Hague, Netherlands.

Imogen Davies was previously Global Adviser on Youth, Gender and Active Citizenship for Oxfam GB.

Khalid Hossain was previously the Economic Justice Resilience Programme Manager at Oxfam in Bangladesh.

Ronald van Moorten works as a researcher at Oxfam Novib in The Hague, Netherlands.

Lien van Mellaert was previously Monitoring Evaluation Accountability & Learning (MEAL) Lead for Empower Youth for Work at Oxfam Novib.

References

Adams, Nathaniel (2015) *Religion and Women's Empowerment in Bangladesh. Occasional Paper*, Berkley Center for Religion, Peace and World Affairs, Georgetown University, Washington, DC: Georgetown University

Bangladesh Bureau of Educational Information and Statistics (2017) *Bangladesh Education Statistics 2016*, Dhaka: BANBEIS, http://lib.banbeis.gov.bd/BANBEIS_PDF/Bangledesh20Education20Statistics%202016.pdf

Bangladesh Bureau of Statistics (2013) *2012 Statistical Yearbook of Bangladesh*, Dhaka: Bangladesh Bureau of Statistics

Bangladesh Bureau of Statistics (2017) *Quarterly Labour Force Survey: Bangladesh 2015–16*, Dhaka: Bangladesh Bureau of Statistics

Bloom, David, David Canning and Jaypee Sevilla (2003) *The Demographic Dividend: A New Perspective on the Economic Consequences of Population Change*, Santa Monica, CA: Rand

Chant, Sylvia and Caroline Sweetman (2012) 'Fixing women or fixing the world? "Smart economics", efficiency approaches, and gender equality in development', *Gender & Development* 20(3): 517–29, https://policy-practice.oxfam.org.uk/publications/fixing-women-or-fixing-the-world-smart-economics-efficiency-approaches-and-gend-251931 (last checked 4 October 2018)

The Commonwealth (2016) *Global Youth Development Index and Report* 2016, London: Commonwealth Secretariat

Cronin-Furman, Kate, Nimmi Gowrinathan and Rafia Zakaria (2017) 'Emissaries of Empowerment', Colin Powell School of Civic and Global Leadership, The City College of New York

DAC Network on Gender Equality (2011) 'Women's Economic Empowerment. Issues Paper', Paris: OECD DAC Network on Gender Equality http://www.oecd.org/dac/gender-development/47561694.pdf (last checked 4 October 2018)

Deeba Chowdhury, Farah (2004) 'The socio-cultural context of child marriage in a Bangladeshi village', *International Journal of Social Welfare* 13(3): 244–53

Elson, Diane and Pearson, Ruth (1981) '"Nimble fingers make cheap workers": An analysis of women's employment in third world export manufacturing", *Feminist Review* 7(1): 87–107

Farthing, Rys (2012) 'Why youth participation? Some justifications and critiques of youth participation using new labour's youth policies as a case study', *Youth & Policy* 109: 71–97

Field, Erica and Attila Ambrus (2008) 'Early marriage, age of menarche, and female schooling attainment in Bangladesh', *Journal of Political Economy, Harvard University* 116(5): 881–930

Goetz, Anne Marie and Rina Sen Gupta (1996) 'Who takes credit? gender, power and control over loan use in rural credit programmes in Bangladesh', *World Development* 24(1): 45–63

Government of Canada (2013) 'Women's Economic Empowerment: Guidance Note', Department of Foreign Affairs, Trade and Development, Government of Canada

Heyzer Noeleen (1981) 'Towards a Framework of Analysis', *IDS Bulletin* 12(3): 1–5

ILO (2013) *Decent Work Country Profile: Bangladesh*, Geneva: International Labour Organization http://www.ilo.org/wcmsp5/groups/public/---dgreports/---integration/documents/publication/wcms_216901.pdf (last checked 4 October 2018)

International Planned Parenthood Federation (2016) *Young at Heart: How to be Youth-centred in the 21st Century. An Introduction,* London: IPPF

Kabeer, Naila (1994) *Reversed Realities: Gender Hierarchies in Development Thought,* London: Verso

Kabeer, Naila (1998) *'Money Can't Buy Me Love'? Re-evaluating Gender, Credit and Empowerment in Rural Bangladesh. IDS Discussion Paper 363*, Brighton: Institute of Development Studies

Kabeer, Naila (1999) 'Resources, Agency, Achievements: Reflections on the Measurement of Women's Empowerment', *Development and Change* 30(3): 435–464

Kabeer, Naila (2001a) 'Conflicts over credit: Re-evaluating the empowerment potential of loans to women in Rural Bangladesh', *World Development* 29(1): 63–84

Kabeer, Naila (2001b) *The Power To Choose: Bangladeshi Women and Labour Market Decisions in London and Dhaka*, London: Verso

Kabeer, Naila, Simeen Mahmud and Sakiba Tasneem (2011) *Does Paid Work Provide a Pathway to Women's Empowerment? Empirical Findings from Bangladesh'. IDS Working Paper 375*, Brighton: Institute of Development Studies

Lairap-Fonderson, Josephine (2002) 'The disciplinary power of micro credit: Examples from Kenya and Cameroon' in Jane Parpart, Shirin Rai and Kathleen Staudt (eds.) *Rethinking Empowerment, Gender and Development in a Global/Local World*, London and New York: Routledge, 182–98

Mahmud, Simeen (2003) 'Actually how empowering is Microcredit?' *Development and Change* 34(4): 577–605

Matin, Imran and Hulme, David (2003) 'Programs for the Poorest: Learning from the IGVGD Program in Bangladesh, *World Development* 31(3): 647–65

Moser, Caroline O.N. (1989) 'Gender planning in the third world: Meeting practical and strategic gender needs', *World Development* 17(11): 1799–825

Nazneen, Sohela, Naomi Hossain and Maheen Sultan (2011) *National Discourses on Women's Empowerment in Bangladesh: Continuities and Change. IDS Working Paper No. 368*, Brighton: Institute of Development Studies

Oxfam (2017a) *End evaluation of resilience through economic empowerment, climate adaptation, leadership and learning (REE-CALL) project*, internal unpublished document

Oxfam (2017b) *Baseline report: Empower Youth for work Bangladesh*, internal unpublished document

Oxfam (2017c) *Baseline qualitative study: Empower youth for work Bangladesh*, internal unpublished document

Oxfam (2017d) *Empower youth for work: Social norms diagnostic tool*, internal unpublished document

Porter, Elisabeth (2013) 'Rethinking Women's Empowerment'. *Journal of Peacebuilding & Development*, 8(1): 1–14, http://doi.org/10.1080/15423166. 2013.785657

Rock, Marilyn (2001) 'The rise of the Bangladesh Independent Garment Workers' Union (BIGU)' in Jane Hutchison and Andrew Brown (eds.) *Organising Labour in Globalising Asia*, London and New York: Routledge 28–49

Scales, Peter C. (2011) 'Youth developmental assets in global perspective: Results from international adaptations of the developmental assets profile', *Child Indicators Research*, 4(4): 619–45

Sen, Amartya (1985) 'Well-Being, Agency and Freedom: The Dewey Lectures 1984', *The Journal of Philosophy*, 132(4): 169–221

Sholkamy, Hania (2010) 'Power, politics and development in the Arab context: or How can rearing chicks change patriarchy', *Development*, 53(2): 254–8

UNICEF Bangladesh (2011) *A perspective on gender equality in Bangladesh. From young girl to adolescent: what is lost in Transition? Analysis based on selected results of the Multiple Indicator Cluster Survey 2009*, Dhaka: UNICEF Bangladesh

World Bank Office Dhaka (2017) *Breaking the glass ceiling; challenges to female participation in technical diploma education in Bangladesh*, http://documents. worldbank.org/curated/en/717771486560820977/pdf/AUS2-REVISED-Bangladesh-Female-participation-in-TVET.pdf (last checked 4 October 2018)

World Bank (2017) 'Skills development', http://www.worldbank.org/en/topic/ skillsdevelopment (last checked 4 October 2018)

CHAPTER 11

Empowering youth in rural, up-country Sri Lanka through gender-equitable education and employment

Ruvani W. Fonseka

Abstract

This chapter explores findings from a qualitative case study on how young adults living in tea plantations in rural, up-country Sri Lanka identify and challenge community gender norms, and seeks to understand the role of educational development programmes in advancing gender equality. The study involved qualitative in-depth interviews, conducted over a period of two months, of young alumni and staff of a local non-government organisation that focused on rural youth education and employment in the area. With the support of the organisation, these youth – the majority of whom are female and from low-income backgrounds – have identified and are working to address many gender inequalities within their community. The chapter also seeks to understand how the organisation works within societal constraints, such as social and cultural norms, education, and family expectations, to advocate for the young women in this community. Participants of the study described major challenges to gender equality, as well as the strategies used to combat these issues. This chapter presents the organisation as a case study of rural youth empowering their peers through non-formal education and employment training, as told through the voices of its alumni and staff.

Keywords: Sri Lanka; youth; non-government organisations (NGOs); gender equality; non-formal education; rural communities

Introduction

Education is often regarded as a crucial tool with which to achieve development goals and gender equality within society. In 2005, the third Millennium Development Goal, to 'promote gender equality and empower women',[1] included decreasing the gender gap in education as one of its major indicators of success. Gender gaps are present at all levels of education, and contribute to widening the disparities between girls and boys and, later, women and men, throughout their lives. Addressing these gender gaps has long been seen as a critical element in the empowerment of women and the attainment of gender equality. Education can increase women's and girls' knowledge of their rights, improve their access to services and lead them to challenge patriarchal power relations within their families (Sen 1999). Education of women and girls has also been linked to higher rates of knowledge with regards to family planning, increased access to contraception and greater equity in household decision-making, as well as decreased rates of domestic violence (Jejeebhoy 1995). In addition to empowering individual women, education is an essential factor in collective empowerment, encouraging women to take action to organise and demand their rights. Finally, education is also seen as a key to realise wider social and economic goals: educating girls and women is an economic investment that can help with a very wide range of development priorities, ranging from reducing a country's pollution, to public health goals including reducing HIV rates and fertility rates (Summers 1994).

However, despite education being championed by development agencies using all these rationales, the notion of it as a route to women's empowerment has been questioned by some scholars who argue that formal education in traditional school systems can reinforce gender inequities and perpetuate disempowering stereotypes (Jayaweera 2002; Kabeer 2005). Gendered social norms reinforced by curricula used in schools can constrain social progress, transmitting a binary model of gender and sexual relations that limits the choices and freedoms of all students. Studies in Sri Lanka show that the relationship between education, work, and empowerment is not fixed (Malhotra and Mather 1997), and researchers and practitioners need to consider the additional impact of structural factors, such as family and society.

When formal education systems within patriarchal societies reinforce gender inequities, non-formal education and training – outside traditional school systems – can provide alternative pathways for women and girls to learn valued skills, overcome gender gaps, and access employment. In rural settings, youth are often unable to complete their formal schooling, either because of 'push' factors from the school system, such as teacher absenteeism, linguistic barriers, and strict standardised testing, or 'pull' factors from their environment, such as pressure to earn money or to marry early. Young rural women who have been overlooked in formal school environments can receive more gender-equitable educational experiences through non-formal education and training. These training programmes can help to fill in the gap between urban formal education systems and their less-resourced, rural counterparts, and prepare young women for better employment options. In addition to increasing employability, non-formal education programmes can foster participants' desires to challenge unequal power relations and problems affecting their communities, as in the case of an antiliquor movement started by members of a women's literacy programme in India (Niranjana 2002).

To what extent does informal education allow young adults of both sexes, but in particular young women, to identify and challenge community gender norms that limit their potential, and perpetuate gender inequality? In terms of the concerns of this issue of *Gender & Development*, to what extent are the goals of young feminists served by this kind of intervention, not only through its actual activities but because of the networking it enables between young women who can organise around shared priorities?

This chapter focuses on young alumni and staff of one non-government organisation (NGO) working in rural Sri Lanka. In this chapter, I refer to the NGO using the pseudonym 'Up-country Youth NGO' or 'UYN'. UYN focuses on rural youth education and employment in the up-country tea plantations of Sri Lanka. With the support of UYN, these young people, a majority of whom are female and from low-income backgrounds, have identified many gender inequalities in their community, and are working to address these. The chapter outlines the various strategies that up-country youth within the programme use to challenge prevailing gender norms that limit their potential. These strategies include: postponing early marriage; identifying employment opportunities for young women; challenging gender segregation and gendered divisions of labour; and increasing the number of female leaders.

My research involved nine young women and five young men who were alumni and staff of UYN. Alumni and staff were selected rather than current students because of their familiarity with the full extent of UYN's programming and their fluency in English. More than two-thirds of UYN's current student body (over 100 students) are women and, during the time of this research, over three-quarters of the teaching staff, all alumni of the programme, were women, including two-thirds of the school leadership team. This high proportion of women staff and students at UYN may be due to young women in the up-country having fewer options for employment, relocation, and further study than young men.

My research: aims and approach

An important element of feminist research is taking into consideration the position of the researcher. I am a young Sri Lankan-American woman, raised in the United States as a racial minority. I undertook this research for academic study, but the topic of the research interested me particularly because of my identity as a young feminist interested in the scope of development interventions to support feminist goals, even when these goals are not explicit. I was interested in the ways that young women – and young men also – could take programmes intending to support their individual development and empowerment, and use these in ways that created wider social change in their communities. My similarity in age to the youth I interviewed, my gender and my visible Sri Lankan ethnicity could have, as Mythri Jegathesan posits in her own work studying Tamil women in the up-country, prompted participants, particularly young women, to speak with me in a more open manner than they might have done with a researcher who differed from them along one of these axes (Jegathesan 2013).

However, despite my many similarities to the participants, I am different in some key dimensions, including my socioeconomic status as a Fulbright-funded US citizen,[2] my Sinhala ethnic background (the vast majority of participants identified as Tamil or Muslim),[3] and my non-fluency in Sinhala and Tamil, the two languages spoken by a majority of Sri Lankans. My inability to speak fluent Sinhala or Tamil did not appear to hinder my interviews and interactions with staff and students at UYN, which is an immersion English programme; however, I was not able to communicate freely with community members who had not attended UYN's programming and who did not speak English as fluently as UYN affiliates. This research is therefore a reflection of the perspectives of young people who are affiliated with UYN, and cannot be generalised to represent the views of the entire up-country population.

Finally, my own cultural background as a racial minority in the United States informed how I approached my research with up-country youth, who are mostly racial minorities within Sri Lanka. My background also meant that I was unfamiliar with most traditions and cultural norms taken for granted in the community I was researching. My lack of familiarity with community norms, combined with my visible Sri Lankan heritage, allowed me to ask naïve questions about cultural practices from the position of an 'insider/outsider' (Sherif 2001), and allowed participants to explain in their own words their perceptions of the norms within their community.

In the next section, I outline the context of the study. Following that, I share some details of the study aims and methods, before sharing my findings. I conclude the chapter by drawing out some of the most interesting findings, and consider the scope of programmes like UYN for empowerment of youth – in particular young women – in rural locations in Sri Lanka, with particular focus on how both young women and young men involved in such programmes can support the feminist goal of gender equality.

The context: young women in Sri Lanka's 'up-country'

Sri Lanka is a South Asian island country, with an estimated population of 20.74 million in 2015 (UN 2017). Sri Lanka has recently risen in the Human Development Index to reach 73 out of 188 countries, becoming a middle-income country in 2010 and attaining high human development status in 2015 (UN in Sri Lanka 2017, 15). However, after nearly 30 years of conflict, which ended in 2009, a large proportion of people in Sri Lanka remain living just above the poverty line, vulnerable to economic or climatic shocks, with nearly one in four living on less than US$2.50 a day during 2012–13 (*ibid.*). Sri Lanka is the least urbanised country in South Asia with only 18.2 per cent of the population living in urban areas (*ibid.*, 16). One in four households in Sri Lanka are female-headed (*ibid.*, 15).

Although Sri Lanka has one majority ethno-religious group, Sinhala Buddhists, it has a wide variety of minority ethnic and religious groups, including Tamils, Muslims, Hindus, Christians, Malays, indigenous people, and Burghers, the latter who are descended from marriages between European colonists and the locals they met upon arriving on the island (McGilvray 1982). Now a part of the British Commonwealth, in the past the country faced conflict and traded with three separate European colonial powers: first the Portuguese, then the Dutch, and finally Great Britain, which conquered Sri Lanka in 1815 and named it 'British Ceylon'. Despite Britain granting Ceylon (later Sri Lanka) independence in 1948, British influence remains in many facets of Sri Lankan life, including education, transportation, and government.

The up-country region

Sri Lanka's poor and vulnerable populations are disproportionately found living in three areas: the rural areas in the Northern and Eastern Provinces most affected by conflict until 2009, in the central parts of the country dominated by the plantation sector, and in Uva province (UN 2017). The central highlands, colloquially known as the 'up-country', were significantly affected by British colonial policies. The British identified the cool climate of the up-country as ideal for tea, rubber, coffee, and coconut plantations, which they established in the early 1800s. To cultivate these plantations, the British recruited Tamil-speaking indentured labourers from South India (Balasundaram 2011). Many of the descendants of these workers still live in the up-country today and still work on plantations. While Tamils are the largest proportion of the population, Sinhala and Muslim ethnicities are also represented as minority populations in the up-country.

People living in the up-country, particularly in the plantations, experience higher rates of poverty than the national average (Jegathesan 2015) and historically have had poor educational and occupational opportunities (Bass 2000). One of the major barriers to employment in the up-country is language. Most people in the up-country speak Tamil, which is a minority language in Sri Lanka. Inability to speak fluent English and/or Sinhala greatly reduces most up-country youth's ability to access job opportunities outside the tea plantations (Bass 2000).

Gender relations in Sri Lanka

The social, cultural, and economic status of women in Sri Lanka is complex. Women in Sri Lanka have had many political and educational successes in comparison to their neighbours in other South Asian countries. Sri Lankan women gained the right to vote in 1931, and the world's first female prime minister, Sirimavo Bandaranaike, was elected in Sri Lanka in 1960. Women make up nearly two-thirds of university students (University Grants Commission – Sri Lanka 2016, 38), and literacy rates are high, with no difference between men and women. Maternal mortality is also low in Sri Lanka, in comparison to other countries in the region (Kassebaum *et al.* 2014). These positive statistics suggest that, compared to its neighbours, Sri Lankan women experience fewer gender inequalities.

However, despite these comparative successes, Sri Lankan women still exist in a patriarchal society that limits their opportunities and freedoms (Marecek and Appuhamilage 2011). Although Sri Lankan women are highly educated and in the past have been elected to lead the country, Sri Lanka maintains the lowest political representation of women in all of South Asia, with women never surpassing 7 per cent membership in the national legislature (Inter-Parliamentary Union n.d.). Despite women attending universities in higher numbers than men (University Grants Commission – Sri Lanka 2016, 38), they make up only one-third of the country's labour force, with two-thirds of women not engaged in the formal labour market (Department of Census and Statistics 2016, 3). The most extreme form of gender inequality in Sri Lanka is displayed in rates of violence against women. Multiple studies have estimated rates of intimate partner violence at one in three women (Guruge *et al.* 2015, 134), and a study on violence in Sri Lanka found that over half of men and women agreed with gender-inequitable attitudes that condoned male violence and female subservience (de Mel *et al.* 2013, 23).

In the up-country, women face additional challenges based on their intersecting identities of gender, ethnicity, and class. Women are the majority of tea pickers on the tea plantations. Women tea pickers perform continuous and difficult physical labour for many hours each day, but are paid less than men – who work for fewer hours and are often in less physically demanding roles, such as supervising machinery. Despite the sector's dependence on women's labour, the majority of labour unions in the up-country are led by and are almost completely comprised of male members – who do not prioritise issues of gender equality in their advocacy (Bass 2012). In addition, women's wages are often controlled by male family members (World Bank 2015).

Young women in the Sri Lankan up-country

Very few studies have been done in the up-country that focus specifically on young women and gender equality and, as in many parts of the world, more research must be done to understand up-country youth's gender-equality activism through their own words and experiences (Lewis and Marine 2015). Young women in the Sri Lankan up-country face a large number of gender- and age-related barriers to equality. Young people of both sexes face limited educational and employment options. Young women in particular are often prevented by their families from leaving their communities to seek work – something that is more commonly accepted among their male peers (Kingsolver 2010). Even within their home communities, many jobs, such as waiting tables in a restaurant, are only seen as acceptable for young men, not young women, greatly limiting women's employment options (Bass 2000).

Up-country women are encouraged to marry early and take on the full burden of family planning, and combined economic and societal pressures decrease their control over their own fertility (Balasundaram 2011). A major limiting factor for up-country young women's mobility, education, and job opportunities is the need to remain 'marriageable' (Jegathesan 2013). Young women who extend their studies or consider leaving their communities for work are perceived to be damaging their reputations and lowering their parents' likelihood of finding them an interested husband. Because of the expectations placed on them by their communities, families, and potential or actual spouses, young women in the up-country are greatly restricted in their mobility, work opportunities, and options to delay marriage and motherhood. Similar to national levels, domestic violence rates are high in the up-country, and it has been found that children who are exposed to violence have a higher risk of perpetrating and experiencing violence in adulthood, thus continuing the cycle (Fonseka *et al.* 2015).

Up-country Youth NGO (UYN): creation and activities

UYN was founded in 2009 by two British citizens. The founders, when visiting Sri Lanka two years prior, were disturbed by the poor socioeconomic status of up-country tea plantation workers and concluded that the low status of the workers was a direct consequence of British policies that had led to the establishment of the tea plantations. After consulting with local employers, the pair created UYN to help unemployed youth between the ages of 18 and 25 find secure and stable employment outside the tea sector. UYN was created as a local Sri Lankan organisation, and it is supported by an NGO in the UK whose major function is to raise funds for the programme in Sri Lanka. These funds come from various sources, including private donations, donations from Rotary Clubs,[4] and partnerships with Sri Lankan and international corporations with ties to the Sri Lankan up-country. The programme is managed by the founders, together with a team of staff who are all alumni of UYN.

UYN began as a free, full-time, year-long English and professional development programme for unemployed youth, focusing solely on improving the employability of up-country youth and widening their employment options beyond the tea sector. However, through extended engagement with youth in the English programme, UYN staff identified two further aims as equally important. UYN's second aim is to improve the emotional health of up-country youth. This aim arose from reports of domestic violence, pressure on female students to marry earlier than they wanted, and a number of suicide attempts by students. To help provide UYN students with coping strategies to address gender inequality and the range of other challenges they were experiencing in their daily lives, UYN developed an emotional health curriculum that is taught in conjunction with the English and professional skills development classes. UYN's third aim is to help young people in the up-country effect social transformation in their communities. This priority arose as a response to UYN students who expressed feelings of worthlessness and an inability to help their communities.

UYN works on all three of these aims currently, and has added a community service element also. This aims to develop the agency of up-country youth to help their communities. During their studies, every student of UYN teaches basic English classes to children in community schools who are under the age of 12. Additionally, every UYN main diploma student develops and implements a unique self-directed community service project to address a need in their own community. Finally, the 20 students at the end of each UYN main diploma programme who have shown the strongest aptitude for teaching are invited to receive a second year of free training, which focuses on developing their teaching abilities, spoken and written English, and professional skills.

UYN's teaching staff is completely made up of UYN alumni. The majority of them are female and all under the age of 30, and they serve as role models for the enrolled youth. UYN's programme and site managers are also young adults from the up-country, who studied English with UYN's founders before being recruited to lead the programme. During the time of this study, UYN's programmes in Sri Lanka were completely directed and staffed by young adults aged 21–29, who were alumni of UYN or studied English with its founders. UYN's responsive, youth-led focus on youth employment and gender equality made UYN an ideal site to study youth strategies for gender equality in the Sri Lankan up-country.

Research approach and methodology

Participant recruitment

During the two months of data collection (May–July 2017), I volunteered at UYN by leading teacher training courses for advanced students, substitute-teaching main diploma lessons, and providing professional development lessons to UYN's staff team. I lived in the community, sharing accommodations with some of UYN's managers. By situating myself within the community and volunteering daily at UYN, I became well known to the staff, students, and local alumni of UYN, and was able to develop a rapport with potential research participants.

I recruited alumni and staff who lived locally by approaching them individually and asking if they would be interested in speaking with me about gender in their community. A total of 14 UYN staff and alumni were interviewed – nine women and five men – representing all the major ethnic groups in the up-country (Tamil, Sinhala, and Muslim), and ranging in age from 21 to 29. To protect their privacy, participants are identified only by gender and age range: early 20s refers to ages 21–23, mid-20s refers to ages 24–26, and late 20s refers to ages 27–29. The study received ethical clearance from the Ethics Review Committee for Social Sciences and Humanities at the University of Colombo, Sri Lanka.[5]

Research methods

Over my two months at UYN, I conducted semi-structured, in-depth interviews with alumni and staff of UYN, lasting 30–45 minutes (Kvale and Brinkmann 2009). All quotations below come from these interviews. All interviews were conducted in English, which was possible because of the high level of English fluency fostered among staff and alumni of UYN. I used a directed content approach, both while developing the interview guide and during the resulting analytical procedures (Gibson and Brown 2009; Hsieh and Shannon 2005; Saldaña 2009). All interviews were coded using Dedoose online software version 8.0.42 (Dedoose 2018). Important interview excerpts were organised into potential patterns of association that highlighted major issues of gender equality discussed by participants (Ryan 2005). Finally, the excerpts were grouped to highlight the major challenges to gender equality that UYN has faced, and the strategies it has adapted to address them, with textual examples of each challenge and strategy. The findings are shared below.

Findings

Major challenges to gender equality addressed by UYN

Participants identified five major challenges to gender equality that UYN had developed strategies to address. The four that negatively affect young women are described below.[6] Participants described how these challenges affected young people in their community, and gave examples of how the strategies adopted within UYN helped mitigate these challenges.

Pressure for girls and young women to marry early

Participants spoke of the challenges faced by young women and girls in the up-country to marry when they chose, within the context of community pressures and expectations to marry early, and through arranged marriages (referred to as 'proposals'). While the participants were not against the idea of marrying someone chosen by their parents, many took issue with the extra pressure placed on girls to marry at an earlier age than they wanted. In response to this significant issue facing young women in their community, UYN alumni shared a set of strategies that they and their peers had developed and were using to delay marriage.

One young woman in her late 20s spoke about the skills she learned in UYN's emotional health and professional development classes that she used to negotiate delaying marriage with her family, and how her success has encouraged younger female family members to also delay their marriages and continue their education:

> Here at UYN I [developed] the courage to say no to my family with good reasons to many proposals … next year, I'll be 29. Just because of me,

other relatives have skipped their wedding[s] and have gone to follow higher education. One of my cousins is in India to study her higher education. I am really happy.

A female staff member in her mid-20s, who was also an alumna, credited UYN for helping her to delay marriage by extending her studies past A-Levels, and for even providing employment that allowed her to reject proposals credibly when she did not feel ready, thus postponing marriage by multiple years:

> Once I finished my A-Levels, from then there were proposals. I [gave] different reasons because I didn't want to get married. When I joined [UYN], there was a proposal. I said, 'No, I joined the course. Let me finish this and see.' I didn't want to – no, I don't want to! I joined here as an intern, then I had a job. I said [that] for three years I can't get married. I have signed a contract.

Gender segregation of young adults in schools and community settings

Another challenge to reaching the goal of gender equality that many of the participants described was strong pressure for young men and women to remain in gender-segregated groups, and to not interact with each other.

Despite this pressure that young people in the up-country face to segregate by gender, UYN has found ways, through its programmes and leadership development, to help young women and men to interact and see each other as equals. Although UYN teaches course-work in a classroom setting, the young staff and alumni highlighted the differences in how UYN integrates the genders, with one woman alumna in her late 20s saying: 'Here, students mingle with everyone … we are different than a government school.'

An alumnus of the programme in his early 20s described how UYN changed his perspective on gender and his own friendships:

> My best friend is a woman. When I count my [circle of] friends, there will be a lot of women, more than boys. UYN helped me to [become] closer to girls and to understand them. And it brought the perspective of gender.

Another young woman in her early 20s described how she had overcome her fear of interacting with boys through her time at UYN:

> I was scared, even to talk with boys. When I came to UYN I started to talk with boys. I didn't even smile; they thought I was terrified. At UYN, I learned to smile. I learned to interact with boys.

Some UYN staff shared their strategies for helping students to interact across genders. One woman teacher in her early 20s stated that, 'Girls and boys can sit together and they are friends. They know their limits.' This highlights the trust that UYN staff have in their students, who are also their peers. Finally, one male teacher in his early 20s described how students who are used to single-gender environments can be supported as they transition to mixed-gender interactions, while keeping gender differences in mind:

> It is not always about separating them. It is about teaching them how to be with a girl ... Let them sit together, but teach them to be positive with each other. That is what happens at UYN. We know that females have different stuff in their life and boys have different stuff too. As a teacher I know this.

Gendered division of labour in the home, school, and workplace

A fourth major challenge, described by the alumni and staff of UYN, was the pervasive social norm around the gendered division of labour, which considers men and boys to be better suited for formal labour participation, and girls and women to be better suited for household work. UYN staff participants described multiple strategies the organisation has adopted to challenge the gender-normative division of labour in the up-country. One female staff member in her early 20s described how UYN has actively redistributed roles within the organisation itself to be more gender-equitable:

> In the staff team, when we talked about events and outside responsibilities, most of the time boys take them, and girls take the inside responsibilities. In the school, girls used to sweep the school, but now we have changed it and the boys also sweep. I think teachers changed it. We discussed and we changed it. [The boys' tasks used to be] bringing the generator, finding chairs, poles, things like that. [The girls used to] sweep, decorate, make flowers, things like that. Much smaller [tasks]. People started volunteering [to do different things]. We had conversations about it and we changed it.

Another female staff member in her mid-20s described how, in her role to help co-ordinate employment placements for students and alumni of UYN, she has helped challenge the limitations that parents placed on female students' work opportunities:

> When I want to get good jobs for the girls, they will always tell that we can't go out of [this community], our parents will not let us go. I just need to change that thought. Males can work anywhere. It is easy for me to find jobs for the male students, but it is difficult to find places for the female students. They give a lot of reasons for not going. [I have succeeded] with a lot [of the girls]. I have talked to their parents ... I ask the parents to come and talk to me. I say, 'If you have problems you can call me and I will respond.' That's what I tell.

Gender-inequitable norms limiting opportunities for women and girls

The final feminist issue that youth of both sexes at UYN have actively sought to challenge is the prevalence of gender-inequitable norms in their families and communities that limit opportunities and experiences for women and girls. As part of its commitment to put women's rights and gender issues at the heart of its work, UYN has attempted to increase gender-equal norms and opportunities for girls and women, both within their own organisation and in the community. One female interviewee in her late 20s, who had a position in leadership at UYN, described how the opportunity she was given at UYN has impacted her community's view of women's work:

> In the outer world, these places would only be given to men, but here [at UYN] it is the opposite. All the chances will be given to us. It's good because we can go and make other changes ... Me and my sister are examples ... We can count the number of people who have really good jobs. [Community people] can say [about my sister and me] 'Look at them, we need to send our daughters to [be] educated.'

Female role models in senior positions can inspire not only younger women, but also men. A male participant in his early 20s spoke of the impact female leaders at UYN had on his perspective of women:

> This was where I learned under a female principal for the first time, and had a lot of female teachers. I learned what sort of changes a female can make. My [main] teacher was a female. I understood the improvement that women can give a community.

Another female participant in her mid-20s described the changes in her family that had resulted from her older sister attending classes and then working at UYN:

> In our culture, when the girl is 17, they should get married ... they should go out [to their husband's home] and not work. My sister has changed that completely. I didn't think I would study A-Levels and work. But all of it has happened because of my sister. She brought the change, and [our] parents understood.

Through the interviews, young men and women who had gone through UYN's programmes described how they were challenging community expectations around early marriage, gender segregation, gendered division of labour, and inequitable gender norms. Although never explicitly mentioning the term feminism, they shared the ways that they promote gender-equitable ideas and are working to make their communities more egalitarian for women and men.

Concluding thoughts: local experiences within the global context

The gendered challenges faced by young people in the Sri Lankan up-country, as reported by UYN's staff and alumni, are not unique to these youth. One in three women in the developing world is married before the age of 18, while in South Asia the proportion is higher at 46 per cent (UNICEF 2011). A lower marriage age has been linked to many negative outcomes for young women, including intimate partner violence (Jensen and Thornton 2003), lowered access to health care (Field and Ambrus 2008; Santhya *et al.* 2010), poverty (Otoo-Oyortey and Pobi 2003), and pregnancy complications (Santhya 2011).

Two of UYN's strategies that were particularly empowering to young women were the delay of marriage and the development of female leaders within the organisation. Researchers have linked low educational and employment opportunities to early marriage in many contexts (Bunting 2005). UYN, through its focus on extending opportunities and filling in gaps in education and employment for their majority female students, works to give young women concrete alternative options to marrying upon leaving formal schooling. In addition, UYN's programmes that were specifically developed to develop young people's self-worth and resilience gave some young women the tools to negotiate successfully, with their families, a delay in marriage, and to support younger female family members to make the same decision. UYN has shown what many development practitioners and policymakers suggest – advancing girls' and young women's education can contribute to delayed marriage (Jensen and Thornton 2003) and increases the likelihood of marriages being wanted (Erulkar 2013).

Young women are more likely to consider themselves as potential leaders if exposed to female role models in leadership positions (Hoyt and Kennedy 2008). Studies on female educational leaders have found that the endorsements and support they receive can greatly influence whether they decide to pursue educational leadership as a career or not (Young and Mcleod 2001). Additionally, girls can experience a lack of female teachers as role models as an obstacle to their education (Fentiman *et al.* 1999). UYN, by supporting female alumnae to become principals and programme directors, both supported young women in entering leadership positions typically reserved for men, and created visible female leader role models who could influence UYN students to consider leadership positions for themselves and rethink community limits on women's roles.

The strategies employed by young up-country adults who work and studied at UYN are linked to feminist actions by youth around the world. While discussing young feminists in the United States and the UK, Ruth Lewis and Susan Marine advocate for more empirical examinations of young feminists' actions, along with a more nuanced understanding of the complex environment in which they act – termed a 'feminist tapestry' (Lewis and Marine 2015). I believe that their arguments can be extended to the intersectional challenges faced by these young gender-equality activists in the Sri Lankan up-country, even though, like most of their peers in Sri Lanka, they do not explicitly identify with the term feminism. By sharing their lived realities, challenges, and successes, the youth at UYN give us many examples of how gender equality can be advocated by rural youth in a highly patriarchal environment. Their stories are just one part of the much larger tapestry of how non-formal education can contribute to gender equality for rural youth.

Acknowledgements

Thank you to the following people in Sri Lanka, the United States, and the UK for making this research possible: Malathi de Alwis, Patricia A. Conrad, Krishani Gayanthika, Anu Manchikanti Gomez, Tissa Jayatilaka, Ramya Jirasinghe, Jeanne Marecek, Tim Pare, Yadharshini Selvaraj, Kalinga Tudor Silva, and Kumudu Wijewardene. Thank you to Daniel Bass and Mythri Jegathesan for their insightful comments on a previous draft of this chapter, and to Samantha Hurst, PhD, for contributing her research expertise to the analysis as well as reviewing many previous drafts. This work was supported by a Fulbright US Student Grant, a programme of the United States Department of State, Bureau of Educational and Cultural Affairs [grant number 34162992].

Notes

1. The Millennium Development Goals (MDGs) were a set of eight international development goals set by global leaders during the United Nations' 2000 Millennium Summit (UN General Assembly 2000). The goals were focused on health, gender equality, education, sustainability, eradicating hunger and poverty, and development.
2. The Fulbright Program is a competitive fellowship programme sponsored by the United States to facilitate cultural exchange and improve intercultural relations between people from the United States and other countries (Jeffrey 1987).
3. In Sri Lanka, Sinhala people make up the majority ethnic group in the country. However, ethnic distributions vary across the island, and in the up-country, Tamils make up a majority of the population and Muslims are more highly represented than they are nationally.
4. Rotary Clubs are local chapters of Rotary International, an international service organisation. Clubs meet regularly and often choose charitable causes to support together. One of Rotary's goals is to reduce gender disparity in education. Rotary International's website is www.rotary.org (last checked by author 11 August 2018).
5. Prior to joining the study, each participant read and summarised a detailed information sheet on the study, and provided written consent. The research project received ethical clearance from the Ethics Review Committee for Social Sciences and Humanities at the University of Colombo, Sri Lanka (reference number ERCSSH/16/25).
6. One challenge faced specifically by male UYN students was the pressure for young men and boys to cut their education short and earn money to support their families. In many cases, this expectation has been passed down from fathers to sons, and this pressure is especially high for eldest sons. One alumnus in his mid-20s explained how UYN was able to keep him from dropping out when he was considering leaving UYN's classes for low-skilled work: 'My parents were not telling me to leave [UYN], but, as an elder child, I could understand what was my situation. I wanted to work, and I thought, "Why do I want to stay?" Then I came here and [UYN employed me part-time in a] project. I thought, "What about the money for bus fare?" UYN helped me to study until Grade 12 [by

providing bus fare]. They were really supportive.' In multiple instances, UYN has successfully prevented young men from ending their education early by providing the financial support needed to justify staying in the programme. Youth labour is a strong reason for young people to leave school early in many places, including Ghana (Fentiman *et al.* 2010) and Brazil (Duryea and Arends-Kuenning 2003). The pressure for eldest siblings to work has also been found in other settings, including Brazil (Emerson and Souza 2008) and Peru (Patrinos and Psacharopoulos 1997).

Notes on contributor

Ruvani W. Fonseka is a predoctoral fellow at the University of California, San Diego's Center on Gender Equity and Health.

References

Balasundaram, Sasikumar (2011) 'Stealing wombs: sterilization abuses and women's reproductive health in Sri Lanka's tea plantations', *Indian Anthropologist* 41(2): 57–78, http://www.jstor.org/stable/41921991 (last checked 4 August 2018)

Bass, Daniel (2000) *Malaiyaha (Up-Country) Tamil Identity and Politics in the Twenty-first Century*, Colombo: International Centre for Ethnic Studies

Bass, Daniel (2012) *Everyday Ethnicity in Sri Lanka: Up-Country Tamil Identity Politics*, Abingdon, Oxon and New York: Routledge

Bunting, Annie (2005) 'Stages of development: marriage of girls and teens as an international human rights issue', *Social and Legal Studies* 14(1): 17–38, https://doi.org/10.1177/0964663905049524 (last checked 4 August 2018)

de Mel, Neloufer, Pradeep Peiris and Shyamala Gomez (2013) *Broadening gender: Why masculinities matter*, Colombo: CARE International, http://www.care.org/sites/default/files/documents/Broadening-Gender_Why-Masculinities-Matter.pdf (last checked 4 August 2018)

Dedoose (2018) *Version 8.0.42, Web Application for Managing, Analyzing, and Presenting Qualitative and Mixed Method Research Data*, Los Angeles, CA: SocioCultural Research Consultants, LLC., www.dedoose.com (last checked 4 August 2018)

Department of Census and Statistics (2016) *Sri Lanka Labour Force Survey: Annual Report 2016*, Colombo: Ministry of National Policies and Economic Affairs, http://www.statistics.gov.lk/samplesurvey/LFS_Annual%20Report_2016.pdf (last checked 10 August 2018)

Duryea, Suzanne and Mary Arends-Kuenning (2003) 'School attendance, child labor and local labor market fluctuations in urban Brazil', *World Development* 31(7): 1165–1178, https://doi.org/10.1016/S0305-750X(03)00065-2 (last checked 4 August 2018)

Emerson, Patrick M. and Andre P. Souza (2008) 'Birth order, child labor, and school attendance in Brazil', *World Development* 36(9): 1647–1664, https://doi.org/10.1016/J.WORLDDEV.2007.09.004 (last checked 4 August 2018)

Erulkar, Annabel (2013) 'Early marriage, marital relations and intimate partner violence in Ethiopia', *International Perspectives on Sexual and Reproductive Health* 39(1): 6–13 (last checked 4 August 2018)

Fentiman, Alicia, Andrew Hall and Donald Bundy (1999) 'Comparative education school enrolment patterns in rural Ghana: a comparative study of the impact of location, gender, age and health on children's access to basic schooling', *Comparative Education* 35(3): 331–49, https://doi.org/10.1080/03050069927865 (last checked 4 August 2018)

Field, Erica and Attila Ambrus (2008) 'Early marriage, age of menarche, and female schooling attainment in Bangladesh', *Journal of Political Economy* 116(5): 881–930, https://doi.org/10.1086/593333 (last checked 4 August 2018)

Fonseka, Ruvani W., Alexandra M. Minnis and Anu M. Gomez (2015) 'Impact of adverse childhood experiences on intimate partner violence perpetration among Sri Lankan men', *PLoS One* 10(8): e0136321

Gibson, William and Andrew Brown (2009) *Working with Qualitative Data*, London, Thousand Oaks, CA, New Delhi and Singapore: Sage

Guruge, Sepali, Vathsala Jayasuriya-Illesinghe, Nalika Gunawardena and Jennifer Perera (2015) 'Intimate partner violence in Sri Lanka: a scoping review', *Ceylon Medical Journal* 60(4): 133–38

Hoyt, Michael A. and Cara L. Kennedy (2008) 'Leadership and adolescent girls: a qualitative study of leadership development', *American Journal of Community Psychology* 42(3–4): 203–219, https://doi.org/10.1007/s10464-008-9206-8 (last checked 4 August 2018)

Hsieh, Hsiu-Fang and Sarah E. Shannon (2005) 'Three approaches to qualitative content analysis', *Qualitative Health Research* 15(9): 1277–1288

Inter-Parliamentary Union (n.d.) 'Sri Lanka Parliament: Historical Archive of Parliamentary Election Results', http://archive.ipu.org/parline-e/reports/2295_arc.htm (last checked 10 August 2018)

Jayaweera, Swarna (2002) 'Women in Education and Employment', in Swarna Jayaweera (ed.) *Women in Post-Independence Sri Lanka*, Thousand Oaks, CA: SAGE, 99–142

Jeffrey, Harry P. (1987) 'Legislative origins of the Fulbright program', *The Annals of the American Academy of Political and Social Science* 491(1): 36–47

Jegathesan, Mythri (2013) 'Bargaining in a Labor Regime: Plantation Life and the Politics of Development in Sri Lanka'. Unpublished PhD dissertation, Columbia University, New York

Jegathesan, Mythri (2015) 'Deficient realities: expertise and uncertainty among tea plantation workers in Sri Lanka', *Dialectical Anthropology* 39(3): 255–72, https://doi.org/10.1007/s10624-015-9386-1 (last checked 4 August 2018)

Jejeebhoy, Shireen J. (1995) *Women's Education, Autonomy, and Reproductive Behaviour: Experience from Developing Countries*, Oxford: Clarendon Press

Jensen, Robert and Rebecca Thornton (2003) 'Early female marriage in the developing world', *Gender & Development* 11(2): 9–19, https://policy-practice.oxfam.org.uk/publications/early-female-marriage-in-the-developing-world-131524 (last checked 4 October 2018)

Kabeer, Naila (2005) 'Gender equality and women's empowerment: a critical analysis of the third millennium development goal 1', *Gender & Development* 13(1): 13–24, https://policy-practice.oxfam.org.uk/publications/gender-equality-and-womens-empowerment-a-critical-analysis-of-the-third-millenn-131574 (last checked 4 October 2018)

Kassebaum, Nicholas J., Amelia Bertozzi-Villa, Megan S. Coggeshall, Katya A. Shackelford, Caitlyn Steiner, Kyle R. Heuton, Diego Gonzalez-Medina,

Ryan Barber, Chantal Huynh and Daniel Dicker (2014) 'Global, regional, and national levels and causes of maternal mortality during 1990–2013: a systematic analysis for the Global Burden of Disease Study 2013', *The Lancet* 384(9947): 980–1004

Kingsolver, Ann E. (2010) '"Like a frog in a well": young people's views of the future expressed in two collaborative research projects in Sri Lanka', *Human Organization* 69(1): 1–9

Kvale, Steinar and Svend Brinkmann (2009) *Interviews: Learning the Craft of Qualitative Research*, Thousand Oaks, CA: Sage, 230–43

Lewis, Ruth and Susan Marine (2015) 'Weaving a tapestry, compassionately: toward an understanding of young women's feminisms', *Feminist Formations* 27(1): 118–40, https://doi.org/10.1353/ff.2015.0002 (last checked 4 August 2018)

Malhotra, Anju and Mark Mather (1997) 'Do schooling and work empower women in developing countries? Gender and domestic decisions in Sri Lanka', *Sociological Forum* 12(4): 599–630

Marecek, Jeanne and Udeni M. H. Appuhamilage (2011) 'Present but Unnamed: Feminisms and Psychologies in Sri Lanka', in Alexandra Rutherford, Rose Capdevila, Vindhya Undurti and Ingrid Palmary (eds.) *Handbook of International Feminisms: Perspectives on Psychology, Women, Culture, and Rights*, New York: Springer, 315–33

McGilvray, Dennis B. (1982) 'Dutch burghers and Portuguese mechanics: Eurasian ethnicity in Sri Lanka', *Comparative Studies in Society and History* 24(2): 235–63

Niranjana, Seemanthini (2002) 'Exploring Gender Inflections within Panchayati Raj Institutions: Women's Politicization in Andhra Pradesh', in Karin Kapadia (ed.) *The Violence of Development: The Politics of Identity, Gender and Social Inequalities in India*, New Delhi: Kali for Women, 352–92

Otoo-Oyortey, Naana and Sonita Pobi (2003) 'Early marriage and poverty: exploring links and key policy issues', *Gender & Development* 11(2): 42–51, https://policy-practice.oxfam.org.uk/publications/early-marriage-and-poverty-exploring-links-and-key-policy-issues-131525 (last checked 4 October 2018)

Patrinos, Harry A. and George Psacharopoulos (1997) 'Family size, schooling and child labor in Peru – an empirical analysis', *Journal of Population Economics* 10(4): 387–405, https://doi.org/10.1007/s001480050050 (last checked 4 August 2018)

Ryan, Gery W. (2005) 'What are standards of rigor for qualitative research', in *Workshop on Interdisciplinary Standards for Systematic Qualitative Research*, Washington, DC: National Science Foundation, 28–35

Saldaña, Johnny (2009) 'An Introduction to Codes and Coding', in Johnny Saldaña, *The Coding Manual for Qualitative Researchers*, London, Thousand Oaks, CA, New Delhi and Singapore: Sage, 1–31

Santhya, K. G. (2011) 'Early marriage and sexual and reproductive health vulnerabilities of young women', *Current Opinion in Obstetrics and Gynecology* 23(5): 334–39, https://doi.org/10.1097/GCO.0b013e32834a93d2 (last checked 4 August 2018)

Santhya, K. G., Usha Ram, Rajib Acharya, Shireen J. Jejeebhoy, Faujdar Faujdar, and Abhishek Singh (2010) 'Associations between early marriage and young women's marital and reproductive health outcomes: evidence from India', *International Perspectives on Sexual and Reproductive Health* 36(3): 132–9

Sen, Purna (1999) 'Enhancing women's choices in responding to domestic violence in Calcutta: a comparison of employment and education', *The European Journal of Development Research* 11(2): 65–86

Sherif, Bahira (2001) 'The ambiguity of boundaries in the fieldwork experience: establishing rapport and negotiating insider/outsider status', *Qualitative Inquiry* 7(4): 436–47

Summers, Lawrence H. (1994) *Investing in All the People: Educating Women in Developing Countries*, Washington, DC: The World Bank

UN General Assembly (2000) 'United Nations Millennium Declaration', United Nations General Assembly

UNICEF (2011) *The State of the World's Children 2011. Adolescence: An Age of Opportunity*, New York: UNICEF

University Grants Commission - Sri Lanka (2016) 'Student Enrolment', in *Sri Lanka University Statistics 2016*, 36–83, http://www.ugc.ac.lk/downloads/statistics/stat_2016/Chapter%203.pdf (last checked 4 October 2018)

UN in Sri Lanka (2017) *United Nations Sustainable Development Framework 2018–2022*, Colombo: UN in Sri Lanka, http://lk.one.un.org/wp-content/uploads/2017/08/Final_UNSDF_2018-2022.pdf (last checked 2 August 2018)

UN (2017) 'World Population Prospects. Total Population: Both Sexes', Department of Economic and Social Affairs: Population Division, https://esa.un.org/unpd/wpp/Download/Standard/Population/ (last checked 2 August 2018)

World Bank (2015) *Sri Lanka: Ending Poverty and Promoting Shared Prosperity: A Systematic Country Diagnostic*, http://documents.worldbank.org/curated/en/714211468189526474/pdf/100226-CAS-P152526-SecM2015-0298-IDA-SecM2015-0204-IFC-SecM2015-0149-MIGA-SecM2015-0100-Box393220B-PUBLIC-disclosed-10-13-15.pdf (last checked 4 August 2018)

Young, Michelle D. and Scott Mcleod (2001) 'Flukes, Opportunities, and Planned Interventions: Factors Affecting Women's Decisions to Become School Administrators', *Educational Administration Quarterly* 37(4): 462–502, http://journals.sagepub.com/doi/pdf/10.1177/0013161X01374003 (last checked 4 August 2018)

CHAPTER 12
Resources

Liz Cooke

Young feminisms

Brave, Creative, Resilient: The Global State of Young Feminist Organizing (2016) FRIDA: The Young Feminist Fund and AWID, Association for Women's Rights in Development's Young Feminist Activism Program, https://www.awid.org/sites/default/files/atoms/files/frida-awid_field-report_final_web_issuu.pdf [last accessed 16th April 2020], 90 pp

This report documents the findings of the first global survey into young feminist organising. Undertaken by FRIDA: The Young Feminist Fund – which exists to support young feminist activism around the world – the research was undertaken in order to determine the key characteristics of young feminist organisations (YFOs) globally, with a key rationale being the vital role played by young women, girls, and trans youth activists in 'the strengthening, rejuvenation and sustainability of feminist activism' (p. 13). Findings were based on analysis of applications to the FRIDA: Young Feminist Fund (the bulk coming from Africa, Latin America and the Caribbean, and the Asia-Pacific region) and a questionnaire. Some of the main findings include: the diverse and intersectional nature of YFOs, which work in areas including youth, climate justice, sex workers rights, health and disability, and indigenous rights; that a significant proportion of YFOs are unregistered, either through choice or necessity; that more than half of survey respondents regularly feel unsafe or threatened because of their work; and that, despite working innovatively, as the authors point out, to address some of the most pressing issues of our time, with some of the most vulnerable people, the lack of financial resources and sustainability is by far the most widely shared challenge faced by YFOs.

Brave: Young Women's Global Revolution (2017) Gayle Kimball, Volume 1, Global Themes, ISBN: 9780938795582, 566 pp, Volume 2: Regional Activism, ISBN: 9780938795605, 660 pp, Chico, CA: Equality Press

This thoughtful and informative two-volume work, based on interviews and surveys undertaken across 88 countries, examines young women's activism across the globe. For the author, much of the political activism of the 21st century is notable for being youth-led and electronically connected. The author characterises those in their teens and twenties (at 1.5 billion individuals, the largest youth generation in history) as the 'Relationship Generation', which tends to 'defy or ignore large bureaucratic institutions including government and religion', and 'focus[es] instead on direct democracy on the local level and loving their family and friends' (Volume 1, p. 1). In Volume 1, Global Themes, the author considers the following topics: 'The Future is Female', 'Global Desire for Equality', 'Global Status of Young Women', 'Consumerism Targets "Girl Power"', and 'Global Media Both Helps and Inhibits Girls'. Each of these chapters ends with discussion questions and activities, making the volume useful as a teaching aid. Volume 2, Regional Activism, includes discussion on feminist waves in the global North and in the field of development, as well as young women's activism in Latin America, Africa, the Middle East and North Africa, Russia, China, and India, plus Egyptian women's experiences of the 2011 Revolution.

Rebel Girls: Youth Activism and Social Change Across the Americas (2011) Jessica K. Taft, New York and London: NYU Press, ISBN: 9780814783252, 256 pp.

In this important book, the author addresses what she identifies as the under-explored topic of teenage girls' activism within the growing academic field of girls' studies, and in the literature on social movements in the Americas, seeking to challenge the 'highly prevalent images of girls as either passive victims or empowered consumer citizens' (p. 18). Through research undertaken in the USA, Canada, Mexico, Venezuela, and Argentina, the author explores, in the first section of the book – Building the Activist Identity – the formation of girls' activist identities, including girl activists' complicated relationship to girlhood itself, and in the second section – Making Change Happen – girl activists' social movement strategies and collective political practices. The author argues that some of the shared characteristics of girls' activism – a commitment to learning, building horizontal, participatory activist communities, and a spirit of optimism – mirror elements deemed to be some of the most effective in the literature on adult social movements and social change. Girls' activism, the author suggests, can therefore provide older scholars and activists with valuable insights into working successfully for social change.

'Teenage girls' narratives of becoming activists' (2017) Jessica K. Taft, *Contemporary Social Science* 12(1–2): 27–39

In this article, the author of Rebel Girls (see above) draws further on her research with teenage girl activists in the Americas to explore girls' experiences of becoming engaged in movements for social justice. Common threads in these narratives include outsider status, influential peer relationships, and a growing social awareness, together with age-based ideas around teenage years as a time of self-discovery and of the self-in-formation. For the author, girls' notions of themselves 'becoming' activists rather than 'being' activists is of crucial importance. While this emphasis demonstrates humility, and facilitates openness and flexibility, she argues, it also plays into developmentalist discourses that see young people themselves as 'becoming' rather than 'being', something which serves to define them as 'incapable, partial, and deficient in contrast to an imagined vision of the capable, complete and rational adult' (p. 29). This, inevitably, has implications for political activism undertaken by girls, contributing to its invisibility or dismissal.

'How to become a feminist activist after the institutionalization of the women's movements: the generational development of feminist identity and politics in Mexico City' (2014) Yin-Zu Chen, *Frontiers: A Journal of Women Studies* 35(3): 183–206

This is a fascinating investigation into the attitudes of a group of young women in Mexico City with regard to their feminist identity and activism. The author argues that in contrast to feminists of the 1970s, who had to create women's movements collectively without the support of pre-existing institutions or organisations, young feminists today have grown up with established state institutions and NGOs responsible for gender and women's rights policy, along with gender and women's studies programmes in universities, and a variety of feminist organisations pursuing advocacy and activism. The author found that the bureaucratic nature of these bodies does not offer sufficient opportunity for young feminists working within them to demonstrate their own leadership, or take their own action. While there was no difference in the political agenda of adult and young feminists, creating their own groups allowed young feminists to pursue the kind of spontaneous, imaginative, and potentially controversial collective activism that would not necessarily be endorsed by their institutions, and crucially, represents a demonstration of 'the desire to be recognized as feminists considered equal to their foremothers' (p. 195).

'"I am not just a feminist eight hours a day" youth gender justice activism in Ecuador and Peru' (2015) Anna-Britt Coe, *Gender & Society* 29(6): 888–913

While the theoretical discussion in this scholarly article makes for somewhat difficult reading, the article is nonetheless of interest because of the insights it provides into the distinction youth gender justice activists (of both sexes) make between themselves and the 'professionalized adult feminism' (p. 889) that exists in bureaucratically-structured institutions in Ecuador and Peru. Indeed, the author states that she uses the term 'gender justice' because of the reluctance of some to describe their activism as 'feminist' because of feminism's association with this professionalised sector. While the ultimate aims of the youth activists and professional feminists were the same – addressing violence against women and girls, and advancing reproductive and sexual rights – the youth activists saw their activism as distinct from that of adult feminists through its targeting of the family, household, and intimate relationships, and the fact that the youth activists see themselves operating in a contemporary context of 'blurred gender equalities'. Here, notions of progress in terms of gender equality in education, employment, and politics exist alongside patriarchal attitudes regarding women's traditional roles, and an often violent backlash directed towards women.

'A network of one's own: young women and the creation of youth-only transnational feminist spaces' (2017) Theresa A. Hunt, *YOUNG* 25(2): 107–23

In this article, the author examines five young women's transnational feminist networks (TFNs) to determine the reasons members have chosen to work in a youth-only setting. The author found that despite the wide variation both between and within the networks studied, the key motivation for operating within a youth-only space was the marginalisation young women felt in organisations or networks run by older generations of feminists. Such a 'silencing' has been responsible for young women activists setting up alternative spaces, where voices and ideas can be heard, and 'the presumption of youthful inexperience' (p. 121) is not a factor. Coalescing around youth has also allowed for other differences between young feminists – such as sexual orientation, or secular versus religious values – to be accommodated.

20 Years of Mobilization: The Role of Young Feminists (2015) Ruby Johnson, United Nations Research Institute for Social Development (UNRISD), www.unrisd.org/beijing+20-johnson [last accessed 16th April 2020]

Arguing that '[t]he mobilization, the courage and the experience of this generation have an important role to play in redefining a just development and human rights agenda ahead', this think-piece from the co-director of FRIDA: The Young Feminist Fund, articulately outlines the kind of work young feminist activists are undertaking – for example, on violence against women and girls, LGBTQI rights, and sexual and reproductive health and rights – and the challenges they face. Written in 2015, the 20th anniversary of the Beijing Platform for Action, which embedded women's rights within the development agenda, the author sees the work of young feminists as part of pushing forward gender-just development, having 'the ability to catalyse change from the local to the global level'. The piece provides an excellent introduction to FRIDA's 2016 report on young feminist organising (see below). [See also the author's 2014 piece 'Claiming rights, facing fire: young feminist activists', https://www.opendemocracy.net/en/5050/claiming-rights-facing-fire-young-feminist-activists/ [last accessed 16 April 2020] in which she discusses the work of a number of young feminist activist groups around the globe and the dangers they face as a result of their work.

#NiUnaMenos: Policitising the Use of Technologies (2017) Maria Florencia Alcaraz, GenderIT.Org, www.genderit.org/feminist-talk/niunamenos-politicising-use-technologies]last accessed 16th April 2020]

This short online piece discusses the #NiUnaMenos movement which began in Argentina and has spread across Latin America and beyond. It highlights the importance of fourthwave, digital activism for forging alliances and networks and participating in the media without the intervention of gatekeepers, or the need for permission. Originally a reaction to the 2015 murder of a 14-year-old Argentinian girl by her boyfriend, the author states that #NiUnaMenos means 'no more femicides', but that it is also a demand for the ending of all forms of oppression, from extreme violence and unsafe abortions to unpaid care work and harassment in the street. For the author, this form of fourth-wave feminism is characterised by 'an alliance between technology, social networks, and people on the streets', with, in many instances, online organising leading to mass public demonstrations.

'#MeToo is riding a new wave of feminism in India' (2018) Alka Kurian, *Mail & Guardian*, https://mg.co.za/article/2018-02-04-metoo-is-riding-a-new-wave-of-feminism-in-india/ [last accessed 16 April 2020]

This interesting newspaper article describes the emergence of what the author sees as a new type of feminism in India. Led by young women utilising social media to challenge patriarchal attitudes, and which has grown up since the beginning of the 21st century, the author cites the 2003 Blank Noise Project protesting against sexual harassment in the street, and the 2009 Pink Chaddi (underwear) campaign against moral policing as examples. The author argues that this new form of activism is in contrast to existing mainstream Indian feminism – which has tended to focus on issues such as child marriage, dowry deaths, and sexual violence against marginalised women. Identifying the fatal gang rape of a 23-year-old student in Delhi as a watershed moment, the author outlines the way young women have been pursuing online and offline activism in order to highlight violence against women, especially in public space, and to refute ideas that women invite sexual violence through their clothing and behaviour. This is also in reaction to state and society attempting to keep women safe through attempts to restrict their movement, instead of directly addressing misogyny and ensuring women's safety in public places.

'Movement-building challenges for young women in Southern Africa' (2018) Shamillah Wilson, https://shamillahwilson.com/2018/05/28/the-challenges-of-young-women-in-movement-building-in-southern-africa/ (last accessed 16 April 2020), 5 pp.

In this essay, the author argues that in Southern Africa there is currently a 'dwindling vibrancy' in women's movements, both nationally and regionally. One of the reasons for this, she argues, is the lack of connection between many initiatives and the participation of both poor, grassroots women, and young women. Focusing on the issue of engaging young women, specifically, the author outlines several key challenges; firstly, the heterogeneous nature of young women – e.g. urban and highly educated versus rural and lacking tertiary education, and without access to ICTs. Secondly, with feminism still a contentious idea in many places, and in contexts of rising religious fundamentalisms, she identifies the need for awareness around the issue of framing – while some young women may happily call their activism feminist, it may be problematic, and indeed dangerous for others to do so. Thirdly, problems of multi-generational, power-sharing tensions within feminist movements remains an issue. Finally, the author calls for new forms of activism to be encouraged, especially around digital technology, but that these should not be labelled as 'youth focused initatives', but rather integrated into broader strategies.

'How South Africa's young women activists are rewriting the script' (2016) Ama-ndaGouws, *TheConversation,* https://theconversation.com/how-southafricas-young-women-activists-are-rewriting-the-script-60980 [last accessed 16 April 2020]

Comparing the current activism of young South African female students with that of their predecessors in the anti-apartheid student protests of the 1970s, the author of this newspaper article finds that while race, Eurocentrism, and colonialism are still of crucial importance, today's female students are refusing to ignore the issues of gender oppression and violence. Highlighting the #EndRapeCulture campaigns on university campuses, and associated topless protests, which the author calls the 'politics of the spectacle', the author argues that through their campaigns, these students have generated solidarity with many women across the country, and done more to raise awareness of issues of sexual violence against women, along with LGBTQI rights, than many other, longer-term initiatives.

The Coming of (Digital) Age: How African Feminists Are Using the Internet to Change Women's Lives (2014) Minna Salami, GenderIT.Org, https://www. genderit.org/articles/coming-digital-age-how-african-feminists-are-using-internet-change-womens-lives [last accessed 16 April 2020]

This short piece draws attention to the digital activism carried out by feminists across Africa. Arguing that while most of the international focus on fourth-wave feminism has been on activism in the global North, and that any discussion of digital feminist activism in Africa tends to be seen through a 'development' lens, the article provides examples of the kind of online feminist connecting, organising, and campaigning that has been undertaken across the continent.

'China's feminist five' (2016) Leta Hong Fincher, *Dissent,* https://www.dissent magazine.org/article/china-feminist-five [last accessed 16 April 2020], 9 pp.

In March 2015, Chinese police arrested a group of young feminists planning to hand out stickers about sexual harassment on public transport, to mark International Women's Day. Most were soon released, but five young women were detained for 37 days, and after a national and international outcry they were eventually released on bail, under investigation for 'gathering a crowd to disturb public order'. In this article, the author, through interviews with the women, recounts the experience of the 'feminist five', and discusses the context in which their protest arose. This is one in which, following the economic reforms of the 1990s, levels of gender inequality have increased, and many young and often highly educated women are rejecting the traditional gender roles of wife and mother being aggressively promoted by media and government. For the author, this younger generation of feminists represents a major threat to the Communist Party, which sees the patriarchal family as the foundation for state stability. (See also the author's recently published book, *Betraying Big Brother: The Feminist Awakening in China*, London and Brooklyn, NY: Verso, ISBN: 9781786633644.)

'Youth feminist activism in China: an ethnographic analysis of an innovative action oriented feminism' (2015) Danyang Wu, Master's thesis, Social Studies of Gender, Department of Gender, Lund University, Sweden, http://lup.lub.lu.se/luur/download?func=downloadFile&recordOId=7853550& fileOId=7853555 [last accessed 16 April 2020], 82 pp.

This Master's thesis offers an informative consideration of young feminist activism in China through its discussion in relation to a set of research questions. These are: What is new about youth feminist activism in China? What kind of agency is embedded in this new form of activism, and what is the relationship between it and earlier incarnations of feminism in China? How does the new generation respond to the challenges they are facing? What potential lies in the more radical and visible resistance demonstrated by young activists in the context of power relations in contemporary China? The author frames her thesis – in the introduction and the conclusion – with the arrest and ultimate release of the 'feminist five' (discussed above). She expresses concern for the future of feminist activism in China in the light of this episode (p. 5), but sees as a positive signal for the future the successful mobilisation (which saw co-operation between young and older feminists, students and workers, as well as the national and international feminist community) that led to their release (p. 72).

Solidarity, Safety and Power: Young Women Organizing in Indonesia (2018) Jethro Pettit, Just Associates (JASS), https://justassociates.org/en/resources/solidarity-safety-and-power-young-women-organizing-indonesia [last accessed 16 April 2020], 31 pp.

This report profiles Forum Aktivis Perempuan Muda Indonesia (Young Indonesian Women Activists' Forum), or FAMM, which is a network of diverse, young women from across Indonesia. FAMM works on sensitive issues, such as environmentally damaging development projects, women's and LGBTI rights, and ending gender-based and political violence. The report outlines the growth of the network, which evolved from the movement-building work of civil society organisation Just Associates (JASS), in South-East Asia, emphasising the key principles and methodologies central to the development of the network, including intersectionality, feminist popular education, and power analysis. The report also makes clear the need for mutual support and solidarity when undertaking the often dangerous work of defending rights in the face of increasing religious fundamentalisms, and opposition from large corporations, criminal and armed groups, and politicians. (See also the 2017 report, 'Building safe spaces to support young women's participation in local governance in Indonesia', published by FAMM and the Institute of Development Studies, https://www.ids.ac.uk/publications/building-safe-spaces-to-support-young-womens-participation-in-local-governance-in-indonesia/ [last accessed 16 April 2020], 20 pp.

Postfeminism and fourth-wave feminism

The Aftermath of Feminism: Gender, Culture and Social Change (2009) Angela McRobbie, London: Sage, ISBN: 978-0761970620, 192 pp.

This influential book, published in 2009, argues that political, economic, cultural, and media influences in the UK have combined to bring about what the author calls the 'undoing of feminism', resulting in a postfeminist social and cultural landscape, part backlash against earlier feminism and older feminists, and part reformulation of feminism into neoliberal ideas of individual 'empowerment' and 'choice'. The author offers a critique of what became known as 'girlie feminism', in which corporate consumer culture marketed femininity (with its necessary grooming and cosmetic products) as feminist, in order to exploit young women's rising incomes. Young women are central to the author's analysis, and in her chapter 'Top Girls? Young Women and the New Sexual Contract', she outlines the new focus on young women and their capacities – the educated 'career girl in the West, and her counterpart in developing economies – the "global girl" factory worker'. In this new contract, the recognition of her 'capacity' and the gains she has made in terms of education and employment require that a young woman abandons any criticism of hegemonic masculinity associated with feminism and the women's movement. Given that she may well be engaged in the endless (consumerist) pursuit of 'self-perfectibility' (p. 63), then her attention may well be elsewhere anyway.

'For Western girls only? Post-feminism as transnational culture' (2015) Simidele Dosekun, *Feminist Media Studies* 15(6): 960–75 (author's pre-print available at http://sro.sussex.ac.uk/63369/1/Postfeminism%20as%20transnational-Dosekun.Pdf [last accessed 16 April 2020]

The author of this article argues that characteristics of postfeminism, such as the belief that gender equality has been achieved, and an ethos of individualism and consumerism as empowerment, do not solely apply to the West. Interpreting postfeminism as a purely Western phenomenon means ignoring class differences in developing economies, in which wealthy, educated elites exist. The author contends that if the increasingly dominant neoliberal definition of women's empowerment is understood as access to material resources and consumer goods, many women in the global South are already 'empowered' (p. 15). For the global South, this means that with the spread of postfeminism, via globalised media, while young women may talk about 'choice' and 'empowerment', they are unable to 'articulate their national or local feminist histories or make sense of their personal experiences of pervasive sexism in critical feminist terms' (p. 17). Thus, postfeminism's 'undoing of feminism' (p. 17), as witnessed in the global North, can be seen to have been globalised and in the words of the author, been 'rendered transnational culture' (p. 17).

'Post-postfeminism? New feminist visibilities in postfeminist times' (2016) Rosalind Gill, *Feminist Media Studies*, 16(4): 610–30

With a focus on the UK, but with wider relevance, this article considers the value of postfeminism as a concept given the evident rise in 'fourth-wave' feminist activism and in a context where feminism is increasingly depicted in the mainstream media as 'cool'. Suggesting that there is currently a 'feminist zeitgeist' (p. 615) within the media, the author argues for the necessity of retaining the idea of postfeminism, not as part of a linear narrative in which one idea or wave of feminism displaces another, but to reveal the 'postfeminist sensibilities' (e.g. a focus on physical appearance, and viewing individual 'choice' and consumerism as 'empowerment') of some of the versions of feminism presented in the mass media. She demonstrates this through an examination of the uneven treatment of different kinds of feminist visibility within the mainstream media, with feminist issues and feminist activism often ignored, trivialised or provoking a backlash, while much attention is given to the entrepreneuralist, neoliberal feminism of the Cheryl Sandberg Lean In variety and the 'resolutely *not* angry' celebrity and style feminism (p. 618). For the author, 'the tenacity of what we might characterize as pre-feminist or anti-feminist ideas remains striking, even in this new moment' (p. 622).

'Intersectional expectations: young feminists' perceived failure at dealing with differences and their retreat to individualism' (2016) Julie Schuster, *Women's Studies International Forum*, 58: 1–8

This article argues that while the oft-made criticism of young women's approach to feminism in the global North – that it has become individualised (as opposed collective) partly, at least because of neo-liberal co-optation – is not always justified, where it is true, this trend has been reinforced by the challenges faced by young feminists in, as the author puts it, 'accommodat[ing] women's diversity within their feminist practices' (p. 1). Drawing on research undertaken with young feminists in New Zealand, the author argues that the importance of adopting an intersectional approach (as a response to the critiques of the dominance of white, heterosexual middle-class women within feminist discourse and practice which arose as part of third-wave feminism) has led to the concerns of many young feminists – particularly those who feel themselves to be in socially privileged positions – not to be seen as speaking on behalf of others. For the author, 'issues of women's differences and relative privilege continue to shape today's feminist discourses and lead to conflicts within various branches of young feminist movements, as, for instance, controversies about allegedly ethnocentric and culturally insensitive approaches of FEMEN or SlutWalk, and online campaigns like #SolidarityisforWhiteWomen have shown' (p. 1).

'#Intersectionality: the fourth wave feminist Twitter community' (2017) Tegan Zimmerman, *Atlantis* 38(1): 54–70

This article is an interesting discussion in which the author suggests that intersectionality (which includes race and ethnicity, class, religion, ability, sexuality and other aspects of identity, alongside that of biological sex as intersecting aspects of discrimination or privilege) is central to fourth-wave feminism, using an examination of the #SolidarityisforWhiteWomen hashtag on Twitter as an example of this. (#SolidarityisforWhiteWomen was a hashtag created in 2013 by the writer Mikki Kendall, challenging the downplaying or dismissing by white feminists of the racism experienced by women of colour.) With digital technology and online activism a defining feature of fourth-wave feminism, the author argues that Twitter plays a crucial role in enabling debate and critical discussion around issues of intersectionality. As part of the article, the author provides a useful 'genealogy' of fourth-wave feminism and makes clear that she sees fourth-wave feminism as not simply existing within the digital realm, 'the fourth wave acknowledges that theory and a web presence alone is not enough to bring about political change' (p. 56).

'Invisible feminists? Social media and young women's political participation' (2013) Julie Schuster, *Political Science* 65(1): 8–24

In 2013, when this article was published, the term 'fourth-wave feminism' was not yet widely used. While the term does not appear in this article, the author can be seen as describing what has come to be called the fourth wave in her discussion of the generational divide in feminist activism in New Zealand. The author found that while younger feminists were highly engaged in online feminist activism – via online communities, blogs, and Facebook – it remained largely invisible to the wider public, and to politically active women of older generations, who worried that there was no younger generation of feminists to pick up their work on their retirement. However, the young women in the study used new media to connect with and support each other, to have political discussions and to organise events in the 'real' world (p. 8). It could be argued that the growth in the use of digital communications across all generations means that the differences identified by the author at the time are not as distinct today as they were. The article remains, nonetheless, a valuable piece of research.

Postfeminism(s) and the Arrival of the Fourth Wave: Turning Tides (2017) Nicola Rivers, Cham: Palgrave Macmillan, ISBN: 978-3-319-59812-3, 174 pp.

This book explores the current resurgence of interest in feminism in the global North, especially within popular culture and the media. Examining different understandings of postfeminism, the author discusses the way that fourth-wave feminism intersects with these, and its relationship to previous waves, with chapters on 'celebrity feminism' and feminist activist group FEMEN helping to illustrate these dynamics. Of particular interest to the author is the idea that there are antagonistic relationships between younger and older generations (and waves) of feminists, something that is promoted through simplistic renderings of each wave, often via the media. In the chapter 'From Feminist Mothers to Feminist Monsters: Tensions Across the Waves', the author questions the utility and indeed accuracy of understanding feminism in this way. She argues, '[s]uch rigid definitions of feminist waves serve to reinforce the pretense of a generational divide, contributing to the sense that feminist subjects hold a static position assigned to them by the arbitrary factor of their age, rather than allowing feminists to occupy multiple positions spanning various waves, or have conflicting opinions based on political differences' (p. 29).

Development perspectives on young women

'"The revolution will be led by a 12 year-old girl": girl power, and global politics' (2013) Ofra Koffman and Rosalind Gill, *Feminist Review* 105(1): 83–102

In this article, the authors explore the current focus on girls within the field of international development. This is often called the 'Girl Effect', a term first coined by the Nike Foundation, which has at its heart the idea that targeting girls – through improved education and livelihood opportunities and integration into markets – is the best way to lift the developing world out of poverty. The authors argue that this recent and extremely prominent focus has been driven by the adoption of notions of 'girl power' current in the global North. Thus, 'the particular fusion of agency, independence, consumerism and entrepreneurialism that has become the hallmark of Western discourses of girlhood' (p. 89) is now applied to girls in the global South. For the authors, a central feature of the 'Girl Effect' discourse is its call to girls in the global North to engage in activism to support girls in the developing world. Portrayed as being educated, empowered, and socially connected themselves, any need for social change in gender relations is displaced on to their less fortunate 'sisters' in the South, playing into colonial, global North–South rescue narratives.

'Galvanising girls for development? Critiquing the shift from "smart" to "smarter economics"' (2016) Sylvia Chant, *Progress in Development Studies*

16(4): 314–28 (author's pre-print available at http://eprints.lse.ac.uk/66231/1/ Chant_Galvanising%20girl_2016.pdf) [last accessed 16 April 2020], 29 pp.

The author of this article views the focus on girls and young women in international development as an extension of the 'Smart Economics' rationale, originally espoused by the World Bank, and rapidly adopted by corporations, multi-lateral development agencies, and INGOs. 'Smart Economics' sees reducing gender inequality as leading to improved economic outcomes, and is characterised by an increased influence of corporate stakeholders and public–private partnerships in development initiatives. The author identifies the Nike Foundation's 'Girl Effect' programme as a key example of what is described as this 'transnational business feminism' (p. 2), in which girls' 'empowerment' is promoted, but as it is instrumental to the alleviation of poverty – rather than as an issue of social and gender justice. A central problem for the author is the emphasis on girls' and young women's individual agency (see e.g. a 'Girl Effect' catchphrase: 'Invest in a girl and she will do the rest'; p. 13). Such an emphasis ignores deep-seated gender and structural inequalities within societies, and the fact that many multi-national corporations are arguably responsible for helping to entrench poverty in the global South.

'"Confidence you can carry!": Girls in crisis and the market for girls' empowerment organizations' (2015) Sarah Banet-Weiser, *Continuum: Journal of Media & Cultural Studies*, 29(2): 182–93.

The author of this article discusses the rise of national girls' empowerment organisations (GEOs) in the USA that has taken place alongside the focus on the empowerment of girls within the field of international development. For the author, issues of low self-esteem and lack of confidence, which have been characterised as a 'crisis in girls', are indeed important for girls and young women, who have been traditionally socialised into being more selfeffacing and submissive. However, she argues that the growth in GEOs is part of a widespread 'marketisation of empowerment', which operates with the same logic that can be seen in 'Girl Effect' international development discourses; essentially, a neo-liberal, market-based logic. This sees young women being encouraged to view themselves as individual, empowered entrepreneurs, and to 'eschew collective feminist politics and coalition as a route to political change' (p. 190).

'Girl power and "selfie humanitarianism"' (2015) Ofra Koffman, Shani Orgad and Rosalind Gill, *Continuum: Journal of Media & Cultural Studies* 29(2): 157–68, authors' pre-print available at http://eprints.lse.ac.uk/62627/1/Girl%20 power%20.pdf, [last accessed 16 April 2020] 16 pp.

Building on ideas they first presented in '"The revolution will be led by a 12 year-old girl": girl power, and global politics' (see above), in which they identify the 'girl-powering' of development, the authors of this article examine what they term 'selfie humanitarianism'. For the authors, this is the turning of the humanitarian focus away from those in need and on to the individual donor. Using the example of the UN's Girl Up campaign as a case study, the authors argue that via a 'cocktail of celebratory "girlafestoes" and "empowerment strategies", often spread via social media, celebrity endorsements, and corporate branding' (p. 2), the desire to help others has been reframed into 'entrepreneurial and narcissistic self-work' (p. 2). The authors are highly sceptical of such campaigns' appeals to sisterhood across the global North–South divide. They argue that the celebration of consumption, branding, and focus on the self inherent in the global North's idea of 'girl power' mean that issues of inequality, injustice, and global exploitation are ignored, and that the humanitarian impetus is dependent on seeing the other as 'like me', not on her own terms (p. 10).

Youth Leap into Gender Equality. UN Women's Youth and Gender Equality Strategy: Empowered Young Women and Young Men as Partners in Achieving Gender Equality (2017) New York: UN Women, https://www.unwomen.org/en/digital-library/publications/2017/5/youth-leap-into-gender-equality [last accessed 16 April 2020] 28 pp.

The interest in girls in international development, as discussed above, has been paralleled by a growing focus within the sector on youth more widely. This is, in part, a recognition of the 'youth bulge' in the current global population, with the largest generation of young people ever making up nearly one-third of the world's population. Almost 90 per cent of these live in developing countries. The participation of these young people is seen as being crucial to achieving the Sustainable Development Goals by 2030. The UN has been holding Youth Forums since 2012, as have many other development agencies, most of whom have also been developing youth policies over recent years: see e.g. USAID's 2012 policy document, Youth in Development: Realizing the Demographic Opportunity, https://www.usaid.gov/policy/youth [last accessed 16th April 2020]; DFID's Putting Young People at the Heart of Development: The Department for International Development's Youth Agenda, https://assets.publishing.service.gov.uk/government/uploads/system/uploads/attachment_data/file/550229/DFIDyouthagendaapproach4.pdf [last accessed 16 April 2020]; and Investing in Youth in International Development Policy: Making the Case, from UK think-tank Overseas Development Institute, https://www.odi.org/sites/odi.org.uk/files/odi-assets/publications-opinion-files/8413.pdf [last accessed 16 April 2020] This strategy paper from UN Women is a reflection of this increasing focus on youth. It sets out the strategy's rationale, and its framework for achieving gender equality in the key areas of leadership, economic empowerment, and ending violence against women and girls through promoting the agency and leadership of young women.

Young Women and the Demographic Dividend in Africa: Defining and Spelling Out the Gender Dynamics Within the Demographic Dividend Discourse (2017)

Nairobi: The African Women's Development and Communication Network (FEMNET), https://femnet.org/2017/06/young-women-and-the-demographic-dividend-advocacy-brief/ [last accessed April 2020], 25 pp.

This paper is a response to the African Union's *Roadmap on Harnessing the Demographic Dividend Through Investments in Youth*. (The Roadmap is the continent-wide youth strategy for capitalising on what is termed as the 'demographic dividend' for achieving Africa's development goals. The 'democratic dividend' referred to relates to the economic benefits that derive from having a large percentage of the population of working age. They are then able to support the smaller, non-working population. Sixty per cent of Africa's population are currently below the age of 24.) Arguing that mainstream discourses on youth tend to focus on and be dominated by young men, this paper highlights issues of key importance for young women and girls – sexual and reproductive health and rights, gender-based violence, employment and mobility, and education – maintaining that a gendered understanding of these areas is vital, so that young women and girls are not excluded from youth-focused development. The paper also reproduces the four 'Pillars' of the Roadmap, providing key 'accountability points' for use in advocacy, so that the Roadmap delivers for young women and girls.

Young feminist activism

There are many young feminist groups and organisations around the globe, practising solidarity and undertaking activism across a wide range of issues. Given the limits of space, we offer a short list of groups that have an international scope.

The Association for Women's Rights in Development (AWID), Postal address: 215 Spadina Avenue, Suite 150 Toronto, ON M5T 2T7, Canada, email: via the website, website: www.awid.org (available in English, French, and Spanish), Twitter: @AWID

AWID is an international feminist membership organisation made up of organisations and individuals working in the areas of gender equality, sustainable development, and women's human rights. As well as bringing together feminists from around the globe at AWID Forums every four years (*the* major international event for feminist activists, gender and development practitioners, and many others), one of AWID's key focuses is Young Feminist Activism (see https://www.awid.org/special-focus-sections/young-feminist-activism last accessed 1 August 2018). This programme seeks to address the particular constraints facing young feminists – such as lack of funding and opportunities, and violence and intimidation – and develop strategies to promote multigenerational organising, young women's access to international forums and processes, and to influence decision-making that affects their rights.

FBomb, www.womensmediacenter.com/fbomb/

Part of the US-based Women's Media Center Web platform, the FBomb is an online space run by and for young feminists. Offering the chance for teen- and university-age writers from around the world to have their work published, it features reactions to and reflections on current news stories, interviews, and personal essays, all from a young feminist perspective. The editorial team welcomes pitches for submissions or full-length submissions, which should be sent to fbombsubmissions@gmail.com.

FRIDA | The Young Feminist Fund, website: https://youngfeministfund. org (available in Arabic, English, French, and Spanish), Twitter: @FRIDAfund

Launched in 2011, FRIDA exists to fund feminist organising by girls, young women, and trans youth who are leading social justice movements, particularly in the form of smallscale start-up groups that may otherwise struggle to gain financial support. FRIDA has produced a helpful guide to generating resources – both financial and beyond – for young feminist activists, the *Resource Mobilization Toolkit for Girls, Young Women and Trans Youth*, https://youngfeministfund.org/wp-content/uploads/2017/11/FRIDA-RM-Toolkit-2017.pdf [last accessed 17 April 2020]. As well as providing information on how to apply for a grant (and to donate to the fund), the website, via its list of grantees and their work, provides a wonderful overview of the kind of young feminist activism – across a wide variety of issues – that is currently being undertaken across the globe.

Hollaback!, email: holla@ihollaback.org, website: www.ihollaback.org, Twitter: @iHollaback

Founded by young feminists in New York in 2005, Hollaback! has grown into a worldwide network of activists who are challenging sexual and other forms of harassment in public space. This umbrella website provides links to all Hollaback! groups, or chapters, globally, and is a space where activists can share their experiences of harassment, and news and more from their local group. Activists pledge to educate themselves on the issue of harassment and how it affects people, to take action if they see someone being harassed in the street, and to share their personal experiences of harassment. The organisation provides training and support for young community activists who wish to set up a Hollaback! Chapter in their part of the world, and a Hollaback! app is available to allow those who have experienced harassment to map and document the incident.

Take Back the Tech!, email: info@takebackthetech.net, website: www.take backthetech.net, Twitter: @takebackthetech

While not explicitly a youth-oriented project, it is possible to see Take Back the Tech! as an example of the kind of digital activism engaged in by young feminists that has come to characterise fourth-wave feminism. Take Back the Tech! is a global campaign network promoting the use of ICTs to challenge online violence against women and girls, and brings together activists working on women's rights, the digital environment, freedom of expression and more, in many countries across the world. While much work – such as training, solidarity actions, media monitoring, etc. – is done by members at a local level, Take Back the Tech!'s biggest annual campaign happens globally, during the annual 16 Days of Activism Against Gender-based Violence.

World Association of Girl Guides and Girl Scouts (WAGGGS), Postal address: World Bureau, Olave Centre, 12c Lyndhurst Road, London NW3 5PQ, UK, email: wagggs@-wagggs.org, website: www.wagggs.org, Twitter: @wagggs_world

WAGGGS is the umbrella organisation for the international girl guiding and scouting movement, with member organisations in 150 countries. While the Girl Guides might not immediately spring to mind as a hotbed of young feminist activity, in recent years the movement has begun to address what might be thought of as 'feminist' issues. Alongside the pre-existing focus on outdoor activities, community service, and the development of leadership skills for girls, WAGGGS runs campaigns on, for example, ending violence against girls and women, body confidence, the Sustainable Development Goals, and a nutrition programme in Bangladesh, Madagascar, the Philippines, Sri Lanka, and Tanzania, which seeks to educate girls about gender disparities in nutrition and tackle malnutrition. WAGGGs regularly sends delegates to the UN's annual Commission on the Status of Women.

www.ingramcontent.com/pod-product-compliance
Lightning Source LLC
Chambersburg PA
CBHW070923030426
42336CB00014BA/2515